The Accidental Capitalist

THE ACCIDENTAL CAPITALIST

A People's Story of the New China

Behzad Yaghmaian

PlutoPress

www.plutobooks.com

First published 2012 by Pluto Press
345 Archway Road, London N6 5AA

www.plutobooks.com

Distributed in the United States of America exclusively by
Palgrave Macmillan, a division of St. Martin's Press LLC,
175 Fifth Avenue, New York, NY 10010

British Library Cataloguing in Publication Data
A catalogue record for this book is available from the British Library

ISBN   978 0 7453 3231 4   Hardback
ISBN   978 0 7453 3230 7   Paperback

Library of Congress Cataloging in Publication Data applied for

This book is printed on paper suitable for recycling and made from fully managed and
sustained forest sources. Logging, pulping and manufacturing processes are expected
to conform to the environmental standards of the country of origin.

10   9   8   7   6   5   4   3   2   1

Designed and produced for Pluto Press by Chase Publishing Services Ltd
Typeset from disk by Stanford DTP Services, Northampton, England
Simultaneously printed digitally by CPI Antony Rowe, Chippenham, UK and
Edwards Bros in the United States of America

I dedicate this book to all those who trusted me with their life stories.

Contents

Photographs

Timeline

1840–1911	Decline and humiliation: the final years of the Qing Dynasty, defeat by foreigners, concessions, and unequal treaties.
1842	Treaty of Nanking (Nanjing): the end of the first Opium War between China and Great Britain. Hong Kong is ceded to Great Britain.
1850–64	Taiping Rebellion: Christian-inspired rebellion against the Qing Dynasty.
1860	Treaty of Peking (Beijing): Signed after British and French troops enter the Forbidden City in Beijing. Great Britain takes control of Kowloon. Russia seizes all lands north of Amur and east of Ussuri rivers.
1884–85	China is defeated in the war with France.
1887	The creation of French Indochina.
1894–95	Treaty of Shimonoseki: China is defeated by Japan in the first Sino-Japanese War. China recognizes Korea as an independent state and cedes control of Taiwan to Japan.
1900–01	Boxer Rebellion: nationalist uprising against foreign domination and unequal treaties. The Eight-Nation Alliance (Austria-Hungary, France, Germany, Italy, Japan, Russia, the United Kingdom, and the United States) attack China, defeat the Imperial Army, and invade Beijing.
1911	Republican Revolution and the end of the Qing Dynasty
1912–49	Transition from dynasty to socialist revolution: warlordism, second Sino-Japanese War, civil war, communist revolution.
1912	The establishment of the Republic of China (ROC) headed by Sun Yat-Sen.
1912	The founding of Chinese National People's Party or Kuomintang (KMT).
1916–27	Warlord era.
1921	Mao Zedong and a small group of revolutionaries found the Communist Party of China.
1922	First CPC–Kuomintang alliance.
1927	Shanghai Massacre: the mass killing of the communists, radical students, and workers in Shanghai by the Kuomintang.
1927	Open confrontation between the communists and the nationalist forces. The communists are defeated and retreat to the countryside.
1927	Kuomintang unifies part of China with Nanjing as its capital.
1931	Japan invades Manchuria.
1935–36	The Long March.

1937	Beginning of the Second Sino-Japanese War: the Japanese invade North China.
1937	Second Communist–Kuomintang Alliance to fight the Japanese.
1945–49	Civil War: final and decisive war between the Communist Party's army (People's Liberation Army) and the Kuomintang forces.
1949	The communists defeat the Kuomintang. Chiang Kai-shek and his supporters retreat to Taiwan.
1949–76	Experimentation with socialism: land redistribution, passage of progressive laws, political infighting, violence.
1949	The founding of the People's Republic of China on October 1, 1949.
1947–52	Land Reform: distribution of land between the landless and land-poor peasants.
1950	First Marriage Law: abolishing arranged marriage, promoting free choice in marriage, giving women the right to divorce.
1954–56	Collectivization of agriculture.
1956	Nationalization of industry.
1958	The Great Leap Forward and the creation of People's Communes.
1959–61	Years of famine, the deaths of 13–30 million by starvation.
1966–69	The Great Proletarian Cultural Revolution.
1966–76	The decade of the Cultural Revolution.
1969–78	Sending the youth to the countryside to learn from the peasantry.
1976	Mao Zedong dies on September 9, 1976.
1978	The official announcement of economic reform.
1978–present	Period of capitalist reform.
1979–82	The end of collectivized agriculture. The introduction of household responsibility system in agriculture.
1980	The creation of Special Economic Zones in Shenzhen, Zhuhai, Shantou (in the province of Guangdong), Xiamen (in the Province of Fujian), and the entire province of Hainan. The first Special Economic Zones established in Shenzhen in August. China begins experimenting with low-wage export-processing capitalism.
1984	Fourteen coastal cities are made open to foreign investment.
1985	Central government abolishes free higher education.
1986	Deng Xiaoping promotes foreign investment in China.
1989	Tiananmen Square Protests: clampdown by the PLA on June 4.
Late 1990s	China in practice (not officially) lifts restriction on migration of peasants to cities.

1990–2004	Increase in the privatization of State-Owned Enterprises (SOEs).
1992	Deng Xiaoping calls for the creation of a "socialist market economy."
1996	Deng Xiaoping dies in February.
2001	China joins the World Trade Organization.
2003	Hu Jintao is elected president.
2006	Hu Jintao calls for the building of a "harmonious society" and the concept of "scientific development."

RUSSIA

KAZAKHSTAN

KYRGYZSTAN

PAKISTAN

INDIA

NEPAL

BHUTAN

MYANMAR (BURMA)

THAILAND

LAOS

VIETNAM

MONGOLIA

Sea of Japan

JAP

NORTH KOREA

SOUTH KOREA

Yellow Sea

East China Sea

TAIWAN

PHILIPPINES

South China Sea

Bay of Bengal

Heilongjiang
Qiqihar
Harbin
Jilin
Changchun
Liaoning
Shenyang
Dalian

Nei Mongol

Hohhot
Baotou

Nei Mongol

Beijing Shi
Beijing

Hebei
Shijiazhuang
Tianjin Shi
Tianjin

Shanxi
Taiyuan

Ningxia
Hui
Lanzhou

Gansu
Yumen

Qinghai
Xining

Xinjiang Uygur
Ürümqi

Kashi (Kashgar)

Xizang
Lhasa

Shandong
Jinan
Yantai
Qingdao

Jiangsu
Nanjing

Anhui
Hefei

Shanghai
Shanghai Shi

Zhejiang
Hangzhou

Henan
Zhengzhou

Shaanxi
Xian

Hubei
Wuhan

Chongqing
Chongqing

Sichuan
Chengdu

Hunan
Changsha

Jiangxi
Nanchang

Fujian
Fuzhou
Xiamen

Guizhou
Guiyang

Yunnan
Kunming

Guangxi Zhuang
Nanning

Guangdong
Guangzhou
Shenzhen
Xianggang (Hong Kong)
Macau
Zhanjiang

Hainan
Haikou

120° E

110° E

90° E

POLITICAL UNITS OF CHINA

Autonomous Regions

Other Provinces

0   300   600 MILES

0   300   600 KILOMETERS

China

xii

Introduction
The Greatest Migration

It was dusk. The air was heavy. Thick smog and dust from the nearby factories and construction sites made breathing difficult. Their infants sleeping in the baskets welded to the bicycle handles, and plastic bags full of vegetables hanging from the saddles, men and women rushed home on their old bicycles. They rode fearlessly on the bumpy and crowded streets, negotiated the traffic, and searched for a fast way out of the impenetrable throng of private cars, taxis, rickshaws, and buses. Low visibility did not seem to be an obstacle. Taxis honked, buses charged ahead, and motorbikes zigzagged between them.

I turned the corner onto a wide and empty street sparsely lit by the flickering light from tall streetlamps. The maddening chaos of cars and buses was behind me, and a comforting serenity had filled the air, when a sudden shattering sound broke the momentary stillness. All I could see was the tail end of a bus, speeding away, then disappearing.

I ran after the bus and stopped a few feet away from the turning wheels of an overturned tricycle wagon. A pair of mud-covered and worn-out slippers lay in the middle of the street. Two bare feet stuck out from under the wagon's wooden flatbed. A young man, perhaps in his twenties, lay motionless on the ground. His legs were trapped under the wagon, and blood was oozing from his left ear. His torn black trousers were tied around his waist with a rope, and his unbuttoned and discolored white shirt was soaking wet from heavy sweating. A veil of dust covered his thick black hair. Patches of blood carved through the dirt on his arms and his dark face. His lifeless eyes gazed at the starless sky. With the help of a friend, I lifted the wagon, and pushed it to the side. The young man's legs jerked. He was once again motionless.

"Where do you hurt?" He did not respond. The blood on the ground was slowly drying, darkening.

"Can you hear me? Can you talk?"

The young man's eyes closed.

"Don't sleep. Please don't sleep."

We called the emergency hotline. The phone rang, but there was no answer. A second and third try failed. By now, a small crowd had assembled around us, some on their bicycles, others on tricycle wagons, others on foot. We tried the hotline again, this time with success.

No one would be coming, said an operator on the other end. They were busy, he said. The crowd grew larger. Some left. Others arrived. A few conversed among themselves. Others called friends on their cell phones.

We tried the hotline again, begging for an ambulance. "It is serious. A man is dying." More people arrived on the scene, and the young man's eyes remained shut. Long minutes later, honking to disperse the crowd, a white mini-van parked opposite the overturned wagon. Four skinny, boyish-looking men in uniform left the van and casually walked to the crowd.

"Everyone should leave now," shouted a young officer.

"I was the one who called. We saw a bus …," my friend said.

"Everyone must leave now," the officer interrupted.

"Will an ambulance come?"

"You must leave."

I took a last look at the young man and his wagon and walked away.

* * *

1   A moment of solitude

That was the summer of 2007, and I had just arrived in Beijing to do a research project on the lives and experiences of Chinese people during the period that turned China from a poor country into a rising power. I am an Iranian-born political economist, and I have been studying and teaching globalization and development for more than 20 years. China's epic changes intrigued me, but I found the popular China narrative incomplete. The narrative lacked the voices of the Chinese people, those who were the backbone of the country's transformation, and its march to globalization. The essential human dimension was absent.

China's globalization produced the largest population movement in human history. More than 200 million men and women left their homes for China's new industrial hobs. Migration fueled China's new industries, made the country a rising star, and supplied the world with innumerable consumer goods. Chinese internal migration became an inseparable part of contemporary globalization. Chinese migrants entered our lives in the West and elsewhere in the world, but they remained ghosts, overshadowed and hidden by statistical tabulations and jargon in China stories. I had come to China for *their* stories, and to learn about their contributions to this rising power.

Prior to the 1980s, the Communist Party tightly controlled the movement of people, even between the towns and villages of the same province. It used an elaborate residence registration system to keep millions of peasants tied to the land, and financed China's early industrialization through mandatory low-priced procurement of agricultural products. The system helped the delivery of the promises of socialism to factory workers through generous social benefit unavailable to others.

With the economic opening of the 1980s, however, the people's registration system became an obstacle to the growth of China's export-processing industries. The new China required massive movement of people across the country. The strict control of population movement had to end to feed the private enterprises with workers, entrepreneurs, managers, engineers, and accountants. China's globalization would not have been possible without this epic migration.

I planned to live among China's growing population of internal migrants and write a narrative of the country's transformation through their lens. Beijing was my first stop.

*   *   *

The 2008 Olympic Games were approaching and Beijing was in the midst of mind-boggling construction frenzy. Large construction sites, cranes, heavy machinery, and unmerciful dust overwhelmed the capital's landscape. Migrants from faraway provinces carried heavy loads of dirt on their bent backs, and moved slowly behind the tall scaffoldings like an army of ants orderly carrying their winter supplies. Riding their tricycle wagons through Beijing's traffic jams, some earned a living selling scrap metal and wood and all that they could scavenge from the construction sites. The young man hit by the bus was returning home after one such day. The tricycle wagon accident was my first encounter with the lives of migrants in the new China.

Beijing's booming construction industry brought many traveling migrants to the capital, but I was heading south to the industrial heart of the new China. Shenzhen was my destination. Once an unknown fishing village of a few thousand residents and only a half-hour ferry ride from Hong Kong, Shenzhen became the epicenter of the new China, and its vanguard of change, when Deng Xiaoping declared it the country's first Free Economic Zone on August 26, 1980. By the 1990s, Shenzhen was the heartbeat of the rising China, the crucible of the Chinese model of growth.

When I arrived, Shenzhen had six sprawling districts with state-of-the art skyscrapers, corporate headquarters, wide boulevards, ring-roads, factories, and ghettoes. Its official population surpassed ten million. A few more millions moved in and out of the city and lived without a record.

Shenzhen was home to the winners and losers of China's globalization, those who made a fortune in the new China, and those who lived on its margins. The largest of Shenzhen's districts, Longgang, was home to export-processing factories making shoes, clothes, toys, electronics, and everything we use in our homes and workplaces. A large constellation of migrant ghettoes and neighborhoods, it housed the poorest of the migrant workers in Shenzhen.

Longgang was also one of the most rapidly changing parts of Shenzhen. Supported by the local government, and financed by public and private money, the district was gentrifying. Factory executives, doctors, and other professionals were settling in its modern quarters. By 2007, Longgang was a collage of poverty and wealth, old and new, decaying and thriving. It was a mirror image of China.

I decided to move to Longgang, live there, and make the district and its population the center of my search in China. China is a vast country with diverse cultures, habits, and languages. I had chosen a small corner of the country that represented much of the recent change in China. The decision to live in Longgang, however, worried my Chinese friends.

"Why are you moving there? This is not a place for someone like you."

"Watch out for pickpockets, don't carry expensive items when you go out."

"Longgang is outside the city limits of Shenzhen. There are many migrant workers in Longgang. The inhabitants of other districts are more educated, and the environment is more secure. My friends and I go to the districts within the city limits of Shenzhen; we are more familiar with them," a graduate student in one of the universities in Shenzhen said when I asked her to be my assistant. She requested higher pay for working in Longgang.

Defying the protests of friends, I moved to the Beautiful Rose Garden, a middle-class apartment complex surrounded by luxury condominiums, migrant ghettoes, and workers' quarters, and a short drive to large and small export-processing factories. I met and befriended migrants from different walks of life—rich and poor, young and old, workers and capitalists—and wrote about those whose stories highlighted the quandaries of China's globalization, and the tensions of a nation in transition.

*   *   *

What originally brought me to China was its epic transformation in recent years. I was interested only in the China of now and its prospects for the future. My conversations with different Chinese, however, invariably took a detour to China's past, to a history that continues to influence government policies, and people's perceptions of themselves and the world that surrounds them. Whether through the lingering humiliation of foreign occupation in the final years of the Qing Dynasty, or the years of civil war, or the excesses and the violence of the social experiments by the Communist Party in the first 30 years of its power, the Chinese remain haunted by their past. The heavy dust of history is felt everywhere. The past remains an important influence on people's psyche. Writing a narrative of China's globalization was a journey into China's recent history and the different ways it affected the Chinese people.

The following pages tell a story of China's economic and social transformation through the personal biographies of migrants. The migrant biographies reveal the diverse and unequal human impact of China's journey

2   Migrants waiting for the train

from a poor country to a rising star of contemporary globalization. The stories take us to painful chapters of China's modern history and how they affected the book's protagonists. They personalize events and developments that remain a mystery to most outsiders.

I have organized the book in four parts. Book I tells the life stories of the residents of a migrant ghetto in Longgang. Grandpa's story is a tale of the struggle for a land of freedom, and the benefits that the revolution and the economic restructuring of China brought to millions of farmers. The story of Grandpa's nephew, however, tells of the tragic consequences of the Great Leap Forward and the economic and social experiments by the Communist Party. Hufang and her husband reveal the dark side of China's globalization. Their story echoes the experience of 50–100 million employees of State-Owned Enterprises sacrificed by the government during the privatization movement of the 1990s.

Book II follows the long journey of migrant girls from village to large metropolis. It tells of the excitements, opportunities, and disappointments of city life. Yu Xinhong's story is the tale of just one of China's current farm-to-city migrants, the story of a young woman who has, so far, survived boom, bust, and near-exploitation to make a life that will be far better than that of her parents.

China's globalization began with the rise of low-wage export-processing capitalism in Shenzhen and surrounding cities. Thirty years later, by the time of my arrival, what had earlier made China an economic powerhouse had become a stigma the government was trying hard to dispel. The Communist Party was pouring resources into high-tech and green research and development (R&D) and production to change China from a producer of cheap low-end products to a leader of modern green capitalism.

Book III follows the life story of Zhao Gang, a struggling capitalist coping with the decline of low-wage export-processing industries.

Book IV tells the story of the triumphs of Yue Haitao and his role in the emerging China of the twenty-first century. Zhao Gang's and Yue Haitao's stories weave a narrative of China's journey from the earlier years of the revolution to the first and the second phase of its globalization.

Book I
The Tenants of the Li Family

THE BEAUTIFUL ROSE GARDEN

I would open my eyes to the clicking sound of metal gates being unlocked on every balcony around me. Lying in my bed, I would count them, one by one, until the sounds were distant, no longer audible in my apartment. Not long after, women would appear on the balconies, hanging out clothes, and moving things around. Still in their underwear, men would smoke their first cigarettes of the day. Children would run in and out. Sitting on stools with their hands under their chins, old women would solemnly watch the passersby.

That's how every day started in the Beautiful Rose Garden. They ended with the clicking sound of closing gates, one by one, and on every balcony. My neighbors would withdraw to their TV sets and watch Korean mini-series and Chinese imitations of American shows. Lights would go off, and all noises would disappear until the clicking sound of the opening of the first metal gate the next morning. A new day would be upon the Beautiful Rose Garden.

I had rented an apartment with two balconies on the third floor of one of the many four-story buildings. A thick and heavy floor-to-ceiling sliding gate, and a glass and aluminum door, separated the front balcony from the apartment. Fixed into the wall, thick metal bars protected the kitchen and the bathroom. "Always lock the apartment door and the gate, even when you are home," said the young broker who took me to the Beautiful Rose Garden.

There were gates everywhere in and around the Beautiful Rose Garden. Designing and making window gates was a thriving business. Four workshops just outside the Beautiful Rose Garden made a wide selection of gates: thick and ugly gates, tall and short gates, gates of all shapes, and designer gates. They built straight flat gates that were popular in wealthier communities, and gates that looked like cages sliced vertically in the middle. These were the favorites of poorer neighborhoods and workers' ghettoes.

Sprawling around the Beautiful Rose Garden, luxury condominiums kept their façades unaffected by installing less intrusive and nicer gates from the inside behind their wall-to-wall windows. Not far from the Beautiful Rose Garden, the surrounding workers' ghettoes had thick, dirty, and corroded gates that covered every entry point to the apartments. The gates stood out on the dirt-covered old walls in the narrow alleys and maze-like communities.

My apartment was sparsely furnished. The walls were dirty, and the paint was old and stained, chipping in many places. The bathroom tiles were broken and falling off. My rent was, however, two and half times the monthly salary of most workers in the nearby export-processing factories. A middle-class gated community with swimming pools, private garages, and

3   A tale of two Chinas

well-maintained landscaping, the Beautiful Rose Garden was a fantasy world for the thousands of young migrant workers living eight to ten people in a room in the neighboring factory dormitories.

Sleepy young men and women guarded the four gates of the Beautiful Rose Garden. Skinny and clad in oversized blue uniforms and caps, white socks, and black shoes, the guards looked like skeletons hidden in armor who were in charge of protecting a fortress. They looked bored at all times, watched people go in and out, and did not object even when strangers passed them by

新旧货 买卖
高价回收家私家电
电话：13717093381

4   Caged in: migrant homes in Longgang

and entered the gates they were there to protect. To the middle-class residents of the Beautiful Rose Garden, the guards were mere fixtures that changed every twelve hours. No one would greet them and wish them a pleasant day. I was an exception—I would wave and bow, and greet the guards with a smile. Seeing me from afar, and anticipating my usual greeting, even the grumpiest guards would smile.

A plaza with a dozen or so small shops stood on the southern exterior of the Beautiful Rose Garden. An old man in long boxer shorts and white tank-top sat on a stool and silently watched the passersby from the early hours of the day. Joining him every morning, a half-dozen middle-aged neighbors awaited the arrival of a young man in a white doctor's coat. Rolling up their sleeves, one by one, they would have their blood pressures read before starting their daily games of Chinese chess.

A short and stocky woman in her fifties sat behind a sewing machine in a small fabric shop. She made pillowcases, bed sheets, and curtains at prices lower than those of the nearby department stores. Once a migrant worker in an electronic factory, she was now an entrepreneur. She was her own boss, a "*la ban*," she would say with pride.

At the end of the plaza by the street, the Milano Café Restaurant served an assortment of coffees—always sweetened unless requested otherwise, and whitened by a suspicious cream-like substance—Western food, and Chinese and other Asian dishes. One among the half a dozen or so other Western restaurants surrounding the Beautiful Rose Garden, the Milano Café Restaurant catered to the better-off families in the area.

*　　*　　*

I greeted the young guard at the south gate and left the Beautiful Rose Garden for a stroll in the neighborhood one early evening. A petite young woman sat on a stool outside a small shop selling cell phones. With her right arm under her chin, she gazed at the passersby. I waved to the woman behind the sewing machine, said hello to the waitress standing outside the Milano Café Restaurant, and entered the plaza.

I was near the main road when, for the first time, I noticed a young man lying on his side under the shade of a large tree at the edge of the plaza. A bottle of green tea, two black plastic bags, a brown shirt, and a long wooden stick were scattered around him. I walked towards him. He sat up.

"Haaallo," he said, with a big smile on his face.

He was unshaven and wore a thin mustache. His thick, straight, dark hair was unruly. His hands and face were unwashed. A layer of dirt had accumulated under his long fingernails. He wore old shoes with missing shoelaces, a striped cream-colored shirt, and brown pants. He looked to be in his early twenties.

"Hello," I replied in English.

He smiled again, and I left the plaza.

The plaza was unusually quiet when I returned home late that night. I proceeded to the Beautiful Rose Garden, not paying attention to things around me.

"Haaallo," I heard from behind me. I stopped and turned around. The young man I had seen earlier gave me a military salute. I waved goodbye.

Next morning, I returned to the plaza with my camera, approached the young man, and gestured a request to photograph him. His jumped up, combed his hair with his fingers, straightened his wrinkled shirt, and tucked it in his pants. The young man stood ready, smiling. As I continued to take

5   Homeless

pictures, he changed his position, moved his hands, stared at the lens, sat down, stood again, leaned to the left, saluted, bent down, and played with the long stick, always maintaining his big smile. I stopped shooting and showed him his photos on my camera's monitor. He posed again, and I shot more photos.

We would exchange greetings each day. I had purchased beautiful big peaches—Chinese peaches are especially big, juicy, and tasty—from a vendor on my way home one evening. I stopped and offered him some. He delved into the plastic bag in my hand, took one, and then another at my request. I brought him pears the next day. He took one, nodding.

A few days passed. Wishing to know his story, I asked my interpreter to speak with him and start up a conversation, one Chinese to another.

"Where are you from?" my interpreter asked him after the usual greetings one morning.

"Paris. No Taiwan. No Japan," he replied and turned his back to her.

"He is not interested in talking to me. He prefers you," my interpreter told me.

As the days passed, our smiling, waving, and greetings became a routine. I would look for him in the same spot, wave, and go on with my business. Signs of change were slowly appearing in the young man. At times he would be withdrawn and tired-looking. The child-like joy disappeared from his face. His cream-colored shirt grew darker, and the dirt under his fingernails became thicker. His hands and face had been darkened by sweat and dirt. Always lying down, often asleep, he would respond to my usual greetings with a gentle wave of his hand, and only a faint smile. I would wait for the "haaallo," and his moving around, but he would close his eyes.

Day after day, I would see him in the same spot, curled up like an unborn child in the womb. Gradually, even the occasional smiling disappeared. He no longer noticed my walking by, did not respond to my greetings. The stripes on his cream-colored shirt disappeared. He was filthy.

Then, one evening, I saw him in the middle of the plaza. He was making strange gestures a few feet away from half a dozen middle-aged women talking waltz classes from a slender man, dancing to tunes from a small portable CD player. My friend was moving his hands and legs in a mix of karate and Tai Chi movements, and making incomprehensible sounds. The women ignored him. Passersby moved in and out of the plaza, none paying him any attention.

That was the last time I saw the young man. His usual spot was empty the next morning, and his bags and dirty clothes were gone.

*   *   *

6   Taxi in a migrant quarter

The Beautiful Rose Garden was in the heart of Longgang's new district center. Wishing to change the public image of Longgang and turn it from a dangerous district into a new magnet for the middle classes, the local government in Shenzhen designated the area around the Beautiful Rose Garden for urban renewal and gentrification. Millions of dollars of public and private money financed new residential buildings, commercial space, parks, and hotels. Luxury condominiums, grand government buildings, and shopping malls replaced poor neighborhoods and migrant ghettoes. By 2007, thousands of doctors, lawyers, factory managers, and others were living in gated communities with swimming pools and underground parking. They surrounded the remaining poor neighborhoods and ghettoes that housed the migrant workers laboring in restaurants, malls, and stores.

Only a short walk from the Beautiful Rose Garden, the Longgang World Trade Center was among the first public attractions in the new district center. A simple two-story complex housing a department store, a supermarket, and a handful of fast food and other restaurants, it attracted locals from all walks of life. It was a public space shared by the low-income factory workers and their well-off neighbors.

Modeled on American steakhouses, the San Diego restaurant brought the ultimate American experience to its customers, with waitresses dressed in black pants, patterned red and black shirts, oversized black cowboy hats, and red bandanas around their necks. Crowded, noisy, and bustling with activity, McDonald's and KFC attracted eager middle-class families hungry for these marvels of popular American culture. Those with meager means purchased prepared noodles, pork chops, and chicken from the supermarket, sat at the sidewalk tables, and enjoyed their eating out. Others strolled back and forth on the sidewalk, in and out of shops. Young mothers breastfed their infants. Squatting by a tree, or in the middle of the sidewalk, and amidst the crowd of people passing them by, others held their babies to urinate. Beggars held out their small metal cups, moved from table to table, and persisted until they were given money.

The department store at the Longgang World Trade Center was an important source of employment for young female migrants in the area. With product lines that were out of the reach of migrant workers, and not suited to the expensive tastes of those living in nearby luxury condos, the store was empty of customers most of the times. Young salesgirls in colorful work uniforms always outnumbered the shoppers.

I would sit by the window on the second floor of McDonald's and watch the girls come to work from different directions. Clad in yellow shirts and purple trousers, and carrying their breakfasts in small bags, they would assemble on the sidewalk, greet one another, sit on the benches or curbs, and nibble on their first food of the day. While waiting to begin their new day of work, jubilant young women would pack the sidewalk. By 9 o'clock, the sidewalk would be empty, but a thunderous sound of salutations by a few-hundred-strong army of salesgirls from the corridor between McDonald's and the department store would fill the air. Stern and combatant, with their heads up and their arms straight down and touching their thighs, the young migrants would stand to attention, repeat slogans after their leader, and take to heart their instructions for the day.

"Good morning. Take care of your receipts, calculators, and pens. Clean your areas in a timely manner. The training list is posted inside. Review it when you are free. Pay attention to your safety. Be spirited and energized," would shout a diminutive group leader. The salesgirls would clap with each statement, salute, shout in unison, and repeat after their leader. They would return the next day, and the day after, repeating the same routine before every shift. That is how the days began at the Longgang World Trade Center.

Vendors assembled with their products on the sidewalk at one end of the Center. A mere handful in the morning and afternoon, they mushroomed at night. Some sold cheap earrings and necklaces, batteries, and all sorts of inexpensive souvenirs. A short woman with a few missing front teeth sold sliced watermelon from her bicycle-cart. A scruffy-looking man enticed the passersby with baked potatoes and soft drinks. Deep-frying meat and seafood filled the air with thick and heavy smoke from burning oil. A short middle-aged man whetted the appetites of the passersby with "smelly tofu", a specialty loved for its rotten smell.

Filled with migrant workers indulging themselves with inexpensive products and affordable food, the sidewalk buzzed with activity and energy in summer nights. They clustered around different vendors, bargained, chatted with friends, and watched the passersby.

*   *   *

Adjacent to the Longgang World Trade Center, to its south, a beautifully designed park provided open space, greenery, fresh air, and entertainment for the migrant workers living in nearby dormitories or small one-room apartments. A statue of a giant dragon stood by a large fountain in the middle of a pool in the park. Lit by a rainbow of colors at night, the dragon and fountain attracted visitors fascinated by the spectacle. Workers from nearby factories took pictures with their cell phones, or paid for the services of photographers standing around with their digital cameras. With the dragon behind them, some would pose before the tiny lens of a friend's cell phone camera.

The park was a refuge for migrant workers from nearby factories. Most factory dormitories lacked areas for public gathering, TV rooms, and any place for socializing. For many workers in the area, television was a dream. Some had small radios. Others listened to music on their cell phones' MP3. For these workers, the park, with its vast clean space, grass and trees, and the open air it offered, was the only affordable recreation.

Soon after the sunset, hundreds of workers assembled for the big event of the night. Some would rest on their bicycles; others would squat. Unshaven, shirtless, their trousers covered in dried mud, they carried the dust and the fatigue of a day of work on nearby construction sites. Escaping their tiny mobile dormitories packed with bunk beds, bags, and other belongings, they would sit before a giant screen fixed high up on two tall metal poles, and eagerly watch programs broadcast by the local television station.

They were farmers from other provinces. To many, the giant screen brought nostalgic memories of the traveling opera troupes that moved from village to village and entertained the farmers and their families. As if they were watching their favorite opera, they sat attentively and respectfully. No one moved; no one spoke. They came night after night, and watched the news, popular TV series, movies, commercials, and all that they lacked in their dormitories. Among the eager spectators were also the friendly residents of the Li Family Village.

THE LI FAMILY VILLAGE

All one could see from the outside was an old whitewashed wall with algae-covered clay tiles on the top. A tall wooden gate stood in the center, a short watchtower on the left corner, and a small entrance on the right. Inside was mystery.

A walled-in ghetto behind the Longgang World Trade Center, this was a constellation of old houses built in five rows facing a big gate more than a century ago. It had once housed members of the extended Li family, owners of vast areas of land in the area. Its current residents called it the Li Family Village.

7   The Li Family Village

Long after its glory days, when I first visited in 2007, the Li Family Village was a migrant ghetto housing construction workers, street peddlers, security guards, and waitresses from impoverished villages from faraway places in China. "Most of us are from Sichuan," a resident told me. She had left Sichuan with her husband and four children in 1990. For the past eight years, she had been sharing a house with another family of five in the Li Family Village. When I met her in 2007, she was worried about the potential demolition of her home. Rumors were rife about a plan to clear the area—the village, and the old apartment buildings and abandoned factories around it—to build new luxury housing complexes. "Where can we go if they do that?" she said. A neighbor disputed the rumors. "I have been living here for ten years. Every year people said the government was going to destroy our homes. We are still here, as you can see. Don't believe what you hear."

Except for the algae on the walls, and a few dead potted plants, there was no greenery, no trees, or flowers in the Li Family Village. Children ran after stray cats and dogs. Big rats scurried in and out of the piles of garbage. The air smelled of burning wood mixed with the dampness from frequent torrential rain. Potholes collected rainwater, dirt, mosquitoes, and flies. The alleys were narrow. A makeshift wood-burning stove stood in front of most homes. Women sat outside, cooked, sewed, and made cheap items that they sold on the market outside the village. Teenage girls shampooed their hair outside their homes, and small boys played in the stream of foam.

There were 92 brick and stone houses with bare cement floors, whitewashed walls, and tile roofs in the village. The homes along the sidewall opposite the tower were tiny two-room residences, each with a low door and small window in the front.

The insides were dark and musty. Plastic and plywood had been used to partition the homes and make room for more migrants, both individuals and families. Three or more families lived in the larger homes—privacy was a luxury most residents could not afford. Dire economic conditions forced them to live communally. No one complained; that is how they had lived in their villages before they came to Longgang. "At least we eat regularly here," one resident told me.

*   *   *

No one knows who laid the first brick of the first home in the Li Family Village. The first members of the Li family built their homes on the last row. They built more homes with the arrival of other relatives, and the growing up and marriage of their children. In the early years of the twentieth century, they built the ancestral home in the center of the village. Once all the rows were finished, they erected a wall with a watchtower around the village. The Li Family Village was completed.

The Li Family Village and its history mirrored China's own tormented past—landlordism, dying dynasties, civil war, the rise of communism, and market reform. "I have lived here all my life. I remember seeing Japanese planes dropping bombs on the hills there," said a 75-year-old man, pointing to the hills behind the Longgang World Trade Center. He was the last member of the Li family living in the village.

His home was small, clean, and tidy. An old sofa covered by worn-out blankets faced a small television in a corner of the living room. A wooden ladder, an old fan, and a chair stood against the opposite wall. A ray of light from the small window behind the sofa illuminated the dust in the air. Faded layers of red, yellow, blue, and green paint told stories of the wall's old age, older than the old Li.

"I was born and raised in this house. This was already an old house when I came into this world. My grandparents and my parents lived in this house. My children grew up here. Now they live in apartments outside the village. I don't want to move. I have lived my whole life here," the old Li told me the day I visited his home. "Everyone knows me here. When I go out, children gather around me, older men and women come to greet me." The old Li resisted pressure by his children to move to an apartment in one the four-story buildings outside the village. "I want to die in my ancestral home," he said.

*   *   *

Accident had brought me to the Li Family Village. I was returning from a factory visit one afternoon when I noticed the wall and stopped. A middle-aged woman selling fresh produce and fruits outside the wall noticed my interest. Short, plump, and balding, and clad in black pajama pants and a purple shirt, she smiled, offered me an orange, and invited me in. I went through the gate and wandered amid the gaze of men and women lazily passing their time. I returned day after day.

Soon I was a regular there. Children followed me around, played ball with me, and performed for me. "Foreign uncle," some called me. Others screamed, circling me, jumping up and down. Some posed for pictures. Clad in a white dress with orange flowers and pink sandals, and with her black hair pulled up and tied with a red ribbon, a ten-year-old performed acrobatic moves. Staring sternly into the lens of my camera, her friend performed classical Chinese dance movements. She held her positions as she waited for me to press the shutter release.

Sleeping with his head down in a tiny seat fixed to the corroded handle of his father's tricycle wagon, a small toddler stole the children away from my camera. They shouted with excitement, played with the sleeping child, poked him, and tried all they could to awaken him. Oblivious to the noise and the action around him, the child continued his midday nap. I walked to a man fixing the flat tire on his tricycle wagon near the ancestral home. A shirtless neighbor rested on an old armchair beside him. His playful son asked him to pose for a joint photograph. Reluctantly submitting to his wishes, he left his comfortable chair, placed the boy on his shoulder, held tight to the boy's feet, and smiled for the photo.

THE PORTRAIT OF MAO

A large portrait of Chairman Mao looms over Tiananmen Square in central Beijing. His receding hair neatly combed back, and clad in the famous blue Mao suit, the Chairman solemnly gazes at the world below him, making his presence felt by those who visit the square every day. A copy of the same portrait, albeit a lot smaller and printed on glossy paper, hangs on the wall of the humble home of Hufang and her husband in the Li Family Village. A soft drink advertisement, a wall calendar, a world map, and a certificate of good performance from a local elementary school surround the Chairman's poster. A bare ceiling lamp strung at the end of a three-foot cord illuminates his face.

A long time has passed since the Chinese, willingly or through fear of persecution, decorated their walls with Mao's photos. Today, vendors in touristy places in Beijing and other big cities sell Mao's posters alongside those of Che Guevara, Sylvester Stallone, Arnold Schwarzenegger, Jackie Chan, and other international celebrities. His face, however, has all but disappeared from people's homes. Hufang's is among the rare exceptions. "Life was a lot better when Chairman Mao was alive. We had stability. We all miss him very much," Hufang said as she gazed at the Chairman's poster one hot afternoon in August 2007.

To Hufang and her husband, the small portrait of the Chairman is like a cherished photo of the past in an old family album. It helps them remember and relive the good times that are long gone, the time when "a pound of pork cost two yuan, and rice, less than one." That was the time when the couple lived, "with no worries," in a small apartment that was provided by their work unit. "Not a bed in a dormitory. We had our own apartment," Hufang's husband said. They enjoyed all that the Communist Revolution had promised the new Chinese working class. "Oh, we were very young," he recalled.

8   Hufang's husband

Hufang's husband was born in a small town in Jiangxi Province in the early 1950s. When he turned 18, ready to begin his independent life, he joined the ranks of socialist workers in a government-owned food-processing factory. His first monthly salary was a meager 36 yuan, but the perks were many. He was among the vanguards of socialist China. For that, the state rewarded him dearly. "Pay was not very high, but things were cheap then, and many things were free." That was 1970.

Like millions of state employees, he was a member of a *danwei*, a work unit that gave him free housing, healthcare, and schooling, ration coupons for rare food and household goods, and a lifelong job with pension. The work unit was the realization of the material promises of socialism. The factory job also gave him a prestige his parents had not enjoyed in their time. This was during the Great Cultural Revolution, and factory workers like him were celebrated as the champions of socialism. He was a proud worker, proud of helping build a new world and enjoying its immediate benefits.

Secure, and full of optimism about the future, the young factory worker decided it was time to have a family. He was in his prime, and did not need to wait. A generation or two earlier, men his age needed money to buy a wife in China's poor villages. That ended with the revolution. He did not have to buy a wife. His factory job gave him the material power many lacked back in the village.

With permission from his work unit, he returned home to search for a wife. A young woman from a nearby village accepted him without question. She was one year his junior. "We fell in love," he said. Hufang smiled gleefully as she listened to her husband recount the story of their marriage. After all these years, she was still in love with him. They were inseparable. "We have gone through a lot together," Hufang said.

The decision to marry the young factory worker opened new doors for Hufang. These were turbulent times in China. Political tension and infighting overshadowed life everywhere, and Hufang's village was no exception. She wished to escape, leave everything behind, and start a new life. The man who could deliver her liberation had come knocking on her door.

"I took her away with me. Her family was happy." Hufang followed her husband and said farewell to her family and village life. Soon, she started work in the same factory. "We worked in different departments," Hufang said. The couple began their shared life in the small home in 1975, a year before Chairman Mao died. "Everyone in the factory wept," the husband recalled about the day he heard the news of the Chairman's passing from his factory's loudspeakers. "We lost a father," said Hufang.

A year after the Chairman's death, Hufang gave birth to a son. She was happy.

Fundamental changes had begun in China following Mao's passing, but life in the factory and the work unit proceeded, largely unaffected. Then, in 1988, the earth shattered beneath their feet. The secure life Hufang and her family had come to enjoy ended abruptly: Hufang and her husband became two of the first victims of China's reforms when the government began the widespread privatization of public property. Their factory shut down, and their jobs disappeared overnight.

Across the country, the government shut down large State-Owned Enterprises, or sold them to foreign and domestic firms which, in turn, fired workers to cut costs. Some 50–100 million Chinese lost their jobs. With that, they lost their homes and everything else they had regarded as natural to their lives. The change was rapid. "We were shocked," Hufang's husband recalled. "We didn't know what to do. We had nowhere to go."

As the socialist dream ended, many became vagabonds and moved between provinces in search of new opportunities. Hufang and her husband packed their suitcases and said farewell to the factory and their cherished home.

The factory gave each a severance package of ten months' salary. They were homeless and without work, but they knew that returning to the village was not an option. They had to move on.

By then, the government had set up four Special Economic Zones in China to attract foreign investment and launch China on the road to export-processing industrialization. One of the four, the province of Fujian, was a magnate for many migrants from across the country. "We decided that was going to be our new home," Hufang's husband said. Fujian's warm weather attracted the couple. "Fujian is very beautiful," Hufang recalled. It had more job opportunities than many other provinces in the country. Finding a job, however, proved difficult for Hufang and her husband, even in Fujian.

"I was 40 when I arrived there. I wasn't too old, but I wasn't young either," Hufang's husband said. Faced with a flood of younger migrant workers from China's rural areas, factories were not interested in men and women their age. "Not finding a job was so embarrassing to me. I couldn't look into my son's eyes," Hufang's husband told me. They looked everywhere, applied for every possible job. Even working as a cleaner, a job usually left for older uneducated migrants, proved difficult. "They wanted younger and stronger people."

Across the country, many laid-off workers faced similar conditions. The lucky ones had become vendors, construction workers, or taxi-drivers. Others were on their way to permanent unemployment. "We had to find something. We had a son," said Hufang.

For the next few years, the couple worked odd jobs. For a time, he sold vegetables, and she cleaned rich people's homes. Life proceeded. The family had found a renewed sense of normality and relative comfort. But for their son, now 15 and restless, life in Fujian was a waste of time. He knew of friends who had dropped out of school and migrated to Shenzhen. They would occasionally send money to their families, and brag about their new life and the opportunities they had found in Shenzhen. There were many more job opportunities in Shenzhen. The city had already become a center of China's industrialization. It had an unending thirst for new workers. Everyone had a chance in Shenzhen. There were no losers. Shenzhen was in the news all the time, and it was only an eight-hour bus ride from Fujian.

The young man was envious of everyone who had already left for Shenzhen. His time arrived one early fall day. He packed a small bag, said farewell to his mother, and walked to the bus station. "It was before noon. His father was out. He did not wait to say goodbye to him. I knew I could not keep him anymore," Hufang remembered. Her son never returned to Fujian. "He did not write for months," Hufang said.

Occasionally, Hufang's son sent word about his whereabouts through friends. He moved between jobs, until he married a girl from Hunan. "You are a grandmother," he wrote in a letter to Hufang after the birth of his son. "I cried," Hufang said. The husband and wife were lonely. They missed their son. "I wanted to meet my grandson." Finally, in fall 1997, the couple decided to move to Shenzhen to be closer to their son and his boy. Soon after, they settled in their current home in the Li Family Village. A year later, Hufang's grandson moved in. "My son and his wife are too busy working. The boy needs guidance and care. We are happy he is with us. He brightens our lives," Hufang told me. "He is a good boy," her husband said. "He is a very good student," Hufang said, pointing at the certificate of performance besides the poster of Chairman Mao.

*   *   *

Three rows of twisted shiny yellow ribbons hung from the ceiling, and a wrinkled picture of Santa was next to the poster of Mao Zedong when I visited the couple three days after Christmas in 2007. Hufang laughed when she noticed the surprise on my face, and told me how their grandson had decorated the house for Christmas from material he had collected in the streets.

The boy came home early on Christmas day, went directly to his grandfather and asked for his Christmas present. "A Christmas present?" his grandfather said, laughing. Disappointed and hurt, the boy retreated to the home's only bedroom. He did not eat for the rest of the day, and did not do his homework. To calm him, his grandfather offered some meager cash. "No, I want a Christmas present," the boy protested. Two days later, a pair of new ping-pong bats and a red-and-white Christmas card awaited the grandson. "This is what we got for him," Hufang's husband said, showing me the bats, still in their original wrap.

"Children are very smart these days. They watch television and know about every American festival," Hufang said.

Smart and sociable, the boy had many friends in the Li Family Village. They ran in and out of the house, took food, and made Hufang smile with joy. "Children," she would say with affection.

"The boy had a birthday party last week. We knew he had planned to have a party, but we didn't expect it to be so big. This was a surprise for us," the husband told me. "A very big party!" he repeated. "My grandson came home from school and told me that some friends were coming for a visit. In one hour, the house was full of little boys and girls. They were so many. They danced, sang, and laughed. That was a very happy night. My son came later that night. He also brought friends and a big birthday cake. That was a good night," Hufang said.

I was ready to leave when, followed by his friends, the boy came to the house carrying a small bucket, with two baby turtles inside. He fetched a few leaves of lettuce from the kitchen, placed them in the bucket, filled a small bowl with water, and rushed out of the house.

"He caught the turtles from the reservoir one day. The reservoir is deep. He could have drowned. I gave him a little beating when he came home. Sometimes you have to be strict with them," Hufang's husband said.

"He is a great boy. I let him do anything he wants. Maybe I should be stricter with him. But he is fine," said Hufang.

"She spoils the boy. A little discipline doesn't hurt. He wants everything he sees. We don't have much money. His father has to watch how he spends money. He doesn't have much either," Hufang's husband said.

In December 2007, the boy's father was unemployed, moving between jobs. A security guard in a factory in Shenzhen for three years, and an assembly-line worker in a number of facilities before that, he had quit his job to pursue his big dream. He was searching for an opportunity to begin a private business. Hufang's son wished to be his own *la ban*, boss. Hufang was not happy with the decision. Being a security guard was a good job, she thought. "It paid a good salary." Hufang and her husband worried, and for good reasons. Their son did not have the money, or any idea about business. He had just given up a good job for a dream.

From the factories to the apartment complexes, department stores, McDonald's, and KFC, every business hired security guards. In factories, the guards controlled the traffic in and out of the compound, and kept an eye on the workers. In McDonald's, friendly young men in security uniforms helped customers carry their trays, cleaned tables, and assisted other employees with their work. In apartment complexes and gated communities, shopping malls, department stores, and many other businesses, the guards stood at their posts, dozed off, and napped when they could. They brought home less than 1000 yuan a month. Most spent their earnings on housing and food, cell phones, and other necessary daily expenses. There was no saving, and no future in their jobs. But someone always needed a security guard. The job was easy—anyone could do it. It did not require education or skills. Hufang's son, however, had better dreams for his future, and the future of his son. He was not going to be a security guard all his life. Not him!

* * *

I first met Hufang on a lazy afternoon in the Li Family Village. Dressed in clean green trousers and a white polyester shirt with red-and-blue flowers, she sat on a stool outside her home, and leaned against a wide-open light-green metal door. Her brown sandals were spotless, not covered by the dust or dried mud common in the Li Family Village. She had short, thick, straight black hair that covered her forehead in a neatly cut bang. She was average height, in good physical shape, and smiling. "We are the oldest tenants here," was the first thing she told me. Her slender husband rested with his legs crossed on an old and discolored brown chair. His rolled-up sweatpants exposed a long scar on his left leg. He sat solemnly, staring into the distance, the opposite direction from Hufang.

Hufang's home was small, but unlike the homes of other tenants in the Li Family Village it was tidy, and very clean. Its bare cement floor lacked the cigarette butts, food crumbs, and random objects found in other homes. The woks, bottles of oil and soy sauce, and everything else were placed neatly on two opposite counters in the area behind the green metal door at the entrance. A solid and unbroken wooden dining table stood in the "living room." A few plates of food lay on the table under thin nets at all times. Neighbors went in and out of their home throughout the day.

"Most of us are from Sichuan. We like the weather here. I used to live in the mountains back home. We were very poor. Life is a lot better here."

"My daughter is a factory worker."

"My son works in a shoe factory."

"My son makes glasses."

"We are all migrants here. Everybody is the same."

"They like my cooking. They always come in when they smell the food," Hufang told me.

"She is a great cook," said a neighbor.

"We never had this food before."

"'Let's go to the Jiangxi auntie's home,' I say, anytime I see guests in this house. 'There must be delicious food,' I tell everyone," another neighbor said.

Hufang was among the very rare tenants who learned Cantonese, the language of Shenzhen, and could communicate with the locals. She befriended, joked with, and confided in the old Li. The old Li visited her home frequently. He too liked her food. "He doesn't have anyone to talk to. Not many people know his language," Hufang told me.

A woman of about 40, from Hunan, was a regular visitor in Hufang's home.

"Do you like Chinese food?" the woman once asked me.

"Have you had smelly tofu?" she inquired later.

"Yes. But I have to confess I did not like the taste or the smell. The smell repulsed me." Laughter erupted.

"It smells bad, but tastes very good. You should try it in my province. Hunan is where smelly tofu originated. Ours is the very best," the woman said.

*   *   *

After ten years in the Li Family Village, Hufang and family still did not have a local *hukou*, or residence permit. This was an old practice from centuries ago, and the Communist Party made effective use of the system after it came to power in 1949. Through the registration of citizens by their places of birth, occupation, and residence, the *hukou* system allowed the authorities to keep millions of peasants tied to the land. It forced the peasants to stay in their villages, and helped finance China's early industrialization through mandatory low-priced procurement of agricultural products. A rural *hukou* holder was given a parcel of the publicly owned land, and denied access to the multitude of benefits the Communist Party granted to urban *hukou* holders. Travel to the city required written permission from multiple levels of local and regional governments. Migration to the city was impossible. Even buying food in the city was not possible without an urban *hukou*.

The economic reforms after Mao's death, and the need for massive population movement to feed the growing export-processing industries, made the *hukou* system an obstacle. Chaos ensued when peasants left their villages in massive numbers, and moved to the coastal areas to take advantage of

9   Hufang and her husband

the new job opportunities in the 1980s. In the early years of reforms local governments frequently jailed migrant workers, and forced them to return to their villages. Meanwhile, the sprawling private businesses demanded new workers.

A more pragmatic system emerged in time. The ban on population movement was lifted in practice without changing the *hukou* law. Hufang, her husband, and their neighbors in the Li Family Village were among the millions of migrants who moved around the country without a new *hukou*. They remained excluded from the subsidized healthcare, education, and other social benefits that provincial governments granted their local *hukou* holders. They were on their own.

Except for occasional difficulties, life proceeded without serious problems, even without a local *hukou*, for Hufang. Soon after they arrived in the Li Family Village, Hufang's husband started a small business selling fresh produce on a street corner not far from home. With help from their son, and the money from the business, the couple lived a life better than most neighbors did. Food was plentiful. Comfortable and content with their new environment, they almost forgot their life in the food-processing factory. Then, one early morning in the summer of 2006, everything changed abruptly. "It was the second time that tragedy hit us," Hufang recalled.

It was still dark. Hufang's husband had left the village to purchase his daily produce from the wholesale market. There were few passersby, and even fewer cars in the street. He was crossing a wide boulevard when he saw a big truck. It happened quickly, in the blink of an eye. He had no time to react. "I saw it come towards me. It was very fast. I could not run away." That is all he remembered when he opened his eyes. He was in a hospital room, motionless. A police patrol had found him unconscious and bleeding. He had broken bones, including ribs, and needed an operation immediately, the doctors said.

Without a local *hukou*, or private insurance, the couple had to pay for the operation and everything else from their own money, money that they did not have. "The hospital asked for 10,000 yuan up front before they even registered him," Hufang said. She was desperate. This would not have happened when Hufang's husband labored in the food-processing factory. The work unit was responsible for all the medical costs of its workers. Healthcare was automatic—it came with the job. "I never thought we would face anything like this," Hufang said.

There was no time to mourn the lost paradise, Hufang thought. Her husband needed an immediate operation. That was all that mattered. She had to raise the money by any means necessary. Pleading with the hospital was of no use. Hufang began calling everyone she knew—neighbors, close friends, acquaintances. "I could only rely on the people I knew," she said.

Friends called other friends, neighbors talked to neighbors. The word was out that the good auntie from Shanxi was in need of help. "Many people know us here," she told me. Hufang's son contacted everyone he had met in those years of laboring in Shenzhen. Before the day's end, "They were all in the hospital with money. Some people brought all their savings," Hufang said. By the time Hufang's husband left the hospital for the Li Family Village, his operation and hospitalization costs had reached 40,000 yuan. "We owe a lot of money. My son is paying them back slowly."

With her husband bedridden for a year, Hufang stayed home and took care of her man. "His leg swelled bigger than his body. He couldn't move at all," Hufang told me. He was in the final stages of his recovery when we met in the Li Family Village. "He limps now, and cannot do much. The doctor advised him to be careful while walking or doing other things. He broke so many bones. It takes time to fully recover. He could break them again if he makes a wrong move," Hufang said.

Disabled, and without pension or any other form of support from the government, Hufang's husband relied on help from his son to survive. Without him, the couple "would have been begging on the street." Her husband was in debt, without work, and unable to walk much, or do any serious task. "We have to wait until he gets better. We have no other option. I have to stay home with him. We are both too old for anyone to hire us," Hufang would tell me. "He is getting better. We just have to wait." And they waited.

The husband's conditions improved slowly. He regained his strength, walked more every day, until he was ready to start afresh. It took two years for him to fully recover from the devastating accident, but Hufang and her husband were back in business in the summer of 2009. This was, however, a different business, and did not require much moving around. The former factory workers were now the food vendors of the Li Family Village.

*   *   *

It was August 2009, and I had gone to visit friends in the Li Family Village when I saw Hufang and her husband push a vending cart full of cooked pig feet, chicken, ribs, and jars of pickled vegetables, scallions, cucumbers, and wild onions. Shirtless, in navy blue sweatpants, and as skinny as the first time we met, Hufang's husband greeted me with a warm handshake. Clad in a black T-shirt and a blue apron with a red teddy bear, Hufang approached me with a big smile. "Where have you been? Did you go home? We missed you," Hufang said. I had not seen the husband and wife for some time. "We just finished cooking for today," she said. I helped push the cart and set up shop by the main gate of the Li Family Village.

Soon, neighbors arrived, haggling, joking, and buying the auntie's delicious food. A skinny middle-aged woman brought two white plastic stools. "Your bag must be heavy. Put it on the stool," she said, taking my knapsack from me. "Sit here," said Hufang. Her front gold-plated teeth gleaming, a short woman in her fifties greeted me and offered me a can of Coke she had bought from a nearby store. "I remember you. Welcome back," she said. A skeleton of a man gave me a cigarette. In no time, a half-dozen people had gathered around Hufang's food cart. Hufang's husband shuttled back and forth. Each time, he brought more food, utensils, and other accessories from the house. Hufang served customers and chopped more vegetables. "Before, everyone came to our home, now they come here. We are never alone," she said, laughing.

*   *   *

Hufang rarely visited Jiangxi, not even during the Spring Festival, when most migrants, rich or poor, returned home to be with their families. After years of separation, and the hardships they had experienced, the couple felt at home in the Li Family Village. The love and assistance they received after the husband's accident had strengthened the bond between them and the tenants of the village. They felt at home. "Ten years is a long time," Hufang would say.

Hufang's son had been pleading with them to move to an apartment in Dongguan, a popular factory town near Shenzhen. He wished to be closer to his young boy, and to provide a better life for his parents. Hufang would not have it. "We are used to it here now. We like our neighbors. They are very good to us." But they knew that, sooner or later, they would have to say farewell to their good friends, pack their meager belongings, and return to Jiangxi, a place that had lost much of its significance to them by now.

We were sitting around the dining table one afternoon. Hufang's grandson and a few of his friends ran in and out of the house. Leaning forward, her elbow on the table, her hand under her chin, Hufang said, "He is very smart. All his teachers like him, but we have to take him back."

Hufang and her husband did not have much education. Not having finished middle school, their son was trapped doing dead-end jobs. The boy was different. He was a good student, and had "a bright future." Hufang dreamed of seeing her grandson at university someday. "Yes, that's my dream," she would declare. She could not see her dream realized if the family stayed in Shenzhen. Hufang had no illusions. "We cannot afford to send him to high school here. It is too expensive without a *hukou*," she explained. Not having a local *hukou* was going to haunt the family for ever.

Hukou was hereditary. Despite being born in Guangdong Province, the ten-year-old grandson could not get a local *hukou*, because his father did not have one. He would remain a second-class citizen, excluded from many advantages the local kids enjoyed, as long as he remained in Guangdong. That did not seem to be a problem when he was younger. "He is innocent," Hufang said. "So smart," she said, patting the boy on the head and playing with his hair.

Nearly everyone in Longgang was from another part of China. Hufang's grandson was unaware of his grandmother's worries. "He is just a kid. He has no idea." His life proceeded without complications. Hufang, however, was thinking about the boy's future. And that was a different story altogether.

The first nine years of schooling in China remained compulsory and free, everything paid for by local governments. However, city and provincial governments resented having to pay for the education of the children of their migrant workers. They received no support from the central government. The children of the migrants were a drain on already tight resources. No one wanted them. The presidents and teachers of public schools did not welcome children of migrant workers.

Parents with local *hukou* saw the migrant workers as an intrusion of rural China, the poor and uncultured China, into their lives. Some felt embarrassed by them. Others were hostile. Few wished to send their children to school with the children of migrant workers. Migrant children were unwashed, dressed shabbily, and had bad habits and social norms the new Chinese middle class despised.

Public schools often demanded a mountain of certificates, legal papers, and documentation in the hope of pushing away and denying entry to the children of migrants. Hufang's son prepared all the required papers and registered his boy in a school near the Li Family Village. Tuition was free. However, there were other fees that the school demanded frequently. Hufang's son bought the boy's books, and paid random fees that surfaced throughout the year. "He always comes home with a new request to buy this or that. There is no end to it. My son pays for everything. I don't know exactly how much he pays, but I know he always complains," she said.

Many boys and girls in the Li Family Village could not even attend public school. Unable to obtain the necessary documents, their parents registered them in special migrant schools, and paid more for tuition and fees for a much worse education. Hufang's grandson was lucky among his friends, and things were manageable for now. However, Hufang could not stop worrying about the boy's future.

It was not possible to send the boy to high school in Shenzhen. There was no help for pupils without the local *hukou, and* Hufang's son was responsible for tuition and the other fees. He could not afford this, especially after his father's accident. "We still owe money to friends. We cannot send him to high school here. My son doesn't have that kind of money," Hufang said. High schools were a lot more expensive.

Hufang's grandson was bound to be a low-skilled migrant worker, following the path of his extended family, if he remained in Longgang. Playing with his friends, enjoying himself, he was unaware of his bleak prospects. "We have to plan for his future now," Hufang said.

Young, and unaware of these prejudices, the boy was soon to be a victim of circumstances beyond his control. He was born to a poor migrant family. He could not change that. "We need to do something," Hufang said.

Now older, Hufang's grandson was more demanding. Unaware of the limitations of his family, he demanded a better bicycle, new clothes, and even a computer. "Every day, for a whole year, he kept asking for a computer. Children want everything these days," Hufang said. The boy's wish was realized when his father visited with a used desktop computer on his last birthday. "I have never seen him so happy."

For most of his life, the boy had lived in the Li Family Village. He had many friends, and was unaware of the difficulties of his grandparents, and the hard choices before the family. "He is just a boy, doing his thing. He is a good boy," Hufang would say. Soon, however, a new life, a strange place, and strange people would be awaiting him. "He doesn't know anybody there. We have lost all our connections. We don't even know what to do there."

The food business had turned around the family's finances, but the income covered only their daily expenses. "How can we save? We have a lot of competition." Out of work, other neighbors had also started food-vending businesses. All sold similar items not far from the Li Family Village. Hufang's only advantage was her love of cooking, and her special touch. That brought her loyal customers, but far from enough.

Without any savings, and with a large debt left for their son to pay, Hufang and her husband would be leaving the Li Family Village and heading to Shanxi empty-handed. They would return home with less money than when they had said goodbye to friends and family. Many had come back with savings, bought a home, and started a business. Hufang would return with her clothes and a few old belongings. She was embarrassed.

"We are still here with my grandson and my friends. My husband is working again and we can pay for ourselves. I will worry about the problems of the future when the time comes," she said the last time I ran into her by the food cart. A half-dozen neighbors had surrounded her cart. Hufang was smiling.

GRANDPA

His neighbours called him Grandpa—I never asked his real name. The first time I met Grandpa was outside the ancestral home in the Li Family Village. The deep wrinkles carved into his rough, leathery skin told of many years of hard work under the sun. His bushy eyebrows protruded above a pair of radiant eyes. He was bold, and his face was unshaven. An old wound from many years back had left a long scar on his right leg. He was clad in a stained, unbuttoned navy blue shirt. A thin rope kept his knee-length light brown shorts from falling down. His fly was open. His brown plastic slippers revealed his crooked toes and his long, dirty toenails.

10   Grandpa

A restless boy sat on the ground beside him and played with an old stroller with a rusty handle and a discolored navy-blue canvas seat covered with stained clear plastic. Two baby bottles, each half full of water and kept inside dirty plastic bags, hung from the stroller handle. The old man reached out to the stroller tray and slowly grabbed a piece of half-chewed steamed bread. Snatching it from his hand, the boy took a small bite and threw the bread on the ground. The old man burst out laughing. He gently patted the boy, picked up the bread, and returned it to the tray.

The little boy jumped on the old man's lap. He patted the boy's head with gentle strokes, and made funny sounds. The boy laughed hysterically and the old man made even stranger sounds. Soon the boy was restless and no longer amused; loud cries replaced the laughter. The old man took out a handkerchief and dried the sweat off his muscular face. He reached for a small black velvet bag tied to the stroller, untied the bag, and took out a small pipe with a brass bowl. His long fingers delved into the bag and he took out a wad of tobacco and filled the bowl. He tied the bag, placed it in the basket under the stroller, lit the pipe, and took three puffs in a row. He paused for a few seconds and watched the boy play with the stroller's front wheels. The old man knocked the brass bowl against the wall and disposed of the burnt tobacco. He reached for the bag, untied it, and returned the pipe to its safe place inside. The boy snatched the bag away with a sudden move. He took out the pipe, waved it a few times, and hit the old man's wrinkled face. The old man patted the boy on his head.

At that point I walked towards him, showed him my camera, and asked permission to photograph him and the child. He smiled. Waving his hand, he gestured his approval while he comforted the child. I offered him a cigarette. He accepted. I played with the child, and we exchanged a few random words.

"All my life, I farmed grain, peanuts, corn, and cotton. These are the main crops in the north," he said.

"Can we meet again? Where would I find you?" I asked before I left for the Beautiful Rose Garden.

"I would like to invite you to have lunch with us if you don't mind the food in my house. Southern people eat a lot more rice; northern people eat a lot of noodles and steamed bread," he said.

We said goodbye.

*   *   *

In the beginning, I approached Grandpa like others I met in China. I would make appointments to see him.

"See you tomorrow at 11 o'clock by KFC," I would say, and wait for him sometimes for more than half an hour then leave without a meeting.

"I'll see you at 3 o'clock after your afternoon nap." The same. I would wait, and he would not show up.

Had I disrespected Grandpa, I would wonder. I became self-conscious and nervous, and he continued to stand me up. Grandpa had an old watch wrapped in a dirty blue handkerchief. I had seen him untie the kerchief and carefully look at the watch to make sure he was not late for the daily ritual of making the fire and boiling water for dinner.

Every afternoon at 5:30, and no matter where he was, Grandpa would return home. He would leave the boy with his mother at the vegetable stand outside the gate of the Li Family Village, and take pieces of wood—broken furniture, doors, and logs from a pile against the wall by his house—to a makeshift stove his family had built across the house against the wall in the narrow alleyway. With a turtle-like walk, he would fetch an old, dented aluminum pot from the house and place it on the stove. Outside the house, leaning against the wall, there were five plastic buckets filled with water at all times. The water came from a well Grandpa's nephew had dug in one of the rooms in the house. In repeated trips back and forth between the stove and the buckets, Grandpa would fill up the pot with water. He would start the fire and wait for the water to boil. Meanwhile, he would bring empty hot-water flasks from the kitchen, and line them up on the ground by the stove. He would later fill the flasks with hot water, one at a time, slowly. Once they were all filled, Grandpa would bring them inside the house and put them on a cluttered counter in the kitchen. Grandpa went through this routine every day. He had a perfect system. Nothing could change that. Why was he not the same with me?

After days of agonizing and feeling self-conscious, I finally found my answer. Grandpa had a routine he would follow every day. His routine would begin after he had his breakfast with the entire family. After everyone had left home to hustle for the day's money, Grandpa would put the little boy in the old stroller and leave the village for a walk around the Longgang World Trade Center. There were two areas he would visit alternately, each within a few minutes' walk from the Li Family Village. A covered corridor cutting through the Longgang World Trade Center was his favorite spot on very hot days. He would sit on a bench, watch passersby, play with the child, doze off, and kill time before returning to the village at around noon.

A nice hour-long nap followed lunch every day. Fresh and energized, he would take the child for the second stroll, this time to the park, under the patches of shade so avidly fought for by other migrants fleeing the heat in their rooms. The afternoon outing would end at half past five, when the old farmer returned home for his next duty.

At times, depending on random events, and his mood of course, Grandpa would alter his route. He would go to the park in the morning and to the Longgang World Trade Center in the afternoon. On occasion, he would take a longer walk and watch people from a bench on the sidewalk not too far from KFC.

Grandpa did not know the world of appointments, scheduled meetings, and all that I was accustomed to. His daily routine—the time to wake up, eating, napping, and everything else—were regulated by nature. He had been a farmer before he came to Shenzhen, and continued to live like a farmer in one of China's most modern and industrial cities. Nevertheless, he was always happy to see me. Each time, he would invite me to lunch in his house, or a cup of tea, or a beer. He did not know he had stood me up.

"I was looking for you. I was hoping to see you. I miss you," he would say after not showing up to what I thought was a confirmed appointment.

As time passed, I would drop by without an appointment. Greeting the men and women in the village, I would go straight to Grandpa's house.

"He is out with the boy," a neighbor would say at times, and I would venture out, looking for him in all the likely places. Meeting up, we would embrace and talk until Grandpa's next chore of the day.

* * *

I learned Grandpa's life story in pieces and randomly. An interview with Grandpa was not possible. He drifted, moved between subjects, told jokes, and talked about what interested *him* the most: the farm, and Chinese history.

"There are 56 nationalities in China. Most minorities live in the south," he said one day, in the middle of lecturing me about Chinese ancient history.

"China has 5000 years of history, and 3000 years of written history," he said. "Did you know that China had 16 dynasties?" He did not wait for my answer. "Let me tell you about the dynasties," he said.

"Qing Shihuang was the first emperor who unified China. After the establishment of the Qing dynasty, slavery turned to feudalism," he paused. "Sun Yat-sen started a revolution against the Qing Dynasty. In Chiang Kai Shek's time land was privately owned. You suffered from poverty and starvation if you didn't own much land. There was a big gap between the rich and the poor," he said and paused again. It was time to smoke. His pipe-lighting routine followed. Three puffs, he emptied the bowl, put the pipe away, and continued his lessons in Chinese history.

"The Communist Revolution abolished private property in land. Land became public property. The quality of life is the best now in China, better than all earlier dynasties. People eat better everywhere."

Land and the ability to eat were always grandpa's main concerns in life. He had spent all his life working long hours on a small piece of land. He was poor, but he had land that could not be taken away. He slept with peace of mind. He knew that, despite all natural disasters and political changes, the land would remain his. He owed that to the Communist Revolution, he told me.

"The difference between socialism and capitalism is the ownership of land," he said one day by KFC. "Our land is state owned, while in capitalism it is privately owned. In capitalist countries such as America, those big capitalists own so much land. Under socialism everyone gets an equal piece of land. You couldn't get too much, but also, you wouldn't lose your land no matter what happened."

"Which system is better?" I asked.

"Of course socialism is better, my son. In capitalist countries the weak people may lose their land, suffer hunger and poverty, and become beggars. But in socialist countries, no matter how weak you are, you will have your land. You could not become a beggar under socialism." An old beggar stopped and asked for money. Grandpa continued his history lessons.

* * *

Grandpa was illiterate, but he spoke with the authority of a learned man when he lectured about war and peace, revolution, and world geography.

"Where did you learn all of this?" I asked one day.

"Hah, where did I learn this? I tell you. I didn't go to school. No, my son. Do you know anything about our traditional Chinese opera?"

"I am fond of the opera," he said. "I learned everything from the opera."

The opera told stories of dynasties, and the battles between loyal ministers and the traitor. "You could tell the characters apart by their makeup, masks, and costumes," he said. A red mask signified a positive character, black highlighted impartiality and fairness, and yellow slyness and treachery, Grandpa told me. He was excited. He would talk, pause, laugh for no apparent reason, and continue his lecture. The opera had taught him about the world. It had filled his free time with music and entertainment in his remote and impoverished village. Grandpa was proud of the opera in his province.

"We have one of the best and most popular operas in China. Opera in the south of China is not as good as in the north. Their tunes are too simple and monotonous," he said.

When Grandpa was young, the larger and more prosperous villages had their own stage and opera troupe. Grandpa's village had a small stage. Traveling opera troupes passed through the village, performed for the public at the village circle, and moved on to the next village. Everyone, old and young, even children, attended the show. The opera troupe brought excitement and joy to the village. Even poverty did not matter when the troupe was in the village. Hungry or with full bellies, all eagerly awaited show time, Grandpa recalled. The opera was the highlight of everyone's life.

"Who invented the airplane?" he said in the middle of his opera stories. "They were two American brothers, right?" I nodded, and he returned to the opera.

Actors were picked up from different villages along the way. It was not easy to find talented performers who could both act and sing. Some were good singers, others fine actors. Only a few were good at both, and could perform well and become famous, he told me. "Most ordinary people can sing a little, but only a few can be opera stars."

Occasionally, the traveling troupes visited Grandpa's village, looking for apprentices, talented children who would receive training from masters. Despite his longing to be in the opera, Grandpa stayed away from the recruiters. "Maybe I could have learned to act, but I was not a singer," he said. Out of every 30 apprentices, maybe one or two succeeded and became performers, the old man recalled. He had no chance, he believed.

* * *

A farmer from Henan Province in northern China, Grandpa left his farm two years before our meeting, took the train south, and joined his nephew and his extended family in the Li Family Village. He lived in a house on the last row of the village. Four generations of people shared the home: Grandpa's nephew and his wife, their son and daughter-in-law and their two children, and a "guest," an 18-year-old construction worker. Grandpa's home was the first built in the village. It was larger than most of the others. While other houses were partitioned and rented to multiple families after the original Li family moved out, Grandpa's house remained undivided. A 100-year-old, high green wooden door was the house's landmark. The door was never locked. It was hardly ever closed in daytime. Thick and dented, its paint fading, its handle aged and tired, the door had witnessed the many changes the village and its residents had endured in war, revolution, and turmoil.

Inside, behind the door, Grandpa's house was a chaotic nest. Its bare cement floor was stained, broken, and uneven. Dirty rags, plastic buckets, toy cars, and large baskets and plastic bags full of onions, lettuce, garlic, potatoes, and large melons were piled in one corner. Rats roamed around freely. They moved between bags of produce, ran back and forth, and nibbled on everything in the way.

The boy rolled on the cement floor, ran around, urinated, and defecated when nature called. Cleaning up the mess was Grandpa's job. Moving slowly, he would take a shovel full of burned coal and dirt from a bucket outside the house, dump the coal on the excrement, mix it, and take it out with the shovel. He would rip pages from an old magazine, pick up the boy with affection and a big smile, and wipe his behind. All done, the boy would resume his activities, playing with the old man's pipe or kitchen utensils on the same spot. The rats minded their own business.

When home, and not sleeping, the old man sat on a low stool by the door inside the house in what was the kitchen, dining room, and a place for entertaining visitors. All cooking was done on the stove outside to "save gas money." Bags of herbs were nailed to a dirty wall with chipping plaster and large and small holes. A dozen hot-water flasks, five or six woks, a jar full of chopsticks, bottles of sesame oil, cooking oil, and soy sauce, and a few half eaten corncobs sat on two wooden counters. Large flies covered the corncobs.

This was a family of chain-smokers. Smoking continued during the meals, and cigarette butts were dropped on the floor. Spitting on the floor was common. Meals were served on a low coffee table made from a salvaged door. The family and guests sat on plastic stools, or wooden stools made from whatever Grandpa's nephew could scavenge from construction sites.

The house had very high ceilings. A one-story home originally, it now had a second floor, a bunk of a sort that was made of plywood and enclosed by brown-painted wood and cardboard. A wooden stairway connected the room to the bunk, where the 25-year-old son of Grandpa's nephew, his wife, and his two children slept at night. Grandpa slept on a sheet of plywood, partly closed off by empty rice sacks. Rags, pants, shirts, and T-shirts hung on ropes, or lay on the old man's bed.

A nine-inch black-and-white television sat on a shelf by the old man's bed. "That's where I watch opera," he said, showing me DVDs of Chinese opera, and inviting me to an evening of opera, beer, and cigarettes.

The old man's house never saw the sun. It had no windows, and was dark day and night. The air inside the house was heavy and stagnant. It smelled of tired dampness, cigarette smoke, and the smoke from the fire outside.

THE COMMUNISTS BURIED THEIR SOLDIERS

Grandpa was born to a family of poor farmers in 1933. His father owned one *mu* (one-sixth of an acre) of land. He was a land-poor peasant. Counting himself, he had six mouths to feed, and the land was hardly enough to produce enough food to fill the stomachs of a family of four. Life was not easy for a farming family in those days, Grandpa recalled years later. There were many worries. Food, any food at all, was Grandpa's family's overriding concern. "We were hungry most of the time," the old man told me.

He grew up with droughts, floods, disease, and unending wars. There was no escape. He was four years old when his sister died of an unknown disease. By then, a bloody war, the second Sino-Japanese War, was ravaging the country.

Sitting on the stool in his usual spot by the green door of the house, the old man told me what he had learned about those years of war from his elders, and from the opera. He repeated the official narrative of the war and peace, word by word. The opera had taught him well. "This is a lesson in history, my son," he told me as he got up to look for a lighter. He filled his pipe, returned to the stool, lit the pipe, and said, "China was a dynasty until 1911."

In 1911, the republican forces led by Sun Yat-sen defeated the Qing Dynasty, China's last dynasty. A new chapter in Chinese history started. China became a republic. The young republic, however, was too weak to last. Soon after its victory, the new government faltered. "Warlords snatched different parts of the country," Grandpa orated, his hands moving around theatrically. China splintered. Sun Yat-sen retreated to Guangzhou, the biggest city in Canton, an hour's train ride from the Li Family Village. Sun Yat-sen led the Kuomintang, the National People's Party, and its army, joined the southern warlords and began the long campaign to unify China under one government.

Meanwhile, young Chinese who had gone abroad to study were returning home armed with Western ideas of liberalism and social justice. They called for the destruction of traditional cultures and values and the creation of a new China based on Western ideas. Some championed Western liberalism, and others called for socialism. They wrote essays, issued political pamphlets, and energized a new generation of radical youth. Among them were the young Mao Zedong and a small band of radicals who founded the Communist Party of China at a secret meeting in Shanghai in 1921. "There were only a hundred of them," said Grandpa. Twenty-eight years later, the communists were ruling this vast country, Grandpa said with pride.

Like the Kuomintang, the communists dreamed of a unified China under a central government. Young and idealistic, the communists sought to follow the example of the Soviet Union, then the only country in the world proclaiming itself socialist. They dreamed of a China without landlordism, a new China that would bring social justice to the country's vast peasantry, and give them land and freedom. The Soviet Union, however, had a different plan of action. This was the time to put aside the battle for social justice, and focus only on ridding China of the warlords and foreign influence, the Soviet Union told Mao and his comrades. Under pressure from Moscow, the young communists formed an alliance with the Kuomintang, "the party of landlords and the rich," said Grandpa. They fought to reunite China. At that time, the communists numbered 300, the Kuomintang 150,000.

These were times of quick changes in China. Three years after the alliance, Sun Yat-sen died of cancer. Chiang Kai Shek, a military commander, rose to the leadership of the Kuomintang. Grandpa disliked Chiang Kai Shek. I have "nothing good to say about him." With Chiang Kai Shek as its leader, the alliance began its campaign to take over Beijing and the northern provinces from the warlords. Meanwhile, the country was slowly radicalizing. Monarchy was gone, new ideas were infiltrating China, and hunger for change had become an epidemic.

There were widespread strikes and student protests. Millions of poor peasants were joining peasant associates in Guangzhou, demanding land redistribution and an end to the landlordism that had remained untouched despite the fall of the Qing Dynasty. As time passed, the communists grew stronger, gaining supporters among workers, peasants, and students, and recruiting new members. Radical and communist-led workers' associations and student groups grew everywhere, particularly in Shanghai. And it is there that the alliance faced its death.

The cooperation between the nationalists and the communists ended when Chiang Kai Shek ordered the massacre of the communist workers and activists. The Kuomintangs forces annihilated student organizations in Shanghai and other places under party control. In a reign of terror that lasted until 1930, thousands of workers, students, and communist sympathizers were killed. Brought to near extinction, the Communist Party retreated and began recruiting for a powerful army, the People's Liberation Army (PLA). Victory was not possible without military might, they now believed.

*   *   *

When we met the next morning outside KFC, Grandpa had all but forgotten about his earlier lectures in Chinese history. He spoke of random things—food, Western inventions, the weather in the north—anything but war and revolution. "Tell me about the Japanese invaders," I said. I had learned how to get the old man going. Talking about the "Japanese invaders" was a favorite pastime of Grandpa's. From the opera he had learned to distrust the Japanese, even more than he distrusted the Kuomintang and the nationalists.

The kid was asleep in the old stroller. It was hot and sunny. The sidewalk was busy with young migrants killing time, and old men and women tending to their grandchildren. A couple of young men stood near us and listened to Grandpa's war stories. Bored with the tales they knew nothing about, they left and gave their place to other curious bystanders. Grandpa had slowly moved into his storytelling mode. For the next couple of hours, he would tell the tale of the second alliance between the Kuomintang and the Communist Party.

The Japanese had fought China during the Qing Dynasty. Years later, they waged a new war. The conflict began as localized and small confrontations in

1931. It became a full-scale war in 1937. The Japanese army took over and occupied large areas controlled by the Kuomintang. "The Japanese invaders took three provinces in the north before they invaded the central plains," said Grandpa.

Desperate to regain the lost areas, for a second time, Chiang Kai Shek agreed to an alliance with the Communist Party. The communists had reorganized and turned themselves into a formidable political and military force, with strong roots among the peasants and the intellectuals. Grandpa was smiling. The impoverished and poorly armed communist PLA had become an army of national liberation and social justice. It was mushrooming, growing by the day.

The newly formed united front needed new blood to fight the Japanese. The Kuomintang and the Communist Party were separately recruiting soldiers where they were stronger and had more influence. In 1938, the Kuomintang forces came to Grandpa's village. "They came to my home and asked for my oldest brother," Grandpa said. Grandpa's brother was 18, the fighting age.

"At that time, you could get a replacement if you gave 6000 pounds of wheat to somebody else who was even poorer than you," Grandpa recalled. Grandpa's father sold one of the two small houses they had built on the land. He paid off another farmer, and saved his son from the war. "Unfortunately, a year later, my brother faced another recruitment drive. This time we couldn't sell our house. This was the only place we had left. We couldn't sell our land either. We would have had no food to eat."

Grandpa's brother finally joined the war against Japan. A year later, while he was in Shanxi Province, he deserted. Unable to return home for fear of persecution—deserters were executed, Grandpa told me—he became a vagabond, working in faraway villages and for other landlords until "Chairman Mao founded the New China in 1949." The brother returned home after the victory of the revolution. He was a hero because he had deserted the nationalist army.

The communist victory came after a bloody war with the Kuomintang forces. It began with the defeat of the Japanese in 1945. When the Japanese finally left China and surrendered to the allied forces, the Communist Party was in practical control of a large part of the country. Civil war was inevitable. "The war lasted almost five years. This was called the civil war," Grandpa said, opening the bag of tobacco, filling the pipe, and lighting up. "Chairman Mao finally defeated the Kuomintang in 1949, and Chiang Kai Shek fled to Taiwan with his tail between his legs," he laughed loudly.

*   *   *

Grandpa became a communist supporter during the civil war. He remained a believer. He had seen nationalist and communist soldiers going through the village, recruiting, and returning for food. He was young, not soldier material. "The Kuomintang wouldn't bury the bodies of their dead soldiers. They just left them to rot. But the communists not only buried their dead, they took care of the dead soldiers' parents for the rest of their lives." The communists treated their soldiers and their officers equally. There were no differences between them. "Only in conferences the officials gave speeches as great leaders. That was the only difference."

As the civil war continued, many deserted the Kuomintang army and joined the People's Liberation Army. There were female soldiers in the communist army, and none in the Kuomintang's, he said. "Did you know that, in those days, the poor families gave their four- or five-year-old girls to other poor families as child brides? Child brides were badly treated if the new family did not have enough food." Many of the child brides escaped and joined the PLA during the war of liberation, Grandpa said. "They actually helped the communists a lot."

After the civil war, the communist soldiers spread around the country, settling down in provinces where they had previously fought. Some PLA soldiers remained in Grandpa's village. He grew to like them, and to respect them for their courage and honesty. "They did not cheat ordinary people," he said. "In the old days, we called each other comrades." Grandpa drifted again. He asked if I knew what comrade meant. "I will tell you. To call someone a comrade means you are very close to each other. It means you have the same ideals, and belong to the same family of people," he said. "How do you say comrade in English? I know how to say it in Russian." During feudal times, people called each other "brother," Grandpa said. "Every dynasty has its own code. We always follow our masters, the kings," he laughed.

*   *   *

Growing up, there were starving people all around Grandpa. War and the old property system had brought widespread destitution to millions across China. "We were very poor in Chiang Kai Shek's time. These were hard times for most peasants. We had little food. Many poor peasants became beggars. They had no choice."

Waging a war to unify China under the nationalist banner, Chiang Kai Shek allied himself with landlords and other propertied classes. Emboldened by Chiang Kai Shek's support, landlords increased pressure on their peasants, squeezing out of them an even higher portion of their output. Meanwhile, promising land and food to the poor peasants, the communists were winning the hearts and souls of millions of land-poor and landless villagers across the country.

"Land was privately owned when I was young. Some landlords owned 20, even 40 thousand acres. Most people owned nothing. There were two landlords in my village, and most young peasants had to work for them. They received only 900 pounds of wheat as payment for a year. You would have got much less, let's say 500 pounds, if you were not very strong." Life was hard, and people wore the same clothes for years, Grandpa remembered. "Oh, let me tell you." He lit the brass pipe. "Getting a wife was very difficult." Many peasants did not marry because they could not afford it. "That's why China's population was small in those days."

Landlessness, poverty, and abuse by large landowners brought millions of Chinese to the communist camp during the war of liberation and the civil war. The communists promised comprehensive land reform. Even during its decisive war with the Kuomintang, the Communist Party began land distribution in liberated areas in northeastern and northwestern China. Following an elaborate and detailed system, peasants and landowners were classified according to the amount of land they owned. By the end of 1952, the communists had distributed some 120 million acres of farmland between 300 million formerly landless or land-poor peasants. After centuries of bondage, the peasants saw their dream realized. They became owners of their own land.

Classified as land-poor, Grandpa's family was among those who benefited from this agrarian reform. In 1951, the family received four additional *mu* of land, one of which was infertile, Grandpa recalled. Life improved for the family. Grandpa's father could not control his joy, he remembered. "We had more food," he said, recalling the jubilance his family and many other farmers felt after the land reform. This revolution was for peasants like Grandpa and his family, and land reform was the first repayment for their sacrifices. One of the fundamental promises of the revolution was fulfilled. Grandpa's family achieved *fanshen*: they "beat the landlords, local tyrants, and the evil gentry," he told me all those decades later. He remained grateful to the communists.

THE GREAT FAMINE

The tenants of the Li Family Village called him Grandpa, but the 75-year-old farmer had never had a child, let alone a grandchild. I never saw him with an older woman, one around his age. His wife must have died, I assumed.

"Oh, she left me a long time ago," he told me one afternoon outside the Longgang World Trade Center. "There are five oceans in the world," he continued in his usual abrupt way, and asked if America had many lakes and mountains.

"America is a capitalist country. China is socialist," he declared.

He opened his small tobacco bag and began filling the pipe. I offered him a cigarette.

"Oh, these must be expensive. You save them, my son. American cigarettes are very good," he said. "I have been smoking for more than 50 years. I don't know how to make wine, but I like to drink," he laughed. "Do you like *bijou*?" he asked. "My father used to make wine when I was young."

"When did your wife leave you?" I interrupted.

The child was restless and demanding Grandpa's attention. "He needs food," said Grandpa, and packed to leave. "I'll look for you in the park later," I said. Waving and pushing the stroller, he left for the Li Family Village.

He looked fresh when we met in the park later that afternoon. His head and face were shaven. He wore a clean blue shirt, and blue shorts too big for him. His bushy eyebrows were more striking than ever, his cheekbones and wrinkles more pronounced. Grandpa looked stronger, more masculine.

"You look young and handsome," I told the old man. He laughed.

Grandpa took the child out of the stroller, sat on the lawn, and slowly filled his pipe with tobacco. The afternoon was hot and humid, and the air stagnant. Nothing moved. A few fatigued bodies lay under the trees. Grandpa gently removed a checkered blue kerchief from his shorts pocket and wiped the sweat off his forehead and neck. I asked him about his wife.

"Why did your wife leave you?"

"Those were hard times, my son," he said.

*   *   *

He was 25 and had been married for five years with no children when Mao and the Communist Party began the new experiment that would change Grandpa's life once for all. "That was 1958," he recalled. Grandpa left home a few months before disaster struck his village. He was dispatched to the coalmines of the dusty and dry Inner Mongolia. Grandpa's family had had a good harvest the year earlier, and with that, he was sure of his wife's wellbeing. She had adequate food. The young man left the village without worries.

Historians have debated the nature and the consequences of the turbulent years that began in 1958 and ended two years later after a disastrous famine that took the lives of millions. We may never know the exact number of people who perished in this period. Grandpa, however, knows *his* losses and the changes in his life. Some half-century later, talking to a foreigner, he remembered.

By 1958, the year of the inauguration of the Great Leap Forward, Chinese leaders were facing serious economic problems in cities and the rural areas. Having inherited a backward economy from the earlier regimes, the new leaders had to deal with the overwhelming problems of job creation, feeding the people, and managing China's vast natural and human landscape. Mao and his close allies were scrambling to come up with an industrialization model that fed, clothed, and housed the growing population of this diverse and impoverished country. It was a daunting task.

The Soviet model of industrialization that China had used earlier had failed on all fronts. Millions of desperate peasants had left their villages in the hope of finding jobs in factories, and enjoying all the welfare benefits granted to urban dwellers. The strict implementation of population movement slowed rural–urban migration. Nevertheless, people found a way to move around. The problem persisted. The population of cities grew from 57,000,000 in 1949 to 100,000,000 in 1957.

By then, Mao had become disillusioned with the Soviet industrialization model of large capital-intensive plants in major urban centers. He did not see the model as suitable for China's growing population and its vast rural area, disconnected from the rest of the country. What China needed was a decentralized, small-scale, and labor-intensive industrialization that would bring the fruits of modern technology to rural areas, he thought.

In 1958, the Communist Party began experimenting with homegrown labor-intensive technologies in rural areas. In addition to the large steel plants now working full force in the northwestern regions of the country, they promoted the development of small-scale light industries across the country. China entered its Great Leap Forward.

Beijing instructed villages to produce their own steel in small backyard furnaces, make light consumer manufactures, and achieve relative industrial self-sufficiency. The new strategy was to spearhead the creation of local crop-processing industries and machine and fertilizer plants, and increase agricultural output. It would bring industrialization to agriculture and make the most efficient use of the unlimited supply of labor in the rural areas, Mao believed.

The diffusion of industry to the rural areas would also lead to the decentralization of economic life, and help reduce the power of the new urban bureaucracy sheltered now in the Chinese Communist Party, a bureaucracy that Mao saw as fatal to the project of building an egalitarian socialist country. The Great Leap Forward was to empower the rural masses, increase their voice in their everyday life, and expedite China's journey to communism. The promotion of light agricultural industries, it was hoped, would increase agricultural productivity. The production of light and inexpensive consumer goods for peasants' consumption was to increase their motivation to raise output and deliver the surplus needed to fuel the expanding iron, machine-building, and other big industries elsewhere in the country. Nothing would stop China's march forward, Mao believed.

The Great Leap Forward was the product of Mao's vision of building communism in a backward country. The victory over the Kuomintang forces, and the expropriation of land from large landowners, were China's first steps on the long road to communism. By the mid-1950s, land reform had eased rural poverty, but China remained poor. Economic despair cast doubt on China's future.

Organized as large State-Owned Enterprises, mines, mills, and factories provided generous housing, education, healthcare, and the promise of a secure retirement for their employees. China's villages remained backward, and life was insecure. Mao was determined to change this.

Through a series of directives from Beijing, in nearly two years, China's agriculture changed from scattered and small privately owned units to agricultural collectives, each including the land, farm animals, and tools and machines of some 246 households, or around 1200 people on average. By spring 1957, all China's rural households had become members of some 750,000 collective farms. Private property in land ceased to exist, and peasants were rewarded on the basis of their work and contribution to their collective's output after the arbitrary deductions for capital improvement and state procurement. And that was only the beginning.

What came next was the building of rural communes across China. Beijing declared the communes to be the ultimate organizational form for the transition to communism, and the agricultural collectives were turned into communes. By the end of 1958, China's rural population was organized in some 24,000 people's communes, each with 5000 households, and 30,000 people on average. Communes were imagined as autonomous and relatively self-sufficient units that organized and combined economics, politics, education, healthcare, entertainments, and culture, and all aspects of their members' social lives. Peasants, workers, merchants, students—all were to be organized as commune members. The utopia that Mao had envisioned was, at last, created in China. The paradise, however, proved to be hell on earth.

The communes were administered and controlled by local party cadres who focused on extracting the highest surplus from the peasants. More surplus output led to favors from higher-up party officials. The Communist Party cadres robbed the peasants and rural workers of their promised self-rule. Far worse, they paved the way for the tragic consequences of the Great Leap Forward.

Arbitrary work assignment by the cadres, mismanagement, and lack of expertise in running the complex affairs of large social and production units created unavoidable chaos and resulted in a decline in output after a short period of production increase in 1958. Massive floods in some areas, and drought in others, compounded the problem. Grain production declined from 200 million tons in 1958 to 144 million tons in 1960. It took more than a decade for per capita grain output to reach its pre-Great Leap Forward level.

While output continued to decline, demand for food increased in the cities, and so did the demand to deliver a larger surplus. Pressured to show improvement in output, local cadres concealed the devastating situation from the central authorities, and inflated the actual production levels in their reports. To meet the demand for a larger surplus, they drastically reduced the availability of food to the locals. Rural consumption suffered. Disaster spread across rural China. By the end of 1962, 15–30 million had died of hunger and disease.

*   *   *

Grandpa's memories of the past always revolved around the struggle for food. Good times were those with ample food, bad times those with hunger. Working in the mines came under the heading of bad times. He had little food, and no water, he recalled. To get drinking water, Grandpa broke and carried surface ice from the Yellow River by camel. "I didn't wash my face for a month. Water was so limited. We didn't even have enough to drink. How could we use the water to wash?" he said.

The mine did not have a canteen, or trailers to sleep in. Grandpa covered himself with "thick canvas" to escape the biting night cold, and slept on the rough earth under the open sky. Even for a farmer accustomed to hardship and hunger, the conditions in the mine were intolerable. Unable to cope, he requested a transfer. Such requests were hardly ever granted by the authorities in those days. Miraculously, however, Grandpa became an exception to the rule. He was dispatched to an iron-making workshop of the Lanzhou Railway Bureau in Ningxia Province. There he ate regularly and had access to all the benefits of an employee of China's State-Owned Enterprises. The job came with housing, a salary, and food coupons. Working for the railways meant good times.

While Grandpa labored in the mines, his elder brothers—one single and the other with a wife and son—tilled the family land and helped their ailing father. Grandpa did not know much about the famine and the problems of the Great Leap Forward until he returned home in 1962.

The life he had left behind not long ago had changed beyond recognition. The mud houses and the fields looked the same as the day he left the village. The people, however, did not. "They had aged." Many were no more. Those remaining had taken different paths and changed their lives to survive the catastrophe.

Facing unbearable hunger, Grandpa's wife had left him for another man in 1961. "You know, the years around 1960 were bad times. A woman couldn't live by herself. There was almost no food. A person could have starved to death in seven days. There were almost three months without any grain. So, the woman had to find a man to take care of her. How could she live as a single woman in such conditions?"

Grandpa was resigned to having lost his wife to another poor soul who promised to feed and clothe her in hard times. He was a practical man, a peasant who understood a person's need to eat. What he encountered next, however, pained him for years to come. It changed his life.

Like millions in China, Grandpa's brothers fell victim to the famine, he would discover. Thirty-three and 35 years old, strong and healthy before the famine, they died of hunger in 1960. In his late fifties, and frail, Grandpa's father had lost his eyesight. Mother was ill. A four-year-old nephew was left without a father. Grandpa had limited options.

"I had come back to the village to take my wife and parents to Province. That was not possible anymore. My parents' health had deteriorated. My wife was gone. And I had a nephew to take care of."

Grandpa remained in the village and devoted himself to his parents and his only nephew. He did not remarry, and never had children of his own. He watched his nephew grow up, become a man and marry, raise a family, and move to Shenzhen in the 1990s. In 2006, Grandpa also left the farm for Shenzhen. He was old and did not wish to "die alone."

THE DECORATOR'S FORTUNE

I met Grandpa's nephew 46 years after the Great Leap Forward took his father. He had dark yellow teeth, half with platinum caps, and a head full of spiky salt-and-pepper hair. Clad in blue trousers that he had rolled up to his knees, and a half-buttoned short-sleeved checkered shirt, he was sweating and covered with dust. He parked his old bicycle in a backroom of his home, offered me a cigarette, then a second, a third, and a fourth, and more every few minutes. Grandpa's nephew was a chain-smoker.

We met frequently. Our meetings would always begin with the offer of cigarettes. He would run to a nearby shop, buy me a can of soda, give me a cigarette, and proceed with his business of the day anytime he saw me talk to others outside the village. There was always an unending supply of Tsingtao beer when I ate with his extended family. He would refill my tin bowl before it was half empty. Smoking would never stop, even during the meals.

Grandpa's nephew settled in the Li Family Village six years before our meeting in 2007. Married for some years, he had a 23-year-old son who worked with him in Longgang, and an older daughter back in his hometown.

We never exchanged names. He was Grandpa's sole nephew. That was all that mattered. To him, I was the foreigner, the writer who frequently visited his home. "He is writing a book about Chinese history," he would tell neighbors.

"Americans always look down on China. They consider China a poor country. They don't understand China at all. Even in the past, China was famous for its silk. It was number one in the world. China was also famous for its fine cotton, which was not produced in any other country," he would tell me.

"I am not an educated man, not an intellectual. But I can tell you something about our history."

"You are a good man. My whole family likes you."

"Fate brought us together. But you live so far away. We would not be able to visit you," he would say.

Chance had brought me to the Li Family Village. The nephew's wife offered me an orange the first time I visited. I was soon like a family member, one they trusted and took into their home with pleasure.

"Will you stay for dinner tonight?" his wife would always insist.

"I have eggs in the house. I can boil some for you. Please wait for me," she would say when she saw me outside the village.

"You don't like our food! I will cook you some meat."

"Are you cold? You are only wearing a T-shirt. I'll get you some warm clothes," she said when I visited one day in December.

"What are you doing for the Spring Festival? You should not be alone. Come to our village with us," she said, weeks before the most important Chinese holiday in February 2008.

"Do you speak Chinese?" she would ask every time we met.

*   *   *

Grandpa's nephew was only four years old when tragedy hit his family. Too young to remember, he told me what the elders from the village told him about the Great Leap Forward. One-third of the people in his village had died of starvation by the end of 1960. "I was a small child when my father died. I grew up without a father," Grandpa's nephew said. He was unforgiving.

"There was plenty of grain in the village, but the farmers could not use any of it," he said. Stored to be shipped for consumption elsewhere, the grain rotted while people died of hunger. No one dared tell the truth. Those who exaggerated the volume of production got rewarded, and those who told the truth were called counterrevolutionary. Desperate, and unable to find food, some survived by chopping and eating the trunks of elm trees. "I still remember collecting wild goose shit, letting it dry, and eating it. That was delicious food for us. It felt like eating a cake."

When it was all over and life resumed a semblance of normality, people coped with their painful memories by telling night-time fables. They healed their wounds by joking about the tragedies they had encountered. "I learned this story from the old people in my village," he said. This is how the story went.

An old woman in the village was asked how much surplus grain she had produced and saved. Knowing that she had to exaggerate her output, she said "nine hundred pounds."

"Where is the wheat?"

"In a jar."

"Where is the jar?"

"I hid it in a hole in the ground."

The old woman was asked to dig and show the grain. She did, and what she showed was only a handful of grain kept in a bowl. Although she did not have much and she had lied, the old woman was not punished. "She had done the right thing. She was actually praised for boasting," the nephew said.

*   *   *

Grandpa's nephew did not have any schooling, but, like Grandpa, he was fascinated by Chinese history. The nephew, however, told a different history of China from Grandpa, especially when it came to Chairman Mao and the Communist Party. Like Grandpa, he spoke with authority. Giving me a lesson in Chinese history was a pleasure he could not pass up. He would invite me for beer and cigarettes and take me on a journey in time. "You have to get the facts straight," he said. Criticizing Mao and teaching me about his wrongdoings were his favorite topics of conversation.

Grandpa had learned history, Chinese history in particular, from the opera. His nephew took history lessons with a client, an ex-Kuomintang general who fled to Taiwan, became a successful capitalist, and returned to set up a shoe factory in Shenzhen in the 1990s.

Chairman Mao hurt the people who helped him during the revolution, said the nephew. A lot of "kind landlords" and rich people gave money to Chairman Mao during the revolution. "But what did he do when he came to power? He took their land and wealth and gave them to others," he said, and lit a cigarette. During the Cultural Revolution, Chairman Mao went against many of the people who had made great contributions to the revolution. He betrayed his loyal friends. "Write a book about the Cultural Revolution."

Chairman Mao lied to the Chinese people about the war of liberation, the nephew wanted me to know. The communists' contribution to the defeat of the Japanese forces was marginal. They were weak and poorly trained and did not have good guns. The Kuomintang received sophisticated arms from the Americans. Without those, the Japanese could not have been defeated. The Kuomintang fought the "Japanese invaders," and defeated them with millions of well-trained soldiers. Chiang Kai Shek signed the treaty when Japan surrendered. The treaty demanded that Japan pay a lot of money for China's losses. But after that, Chairman Mao started the civil war and brought down the government. "So Japan didn't pay anything because the government that signed the treaty was no longer in power."

*   *   *

Grandpa's nephew grew up a farmer. At only seven years old, he began helping with the farm work from the early hours of the day. By his early teens, he had the hands of a farmer, and his skin was rough and darkened from exposure to sun. He saw many changes in his village, new land policies, upheavals, and political movements. By the mid-1980s, most of the men in his village had "gone out" to work in factories in Guangzhou or Shenzhen. Some returned in a few years and changed their mud houses to brick homes, started businesses, and showed off their wealth to their impoverished neighbors. Some were even taking new wives.

Grandpa's nephew was strong and hard-working, and as capable as others were. With very little planning, one summer in the early 1990s, he took his wife and his eight-year-old son and headed south. He was in his mid-thirties when he arrived in Guangzhou. Grandpa remained on the farm.

Grandpa's nephew rented a room for his wife and son and began his new life working in different factories, moving from electronics to clothing and back to electronics. He lived in factory dormitories and rarely saw his family. For the first few years, he worked twelve hours a day, seven days a week, and earned 600 yuan a month. Five years after leaving the farm, his salary was 700 yuan a month. He had come south with the dream of saving enough money to build a nicer home back in the village. That dream would never have been realized with 700 yuan a month. He needed a break, a *new* start, and he found that break in construction. Many were making a "good fortune" in construction in those days. Determined to get rich, he left the factory world for a new life.

He began by helping others in the demolition of old buildings, moving earth, and doing all the odd jobs on construction sites. Soon he was plastering, pasting ceramic tiles, and furnishing bedrooms, bathrooms, and kitchens. In two years, he was a "master decorator," making 300 yuan a day. This was a quarter of the monthly salary of a factory worker, with many hours of overtime. "Sometimes I subcontracted projects from bigger contractors. Last time I did a project in a nearby community I made 4000 yuan in five days. There are a lot of rich people around here. They redecorate their homes every five to ten years. Business is good."

With enough experience as a decorator, Grandpa's nephew moved to Longgang, where a construction boom had started in the new district center. There were new buildings everywhere. Housing prices were doubling, quadrupling. Longgang had an unending demand for qualified decorators. Grandpa's nephew was entering a goldmine.

11   Construction workers in Longgang

By now, his son was an adult and a factory worker. He left his job to be his father's apprentice and help. The family's income grew even higher. And there was more to come. A farmer, who knew the art of growing vegetables, the nephew's wife joined other migrant tenants in the Li Family Village in turning an abandoned construction lot across the village into a collective vegetable farm. They divided the land between themselves and each grew potatoes, tomatoes, lettuce, and other produce that they consumed at home. The nephew's wife bought extra produce every day and began a small money-making business outside the gates of the village. She was soon the main vegetable vendor of the village. More money was flowing in than the family could spend. They were saving an enviable 30,000 yuan a year, nearly three times the yearly salary of a factory worker.

*   *   *

There was an unwritten code of conversation in Grandpa's family. I knew what to expect and from whom to expect it. In his elaborate and theatrical way, Grandpa would take me on a journey into revolution and war, land reform, and the glories of socialism. And, of course, a good dose of Chinese opera always accompanied his stories. The old man was a natural storyteller. I would sit before him, all attention, and follow his narration of events that remained a mystery to many in China, and elsewhere in the world.

Grandpa's nephew also lectured me on Chinese history, and the demons of communism and Chairman Mao. However, he and the old man never told their tales in each other's presence. Grandpa would leave the room and busy himself with his usual house chores when it was his nephew's time to teach me a thing or two about China. The nephew would speak with no emotion, and without the physical gestures that made Grandpa so intriguing to watch. The past had left deep scars on the nephew's soul.

The nephew's wife was jolly and talkative. She was motherly and kind, with a limited repertoire of statements when she spoke to me: "Do you like

Chinese food?" "When will you visit your home?" "Why do you not have a wife?" "Will you stay for dinner?" "Do you speak Chinese?"

The nephew's son stayed in the background for the most part. He would offer me cigarettes, and smile when I greeted him. He did not talk much when I was around. He was married to the slender Liao Yan, who gave him two sons. It was Grandpa's job to babysit the youngest while Liao Yan worked with her mother-in-law, selling produce outside the Li Family Village.

I would only see Liao Yan outside the wall by the vegetable stand. I did not know how she spoke until a very hot day in August 2009, when we conversed for the first and the last time.

*   *   *

I was visiting friends in the Li Family Village. Grandpa was away with the nephew's youngest grandson. Grandpa's nephew was out trying to collect his pay for a job he had done weeks earlier for a Longgang contractor. Payment delays were common—collecting the money was sometimes more difficult than finding a job. The family was all accustomed to the routine.

It was early afternoon, and Liao Yan's husband was asleep in the house, regaining his energy after a long day of work. He had been up since two o'clock the night before, when he left home to buy vegetables and fruits for the family's business. He had returned home for breakfast, before leaving again on a project his father had recently contracted. The nephew's son repeated this routine six days a week.

I had been with the nephew's wife and her daughter-in-law for some time now. Sitting on a yellow plastic stool, I was chatting with customers, sweating from the heat, drinking warm cola, and smoking cigarettes with neighbors. "You stay for lunch," the nephew's wife said. I accepted. "Wait inside. My husband will be home soon," she said, and sent me to her house with my interpreter and her daughter-in-law. The house was always cooler than the outside. The sun never visited Grandpa's house in the Li Family Village.

I took a bag of carrots and a small cabbage and followed the daughter-in-law to the house. Two old and dirty plastic stools stood in a corner. Liao Yan offered one to me, the other to my interpreter, and squatted near the door. We quarreled over the stool. She refused to have her guest squat.

That afternoon, Liao Yan was free of all household responsibilities. She looked pretty and relaxed. It was only going to be the three of us for a while. A minute or two passed without anyone speaking. Liao Yan broke the silence at last. She looked at her arm, examined it, and said, "I am getting so dark. I was a lot lighter before." Liao Yan was tall, slender, and pretty. The exposure to the sun was, however, tanning her skin. She would soon have the rough skin and the darkened face of a farmer. "People tell me I should stop selling vegetables and working outside. I can get a job at the supermarket. I might become lighter. But the pay is not good. I have to work with my family anyway."

To many Chinese, a woman's dark skin was a sign of ignorance, and the narrow-mindedness of rural life. Women in the cities had light skin. They protected themselves from the sun, and avoided exposure to the bitter cold common on the farm. Dark skin was a loud echo of the past, the old China, the China of Chairman Mao, and the thousands of years of ignorance and poverty before the Communist Revolution. A new China was marching ahead, and rapidly. It was a white China. Billboards and television commercials advertised new bleaching and skin-whitening lotions. Women, even the factory workers, protected themselves against the sun by carrying colorful parasols. They wanted to look urban and white. "I cannot carry a parasol when I work outside. I have no choice," Liao Yan said, looking grim and disappointed.

* * *

Liao Yan was born in a small village in Hubei Province in central China. A middle school dropout without much prospect in the village, she left her family and the village and headed for Shenzhen when she was 15. When she arrived in Shenzhen, she had only the phone number of another girl from her village and the address of the toy factory in Longgang where she had been working for the past few months. Liao Yan had to find her way to the factory. That was a journey on its own for a teenage village girl: "I was scared."

Tired from the long train ride and bewildered by the chaos of the city, Liao Yan took three buses and walked a long way. Five hours after arriving at the Luohu train station, she was standing outside the gates of her friend's factory. The next morning, she was wearing a short-sleeved blue uniform and spray-painting little toy trucks for a salary of 400 yuan a month. Later that day, exhausted and nearly unconscious after a twelve-hour shift, she passed out on her narrow bunk bed. "There were 200 beds in a very large room. There were two rows of beds. All of us slept in that room. I had never seen a room that large." Liao Yan was now a factory girl. The village life was all but behind her. "I was happy."

Liao Yan's first job did not last long. Her friend left the factory for another job with better pay. She left after her. Her next job was at an electronics factory, and it was in that factory that Liao Yan met her future husband four years after leaving the village. "He was so skinny," she giggled. At age 19, Liao Yan married Liu Yansheng, the son of Grandpa's nephew. Liao Yan's family was not pleased. Liu Yansheng was from Henan, and she from Hubei. Marrying him meant she would never return to her village, and her family was to lose her to another. Liao Yan's family did not know the boy, or his family. Would he treat their daughter well? Would he earn enough money to give her a good life? Despite her family's concerns, Liao Yan chose Liu Yansheng as her husband. She did not regret her choice.

Months after marrying, her young husband left the world of factories to apprentice with his father. Liao Yan followed him to the Li Family Village. She had been a vegetable vendor ever since.

*   *   *

Liao Yan's new family gave her love and security. They were rich compared to other families in the Li Family Village. Like everyone else, they worked hard. But unlike everyone else, they earned a lot of money. When we first met, the family displayed their produce on pieces of cardboard and fabric on the ground. Not long after, they had four carts on wheels. The business had grown, and there were people haggling and buying vegetables and fruits at all times. Money was good. Sales fluctuated, but they always ended the day with enough money. On good days, they brought home 200 yuan. They used the money from the vegetable stand to pay for their daily expenses. The family ate plenty of pork and chicken. The men drank beer and *baijiu*, and smoked many packs of cigarettes every day.

To earn 200 yuan a day was an unachievable dream for many. Grandpa's family, however, made a lot more from the nephew's decorating contracts. "He is a very experienced decorator," Liao Yan said about her father-in-law. Others in the Li Family Village agreed. "Not everyone can make money like the boss," a neighbor told me once. "Before, he had a team of ten people working for him. Now he only works with my husband. It is better this way. They bring home more money," Liao Yan said about her father-in-law. "Sometimes they make 600 yuan a day if they get a really good contract."

And while their neighbors could barely make a living, Liao Yan's family saved plenty and bought two buildings back in Henan—a four-story building, and a new one-story commercial space for the price of 200,000 yuan, an unimaginable sum of money for the migrants in the village. "We are renting out both of the buildings. The second building is very big. My family rented that to a store." Liao Yan had, after all, made the right choice marrying the nephew's son. Her blood family had fewer concerns now: their daughter had married into money.

With the rent from the two buildings, Grandpa's nephew and his wife had no worries about retirement. They were in their fifties, and ready to quit working. They wanted to return to the village for a quiet and comfortable life. "They are thinking about going back home in two years. They will take the boys with them. My husband and I will stay and take care of the vegetable stand." That meant 16-hour shifts every day. They would begin shopping in the early hours to keep the stand open from six in the morning to eight in the evening. "It will only be the two of us then. We will have to do everything." Liao Yan looked worried. "I have to be outside all the time," she said, staring at her arm.

THE SCENT OF FRESH GRASS

It was a late August day when I saw Grandpa last. I was on my way to Beijing the next morning. He was sitting on the stool at the entrance. Grandpa was limping that day. He had an infected toe, he told me. To protect the toe from dirt and further infection, he had wrapped his whole foot in a black plastic bag, the type used in produce shops. He was wearing his old brown slippers.

I had bought Grandpa a Western-style pipe from the department store at the Longgang World Trade Center. Grandpa had strolled near the department store every day, but he had never ventured inside and walked through the aisles filled with clothes and other Chinese-made products beyond the means of anyone in the Li Family Village. He now had a gift-wrapped present from the Trade Center. Grandpa carefully opened the box, and held the pipe in his wrinkled hand. He investigated its woodcarvings, placed it in his mouth, removed it, laughed, and repeated the motions. "I will always think of you when I use this pipe," he said.

Seeing me in the house, a few neighbors came by to say hello. Village children went in and out. "Hello," a ten-year-old said in English each time she entered the house.

"Let me tell you a story," Grandpa said, repeating the tale of young Huang Shuai, who refused to learn English during the Cultural Revolution. Grandpa's story, however, had a different twist at the end. It was different from the popular fairytale I had heard from Zhao Gang and others.

"I am Chinese, and I do not need to learn English. I don't need the ABC to be a red vanguard," the girl wrote in a poem. Angered by her disobedience, her teacher reported the young girl to the authorities. She was criticized and humiliated. Young and impressionable, and hurt by the harsh reaction to her otherwise revolutionary idea, the girl jumped in the river near her home and committed suicide. A journalist reported the news. The teacher and the school principal were held responsible for this tragedy. The government took care of the girl's parents to the end of their lives, Grandpa said. The story had darkened his mood.

"You will be going home soon. Do you miss home?" Grandpa asked.

"Do *you* miss home?" I asked Grandpa.

"Of course. How can I not?" he said. Lighting his pipe, he took a few puffs, put the pipe away, and began a monolog, a ballad of estrangement. Even the child could not distract him.

"You hang out, and have a good time here in daytime. The buildings are new. They are clean and beautiful. The park is beautiful. Everything is nice. But when you go back home, empty, and alone, you fall into a deafening silence. Your mind returns to the village. You miss your hometown, the people, and the smell of the field. You remember the scent of fresh grass, and the morning dew. You leave the house at night, stand outside, raise your head and stare at the bright moon. You close your eyes, and your nostalgia comes around. The scenery outside is beautiful, but in your heart, you miss your home. One's roots always remain in his place of birth. Strong emotions exist between the village and its people. You never forget your childhood friends. Even if it is only in your dreams, you will always go back home."

There was a noise outside the house. The nephew's wife entered with a big basket of fresh produce. "Will you stay for dinner?" she asked, and put down the basket. "I feel bad. You don't eat with us," she said when I told her about my plans for the night.

"You have been very kind to me. I'll never forget your hospitality," I said.

"In my hometown, we stop working to be with our guests if people come to visit from far away. Next time you come, stay with us. Don't spend money on hotels. They are too expensive around here," she said, and walked to the pile of fruits and vegetables on the floor by Grandpa's bed. She took a plastic bag and filled it with apples. "Your journey is long. You will get hungry. Eat these on the train," she said. Looking at Grandpa, as if asking for help, she began listing the names of provinces I would be passing through on my way to Beijing. Their neighbors and everyone else they knew traveled by bus or train. No one in Grandpa's family had ever flown anywhere. "It is a long way," she said again, and offered me boiled eggs for the journey.

The time had come to say farewell. Grandpa accompanied me to the gate. "Human beings are emotional animals. They are the soul of the universe. You and I live in different parts of the earth. We speak different languages. But we have known each other for a while now. I have affection for you. Fate brought you here from faraway lands. It was my luck that I met you. We met and had long and deep conversations so many times. I am an old man, and I might never see you again in this world. It is sad, but true that we have very little chance to meet again. This will be our farewell," he said. The old man had tearful eyes. Holding my hand, he slowly walked me to the village gate and said, "I wish you good luck in your journeys. I will miss you."

Book II
The Migrant Girls' Long March

THE TOY FACTORY GIRLS

In a factory near the Li Family Village, two high school graduates worked six days a week, twelve hours a day. They spent their free time in the park by the Longgang World Trade Center. They had come to Longgang for the "experience." They were discovering the world. I met them by chance in the park.

It was a hot late Sunday afternoon in July, and I was taking a stroll, looking to strike up a conversation with workers who had filled the park with their laughter and the sound of music from their cell phone MP3s. Sundays were special days. Young workers would arrive from the early hours of the morning, some on their bikes, and others on foot. Dressed in their best, young women would be accompanied by boys with funky hairdos, clad in jeans, T-shirts, or unbuttoned short-sleeved shirts. The couples would take refuge under the shade of the trees, snuggle, joke, and giggle, and take pictures of one another with their cell phone cameras.

Exhausted by the heat, I sat on a small cement bench in a quiet corner of the park and watched the passersby. I was cleaning my camera when I noticed the stare of two girls standing on the corner by a small red bicycle. I smiled. They smiled back, turned the corner, and sat on a bench some three feet across from me.

They were petite and clad in blue jeans and colorful plastic flip-flops. One wore a red shirt, the other a pink blouse. They would look at me with curiosity, turn to each other, look at me again, and smile. Minutes passed. No one spoke. Then, leaning forward, the girl in red mumbled a word that sounded English with a heavy Chinese accent. Gesturing with hands and face, I showed my inability to understand. She covered her mouth with her small hand and giggled. A minute or two later, she spoke again. This time, it was Chinese, I thought.

"I … don't … understand … Chinese," I replied, pronouncing each word slowly, pausing between them, and hoping they would understand me. The girl in red consulted with her friend. They whispered.

"American?" she said in English.

"Yes," I replied.

They whispered again, looked at me, and smiled. Thinking and rehearsing her sentence, the girl in red asked, "How much time in China?"

"Less … than … a … month," I replied

Other questions followed. After long minutes of consultation among themselves, and using broken English and many misplaced words, they asked

12 Migrant workers and globalization

if I liked China, and how long I was going to stay in Shenzhen. Thinking it would be difficult to explain my project, I told the girls, also in broken English, that I was traveling the world, going through China, India, and a few other countries. They watched me with eyes wide open, and nodded each time I named a country that they understood.

"Vietnam!" cried the girl in red, looked at her friend, and said something in Chinese. "India!"

Using her index finger to show me the numeric number one, she asked, "One ... person?"

"Yes, I am traveling alone."

I was traveling alone in China and without speaking any Chinese! The girls were puzzled. They asked more questions, many of which I did not understand. How was I managing in China, they wished to know.

"I am here with an interpreter."

They looked at me with blank faces. I changed my words. Their confusion remained. They said things. I said things. I used a different sentence structure.

"T...r...a...n...s...l...a...t...o...r."

No use. They spoke with each other, talked to me, and finally, after five minutes or so, I believe they understood I was traveling with an interpreter.

Then came more questions, personal questions an American would not dare to ask in the first encounter with someone.

"Where is your wife?" asked the girl in red in surprisingly better English, and with less rehearsing.

Shocked to find me unmarried, they asked for the reason. In China, men half my age were married with children. Those my age were grandfathers. No normal person remained unmarried. They looked at me, puzzled, and waited for an answer.

Miming, holding her hand near the ground to demonstrate her point, the girl in red asked, "Child?"

"No!"

She stared at me with sad eyes. She did not smile.

And as we spoke, a crowd of old and young men and women slowly gathered around us. Some stood as close as inches away from my face. Others sat on the grass behind me. Others leaned on their bikes in the middle of the passway. They all stared at me. Some came closer, and looked as if they understood the words we exchanged. I was nervous, and did not know what to make of the attention and the crowd around me. The girls looked oblivious, undisturbed.

Until now, I had only answered questions they had asked. It was now my turn to ask.

"What do you do in Shenzhen?"

They consulted, looked thoughtful, consulted again, almost said a word, retreated, and told me that they worked in a factory.

"Very hard," the quiet girl in pink spoke for the first time.

"Where is the factory?" I asked.

They pointed to the left, towards a crowded neighborhood away from the park.

"What is the best way to learn English?" is what I understood from the constellation of words the girl in red pronounced after a momentary lapse in our conversation.

"We like to learn English. Our English is very bad."

I told them about the value of conversation, and reading.

"What you are doing now is one of the best ways. Talk to others."

"What do you make in the factory?" I asked. I tried again and again, showed my clothes, camera, and shoes, and everything around me to see if they produced those in their factory.

"Bicycle?" I pointed at the small bike parked behind them.

Using their hands, they showed me the shape of a box, a moving box.

"Children," said the girl in red.

"You make toys, children's toys," I exclaimed.

"Toys," they shouted.

"We like to learn English," the girl in red said abruptly.

"You will be our teacher?" they said together. I accepted.

"When?"

"Tomorrow," I said. They nodded.

"Noon!" I suggested.

Noon was too early.

"We are sleeping."

"Four in the afternoon"

That was also early. I suggested six.

"Not six in the morning!" said the girl in red.

We made plans to meet the next day at six in the evening, at the same spot in the park.

Ready to leave, for the first time, we introduced ourselves. The girl in red wrote their names on a notepad from the factory. Li Lan was her name, and Miao Ging her friend's.

13   Li Lan and Miao Ging

* * *

They arrived on the red bike and with notepads, pens, and a book with sample English passages, partial Chinese translations in the margins, and a long list of words and expressions at the end. We sat on the grass under the shade of a tree, and began our first English class by reading passages from the book.

The first passage was a lesson on the importance of parents in the upbringing of their children. They read together, fast, synchronized, mispronouncing every word, swallowing the last letter or two in most. Following them, I read slowly, pronouncing every word, taking my time.

"This is how you should read. Read slowly. You read too fast. Pronounce each word, each letter. Do not rush. Read slowly."

"Our teacher reads fast. He told us to read fast."

The second passage was a lesson about dangers of firecrackers. Once again, they read with haste and many mistakes. They read the third passage equally quickly.

"This is how our teacher reads," they said.

Tired of reading, they put the books aside and resumed their curious questions about my life.

"Why aren't you married?" Li Lan asked abruptly.

"No babies?"

"No babies."

"Why do you live in Longgang?"

Why would an American live near the factories? I told the girls that I was in the south of China hoping to meet factory workers like them, write their stories, and get to understand their lives and experiences. I wanted to be close to the factories, I explained. As I talked, they paid close attention. I was the first foreigner they had met, the first professor they had befriended, the first writer, and the first person who had been to other parts of the world. I had come from a world they wished to know better, to touch, and to feel. And I was interested in them.

"You are interested in factory workers!" Li Lan exclaimed, and asked if I lived near the park

"That way," I pointed to the direction of the Beautiful Rose Garden.

"Your apartment must be very beautiful," Li Lan said

"Where is your interpreter?" Li Lan asked.

I told the girls about my 23-year-old interpreter, a college graduate on her way to the United States to continue her studies. Fascinated, they asked questions about her life story, her proficiency in English, her pronunciation of English words, and everything else that made her a *special* Chinese woman.

"Does she read fast like us?"

"Where did she go to university?"

"Beijing."

"Beijing University?" Li Lan said with eyes wide open.

"No. She studied in another university in Beijing."

"Your interpreter must be beautiful," Li Lan said. A graduate from a university in Beijing, soon traveling to America, working as an interpreter with a foreign writer, how could she not be beautiful? Li Lan was short, born and raised in a small town in Guangdong. She had never been to Beijing.

"I want to go to university," Li Lan said with difficulty, and after many attempts.

"I admire your interpreter," Li Lan said, and wrote the word "admire" in a beautiful handwriting on a notepad.

"Maybe I can be your interpreter," she said, laughing.

Once again, it was time to return to the factory for the night shift. Departing, we made plans to meet the next day, the same time and place, this time with my interpreter.

"Would she really come?" asked Li Lan.

*   *   *

The initial introduction was fast and uneventful. I spoke. The others listened. Li Lan stood behind Miao Ging and gazed far away. No one smiled. Silence prevailed. I joked. No one laughed.

This was an unbearably hot and humid day, and the park was nearly empty. I asked if the girls wanted to escape the heat and go to the McDonald's at the trade center. No one replied.

"Should we stay here?"

"What do you want to do?"

Everyone, including my interpreter, looked in a different direction.

"OK, that's it. We will go to McDonald's," I said, and we walked towards the World Trade Center.

Ordering food and drinks was an ordeal.

"What would you like to eat?"

"Nothing," Li Lan and Miao Ging replied in Chinese.

"Let's get something to eat and drink. Please tell me what you like."

The answer came in Chinese.

"I don't understand Chinese. You know English. We are here to practice."

I ordered food and drinks for everyone, and proceeded to a table in a less noisy corner.

"Please eat. Your food will get cold."

Clandestinely staring at my interpreter eating her food, Li Lan and Miao Ging nibbled on theirs. No one spoke.

"Let's read," I broke the silence.

"Not today," Li Lan said, and continued to watch my interpreter.

"Are you shy because of her?" I asked.

She smiled with her head down.

"Can we meet tomorrow? Li Lan asked.

This was a Thursday evening, and the next Saturday and Sunday were the girls' free days in the month. Monday was to be the first day of their new morning shift, working from eight in the morning until eight at night. Taking advantage of the free day, I invited them to homemade Chinese food at my apartment.

"Do you know how to cook Chinese?" Li Lan asked with excitement.

"Who taught you?"

"Do you like Chinese food?"

"Do you use chopsticks?"

The silence was finally broken. When we left McDonald's, Li Lan looked me in the eyes, smiled, and said, "I am very happy."

*   *   *

They came with two boys their own age. The boys each carried a small plastic bag.

"These are our friends from the factory," Li Lan said.

"We brought you apples. Do you like apples?" asked Miao Ging.

Tall and skinny, with long straight hair, and wearing a red T-shirt, one boy offered me a bottle of iced tea.

"They brought these for you," Li Lan said.

Li Lan stayed by me while we walked to the store near the Beautiful Rose Garden to buy the ingredients for our feast. Once again, she was talkative and engaging. She asked about my apartment, cooking Chinese food, and my travels. Then, stopping suddenly, she looked me in the eyes and said in perfect English, "I have a dream. I want to become an interpreter in the future. I *will be* an interpreter someday." She had tears in her eyes. "I am very happy tonight. I will always remember you," she said.

*   *   *

With five bags full of groceries, we walked towards my apartment.

"Walk fast, we are late," I said.

"Not fast. Slowly. This is what you taught us," Li Lan said, laughing.

"Always slowly," she said, mimicking me.

Arriving in my apartment, the boys joined my interpreter in the living room, sat in front of the TV set, and quietly watched television for the next hour. Li Lan helped me unload bags of tomatoes, cucumbers, zucchinis, eggplants, lettuce, and spinach. She stored a large watermelon in the refrigerator.

"I want to help. Give us something to do," Li Lan said, and asked the English names for every ingredient I used and repeated after me.

"Po...ta...toes,"

"Egg...plants"

I marinated and cooked a large fish in freshly squeezed orange juice and soy sauce, and made a Chinese dish with eggplants, three types of mushroom, and zucchini. Tossing together chopped pieces of cucumbers, tomatoes, broccoli, carrots, baby corn, and two mangos cut in small pieces, I made a colorful salad.

"How will you cook this?" asked Li Lan.

"I am not cooking this. This is a salad. We will eat it raw."

She put her hand in front of her mouth to hide her laughter, leaned against the kitchen wall, and said, "No cooking?"

Ready at last, I put the large bowl of salad in the middle of a low glass table in front of the only couch in the living room. The fish platter and the Chinese dish on each side, two family-size bottles of Coke, plastic cups, and chopsticks crowded the table. I sat on the floor and waited for the feast to begin. No one moved.

"Please eat, begin with the salad," I said.

The boys stared at the food. Li Lan sat back on the sofa. Miao Ging remained motionless. My interpreter watched television.

"Why don't they eat?" I asked my interpreter.

"They don't know how to eat the salad," she said.

"With chopsticks," I said, and demonstrated how to pick up pieces of cucumber and tomato, bathe them in the salad dressing, and put them in their mouths. The boys looked petrified.

"Come on, Li Lan. You start."

Chopsticks in their hands, they approached the salad bowl slowly, hesitantly picked an ingredient, put it in their mouths, and retreated to their original positions.

"What is it? Why don't you eat?"

"They are not used to eating raw vegetables," my interpreter said.

This was the south of China; no one ate raw food, even vegetables.

"It gives you stomach pain," said the boy in red.

"No, that is not true. Raw vegetables are good for you," I protested, and lectured them on the virtues of eating raw food, and the Japanese custom of eating raw fish. I tried desperately to persuade them to take their chances with my beautiful salad.

"Try the fish at least," I begged.

Cautiously picking up their chopsticks, the boys each took a small piece of my carefully prepared fish. I stared at them, hoping for a smile or a sign of satisfaction on their faces.

"So, do you like it?"

More Chinese words were exchanged.

"It is not salty enough for them. They don't cook fish this way," my interpreter said.

"I added soy sauce just for them," I said, with disappointment.

"Not enough for them," she said.

"There is no ginger or garlic in the fish," the boy in red spoke again.

"I forgot to add them," I said defensively, feeling defeated in my attempt to make my Chinese guests happy.

"Try again. You would like it. Try the eggplants. I promise you would like it."

Eating took a long time. Slowly, more pieces of fish were chopped away, more cucumbers and mangoes chewed, and more eggplants savored. In 30 minutes, the salad bowl was half empty. Twenty or so minutes later, no sign of the salad was left except for the pool of dressing at the bottom of the large bowl. The fishbones floated in my orange sauce, and a few pieces of garlic and ginger remained from the Chinese dish. I smiled.

Stomachs were full, and dirty dishes were cleared away. I joined the boys to smoke on the balcony. Back at the table, everyone was more talkative. There were questions about eating habits in America, the health virtues of not deep-frying, and Chinatown in New York City. The boy in red knew of a neighbor who left his wife and children behind to work and earn more money in Chinatown. The family waited for news, money, or anything from America.

"He disappeared. He never came back, or contacted his family," he said.

I told them of the recent wave of Chinese immigrants trafficked to the United States. "Most work like slaves in restaurants in Chinatown and live in overcrowded rooms to save and pay back their debt to their traffickers," I said. "Life is not easy for many of the new immigrants," I told them.

"Do they work in factories?" the boy in red asked.

I told the story of the 58 Chinese migrants suffocated to death in a trailer in Dover in 2000. Attracted to my stories, their eyes were no longer fixed on the TV screen; they listened attentively. They were saddened.

"Do you care about all these people?" Li Lan asked.

"You are a kind person."

The conversation continued, and, Li Lan translated my words for the boys and theirs for me. My interpreter watched television.

"You are an interpreter tonight," I told Li Lan. She looked at me with a big smile on her face.

*   *   *

Their English was improving rapidly as we continued to meet every week. Li Lan would send text messages in English and ask about my whereabouts. Every week, disciplined and committed, they would bring their books and notepads, and we would read and reread passages.

"I told my mother that we met a writer from America. She is very proud," Li Lan told me.

"I will never forget you," she said every time we met.

"Will you come to visit us?"

"I made up my mind. I am going to study English and become an interpreter."

At our last meeting, the girls came dressed up, wearing clean and beautiful shirts, and nice trousers. They had both gone to a hair salon during the week, getting beautiful cuts.

"You look very nice. I like your hair," I said.

They giggled. We did not read much that night. Li Lan was quiet and withdrawn.

"What is the problem, Li Lan?"

"I have to tell you. We almost did not come tonight. Our boss asked us to work overtime. We told him we had to come to see you. We had to come. The boss did not agree. We insisted. He finally accepted. Two other friends are working for us tonight. We have to work two shifts tomorrow."

Before leaving, Li Lan took out her notepad and asked me to write something for her, something to keep, something to remember me with. I wrote separate notes for each girl.

"Now I want to write something for you," Li Lan grabbed the notepad from me.

"Dear Behzad, I was very happy that we can meet you in Shenzhen and I very thank you for teaching our English, now. I hope you can happy every day, and you can work happy. I think you will become a great man. I will remember you forever. Li Lan."

I WANT TO SEE THE WORLD

It was a lazy Sunday afternoon. Grandpa was resting on the lawn under a tree puffing on his pipe, and I was playing with the little boy. A woman of about 30 in orange T-shirt and jeans looked our way with a big smile. She had short straight hair, and her bangs partly covered her eyes. A purple bag hung diagonally over her shoulder. Grandpa wiped the sweat off his neck with a kerchief, looked towards me, and said, "So, you want to collect materials to write a book. What is your focus—agriculture, or history?" I smiled. "So, you are a professor. How many days have you been here?" he said, and gently knocked his pipe against the stroller to empty the burnt tobacco. He untied the old brown bag, filled the small brass bowl, and said, "You can write a story from a farmer's mouth," The woman in the orange T-shirt came closer, and Grandpa told his story.

Once upon a time, many years back, an old peasant lived with his son in a village in northern China, Grandpa said in his usual oratorial style. It was April, and it rained without a pause. The farmers were happy, although they feared a possible flood. Like everyone else, the old peasant watched the rain, thinking about his crops and worrying about the flood. The farmer's son was never much of a farmer. He knew nothing about the world of crops. He was a man of letters, a writer. One day, during those days of heavy rain, the boy sat by the window and stared at the world outside. He looked puzzled. For the whole day, and the next, the boy stayed by the window and did not move. And the rain continued. The old peasant became concerned. "What is it, my son? What is troubling you?" asked the old man. The son had not eaten for more than a day now. "I am looking for the right words to describe this rain, father," said the son. "The young man was helpless," Grandpa said, and he cracked up laughing. He paused and hunched forward, looked me in the eye, and said, "The boy wanted to write a poem about the rain. But he didn't have the right words." The old peasant was uneducated and ignorant, but he had the perfect answer for his son. "Lo Main rain," he said to the troubled writer, describing the rain using the word for noodles. "Lo Main rain," repeated the son, and continued to write for hours. "Lo Main rain," said Grandpa.

The smiling woman joined our circle. Grandpa lit the pipe. "Yes, the wisdom of an old peasant!" he said, nodding. He untied his checkered blue handkerchief, took out his watch, and said, "The fire is waiting for me."

I invited the smiling woman to join me for a snack at McDonald's.

"I am free. This is my day off," she said, and we left the park for the Longgang World Trade Center.

*   *   *

Wang Chun Ling was born to a poor peasant family in a small village in Hunan Province in 1977. She was five years old when she started to wake up at dawn and follow her parents to work on the farm. Mother was short-handed when Wang Chun Ling began elementary school. Chores awaited her when she returned home. She would spend the next hours cleaning, and running between the family's mud house and the farm. Wang Chun Ling graduated with low grades every year. At the end of the third year, Wang Chun Ling said farewell to schooling. "My parents needed me, and I did not like studying

14   Wan Chun Ling

at all," she told me. Wang Chun Ling's short school experience ended at age ten. She spent the next 19 years working on a small farm before she left in the summer of 2006. Wang Chun Ling was hardly able to read and write, and had a difficult time organizing her thoughts.

In many ways, Wang Chun Ling was a younger Grandpa. Carrying on a conversation with her was not an easy task— staying on the same subject for more than a few minutes was nearly impossible. Grandpa had had less schooling than Wang Chun Ling, but he had had the opera as his teacher. Wang Chun Ling had no interest in the opera. She did not know about emperors and dynasties, war and peace, and all the stories that Grandpa told so passionately. She was a simple peasant. Her dark and leathery skin betrayed her many years of constant exposure to the sun. She wore cheap jeans and T-shirts, and did not follow the popular fashion among most migrant workers, younger and more educated girls like Yu Xinhong and her friends.

We spent the first couple of meetings talking about random matters. As with Grandpa, food was always a favorite subject for Wang Chun Ling.

"Do you like Chinese food?"

"Do all Americans like Chinese food?"

"How is Western food?"

"I would not like that," she made a face, listening to me describe making a green salad.

"Do you like the Chinese people?"

"Do you like China?"

"Welcome to China."

"Do you like sesame oil?"

"I will bring you sesame oil from my farm," she promised one day. "We will cook together. You come to my place," I said.

We made plans to meet at my apartment the next Sunday "I have been looking for a chance to cook since I left my village," she said when she arrived that Sunday morning. "I brought this with me from the village last year. It is yours now," she said and untied a clear plastic bag, taking out a small Coca-Cola bottle filled with thick, dark sesame oil. She followed me to the kitchen, stood beside me, and said, "I am ready. Tell me what to do." I asked her to wash some fruit and began chopping the scallions, eggplants, zucchinis, and mushrooms. "No! Not this way. I show you how to cut vegetables," she protested and took the knife from me. Wang Chun Ling demonstrated the art of cutting vegetables quickly, in uniform sizes, and stirring and flipping them in a wok. "I have not cooked for almost a year," she said again.

*   *   *

We were sitting on the floor, eating oranges and watermelon and resting, when she reached for her purple bag, took out a picture, and said, "This is my son. He is one year old in this picture." I held a studio photo of a little boy sitting on a yellow plastic duck much larger than him. He held on to the duck's neck and stared at the camera with a frightened look. "He is two now. I haven't seen him for a year."

This was the first time Wang Chun Ling had talked about her family. "Keep it. I have another. This is for you," she said and gave me the picture of her boy.

*   *   *

In 1996, when Wang Chun Ling turned 19, most villagers her age had already left for work in factories in the coastal areas. Wang Chun Ling had heard stories about Shenzhen and life away from the farm. The stories were thrilling—if only she could join everyone else, she thought. But that was not possible. Once or twice she mentioned the idea to her aging parents. They would not have it. They needed her to take care of the farm, they said. And they had stories of their own. Shenzhen was a dangerous city, they had heard from those returning home. The city was full of thieves, not a good place for someone like her. Wang Chun Ling was fully aware that she had no chance. She had to stay on the farm. There was no way out. And when a man her age from the next village asked for her hand, she was quick to accept. Perhaps marriage would bring some excitement to her life. Wang Chun Ling became a married woman at age 19, and a mother a year later. Five months after the birth of her first son, Wang Chun Ling's husband packed his clothes and took the train to Beijing "to earn money and build us a house." Wang Chun Ling's husband joined thousands of other migrants moving from one construction site to another, and living in overcrowded makeshift homes in the capital.

Wang Chun Ling continued helping her old and frail parents. To earn extra cash, she worked part-time on a commercial flower farm, picking, trimming, and packing flowers. "There are beautiful flowers around my hometown," she said. She would leave home on her bike at six in the morning, ride for seven miles to the flower farm, and return home with 15 yuan, less than two dollars, after eight hours of work. "It was not much, but the owners also worked hard planting and taking care of the flowers. They hired us to help pick flowers. We were all hard-working people. Our goal was the same. We wanted to earn more money and live a better life," she said.

Wang Chun Ling's husband did not return home for the next three years, even during the Spring Festival. Occasionally, he sent money to his wife and his aging parents. Wang Chun Ling raised her boy, worked on her parents' farm, and helped her parents-in-law with farm work and other needs. During the next seven years, she saw her husband five times, each time for one week. She gave birth to her second son nine months after her husband's last visit.

Then one day, as if she had had an awakening, something sparked in her. "I could not stay anymore." Remaining on the farm was no longer an option. Even her newborn could not stop her from leaving. She had made up her mind: her time had come. The fierce protests of her parents did not matter this time. She left not to be with her husband in Beijing, but to work in Shenzhen.

"What did your husband say?" I asked. "It was my decision," Wang Chun Ling said, laughing. Wang Chun Ling left her two boys with her husband's parents, took a small bag of clothes, and boarded the train to Shenzhen. She was 29 years old and had never been on a train before. The farthest she had ever traveled was to the town less than 20 minutes' drive from the village.

*   *   *

When I first met Wang Chun Ling she had just returned from a three-week visit to Shanghai. A friend from an earlier job had paid for her ticket and other expenses, she said. She left her factory job and boarded the bus to Shanghai "to have fun with her friend." Wang Chun Ling had seen Shanghai's nice streets and beautiful buildings on television. Friends had told her about the "fun life," and all the things she had never experienced. Now was her chance. She quit her job without receiving her back pay. The visit may also lead to a job and a longer stay, she thought.

"Shanghai is beautiful," she told me. Wang Chun Ling loved the malls, the buildings, and the boulevards. Finding a job, however, was a different matter. "Most jobs required taking an exam. I don't have much education. It was impossible to find a job there for someone like me." Disappointed, she returned to Shenzhen after three weeks. "I don't regret going there at all. I had a wonderful time."

Back in Shenzhen she was out of work. Finding a new job was not, however, a concern. All export-processing factories were facing a labor shortage in 2007. Competition was fierce and factories were giving their workers better terms and higher salaries to steal them from others. Wang Chun Ling landed a job at the packaging department of a large toy factory the day after she returned to Shenzhen. She was staying at a small apartment near the Li Family Village with a friend from a previous job. Wang Chun Ling was not sure how long she would stay at the new one.

*　*　*

Wang Chun Ling had had three jobs since she left the village. Her last one before leaving for Shanghai was in a large Taiwanese-owned company that made shoes for New Balance on the outskirts of Longgang. She was one among 10,000 workers living in the factory compound, and found that exciting. She befriended boys and girls from other provinces—until a year earlier, she had not met anyone living even more than an hour away from her village. Wang Chun Ling was experiencing a new life. She was happy, meeting new friends, going to the mall in her free time, and living a life free of responsibility.

Of all the friends Wang Chun Ling made in Freetrend, 19-year-old Fan Xiu Qin from Hubei Province was her closest. Fan Xiu Qin loved to travel and "play." She quit her job without giving notice when Wang Chun Ling told her of her plan to visit Shanghai. "We took the bus together and laughed the whole way to Shanghai," Wang Chun Ling told me. Fan Xiu Qin remained in Shanghai for an extra two weeks after her friend returned to Shenzhen. "Can I bring Fan Xiu Qin to meet you? I have told her a lot about you. She is very curious," Wang Chun Ling said before one of our Sunday rendezvous.

I was waiting outside McDonald's when Wang Chun Ling arrived without her friend. "This girl cannot even take a bus. She is on her way," she said, and dialed Fan Xiu Qin's number. "She is coming," she called again, walked back and forth, and checked every bus that stopped in front of the Longgang World Trade Center. More buses arrived, and Wang Chun Ling made more calls, shouted and laughed more, and paced back and forth. "She will be here in a minute," she said a number of times. "Yes! She is here," Wang Chun Ling shouted as she ran to the bus stop.

"*Nihao,*" said Fan Xiu Qin in a low, gentle voice. She was four feet tall, with short hair and a pretty and girlish face. As we walked away from the Longgang World Trade Center, the two friends quarreled, laughed, and quarreled more. "I am happy to see her," Wang Chung Ling said as she complained about her friend being late.

It was time for lunch, and I suggested a restaurant by the Beautiful Rose Garden. Wang Chun Ling took control of ordering, and selected colorful dishes of pork, chicken, beef, fish, and boiled vegetables. Our food arrived and all conversation stopped. For nearly an hour we voyaged with our chopsticks from one dish to another, and enjoyed our meal in silence. Jokes and laughter, and a random conversation about life and work, started soon after.

Wang Chun Ling: "Do you like noodles? We eat a lot of noodles in my province."

Fan Xiu Qin: "The whole of China eats rice. Only people in your province eat noodles."

Wang Chun Ling: "No, that's not true! People in many parts of China eat noodles."

Fan Xiu Qin: "Potatoes are not good for you. My grandpa had stomach cancer from eating a lot of potatoes. He is dead now."

We had been at the restaurant for nearly two hours when I suggested a stroll in the park. The waitress brought the bill.

"I am paying this time," Wang Chun Ling said and grabbed the bill.

"I feel embarrassed. You always pay in McDonald's. I have money now. I have a job," she said. We began walking to the park.

"Do you have parks in America?" Wang Chun Ling asked.

"Of course. There is a large park near my home. It is 500 times bigger than this."

"Is he exaggerating?" Fan Xiu Qin whispered in my interpreter's ear.

"Does it rain in America?" asked Wang Chun Ling.

"It rains everywhere in the world. Don't say silly things. It's embarrassing," Fan Xiu Qin said.

We sat under the shade of a small tree in a far end of the park. Silence prevailed once again. "I want to quit my job. It is hard working in the toy factory," Wang Chun Ling broke the silence. "I have to work for many years to save money. I wish I had more education. I played too much when I was in school," she laughed again. "Poverty was actually an excuse. You could always study if you wanted to. Even the poorest parents would support their children's studies," she said.

"Neither of my two brothers finished school. I was an average student. I wish I had stayed in school. It is too late to have any regrets now," Fan Xiu Qin said with her head down.

"I feel really trapped sometimes. I will live with my aunt until I get a new job. My aunt has been working in the electronic factory for many years. She cleans the dormitories. The work is hard, but she cannot get anything else. She is 50 years old. Who would hire her? She has a son and a daughter. The son is still in school at home. The daughter works in a factory here," she said.

*   *   *

Fan Xiu Qin dropped out of school and took the train to join her aunt in a small factory in Shenzhen when she reached 16. "I was curious about the outside world," she said. A job at her aunt's factory was waiting. "Twelve hours a day, with only one day off every four weeks," she said. She earned 800 yuan at the end of the first month. Fan Xiu Qin had never had so much money in her life.

This was the first time she had been away from home, her first time working, her first time following orders. She had never even helped her family with the household chores. Fan Xiu Qin was homesick and tired. "I cried every night." Three months after she left home, Fan Xiu Qin quit her job, took her saved money, and returned to the village. But remaining in the village was also not the right thing—even the short time she had spent in the city had changed her too much. She felt trapped between two worlds. Shenzhen was difficult; home was too mundane. Back in the village, she was restless and cranky, arguing with her mother all the time. A few weeks later, Fan Xiu Qin returned to Shenzhen, this time determined to stay regardless of the difficulties.

*   *   *

As the days passed, Wang Chun Ling became increasingly frustrated with the long hours in the toy factory. "I cannot bear this anymore. This job is easy, but the hours are impossible. I don't have enough time to shower some days," she complained. She called home and told her old mother about the hard time she was having. "Come back to your children. They need you," mother told her. But going home was not an option.

"I want to see all over China," she would tell me. To see elsewhere in China, Wang Chun Ling needed money she did not have. She had to remain in the toy factory for at least two months to receive her first pay. That was the norm everywhere in Guangdong. She was constantly on the phone with her husband in Beijing, or her friends, or ex-colleagues from Freetrend and other jobs. Wang Chun Ling had nearly finished all that she had saved from her previous jobs.

One day when Wang Chun Ling was feeling unusually down, a call from a friend brightened her day. "I talked to my boss. You can start working as soon as you get here," the friend told her about a job in a warehouse—one of the lowest-level jobs in the hierarchy of work available to migrant workers—in Zhejiang Province. The day after, Wang Chun Ling left the toy factory without notifying her boss, and without receiving any money for her work. "I am so happy. I feel free again," she told me. She would be on her way to Zhejiang by the end of the week. However, there was a slight problem.

Wang Chun Ling did not have enough money for the bus fare. The friend in Zhejiang had agreed to transfer the money, but she needed a bank account for that. Thirty years old, she still did not have one. She rarely had any business in a bank. She was bewildered.

"Borrow money from someone and go to a local bank with your ID card. They will open an account for you. That is easy," her friend told her. With fear and apprehension, Wang Chun Ling followed the friend's advice. The experience was harder than anything she had encountered in the past. She had to sign papers, fill out forms. "I didn't understand many words. I was so scared," she told me later. "I am happy I did this. I now have a bank account," she said, laughing loud.

Saying farewell was difficult. "We are family now," she told me on the phone. She was leaving the next day. "I will call you as soon as I get a new phone number," she said.

That night, she had a long conversation with her husband. He objected to her going to Zhejiang. They quarreled. Upset, she hung up on him. He called again. They argued. "Why don't you come to Beijing instead?" said the husband. That was an interesting proposition, she thought. Wang Chun Ling had a new plan.

"I am going to Beijing," she said when she called me the next day. I was also leaving Shenzhen for Beijing to meet Yue Haitao shortly after. "I will see you in Beijing," she cried. "I will find you a cheap hotel. Don't worry about anything. I will be there before you. I can take care of everything before you arrive." Not long after, Wang Chun Ling called from Beijing with a list of hotels, their prices, and their locations. "They are all too expensive. Don't worry. I will find you something cheaper," she said.

"When are you coming?" she said on the phone the day after, and every day. I was busy making plans and arranging for interviews when I arrived in Beijing, and did not contact Wang Chun Ling for two weeks. She called my interpreter in Shenzhen every day, dialed my old number, and even looked for me in Beijing.

"I knew you were a professor. My husband took a day off from his work and we went to Beijing University looking for you," she told me when we finally met at a restaurant one October afternoon. They found Beijing University's address by asking random bus drivers and police officers. The couple spent an entire afternoon at the university, walked to every corner, visited every café and restaurant on campus, and asked strangers about me. "Why were you not there?" she asked me. "Why did you go to the university to look for me?" I asked Wang Chun Ling. "You are a professor, aren't you?" she said.

* * *

Wang Chun Ling's husband was average height and skinny, with thinning hair. He was a chain-smoker. He remained quiet during the lunch and throughout the day. Wang Chun Ling ordered the food and made suggestions for things to do. At times, he smiled when she joked.

"How long do you think you will stay in Beijing?" I asked him at one point.

"As long as it takes to save money to build a home in the village," he said.

"How long will that be?"

"You asked me that question in Shenzhen," Wang Chun Ling interrupted. "It is hard to save money I told you."

Three weeks after arriving in Beijing Wang Chun Ling found a job taking care of a "rich" old woman. Although both were in Beijing, the husband and wife continued to live separately. Wang Chun Ling lived in the woman's home, her husband in a trailer dormitory at a construction site. He went without work for many weeks in a row. "This is still better than the village—I cannot make any money there," he said.

When he had work, Wang Chun Ling's husband labored 14 hours a day. He slept the rest of the day. After ten years in Beijing, he had not visited the Great Wall, the Forbidden City, or any of the other places that attracted millions of people to China from across the world. Construction sites were all he knew about Beijing. He got lost moving around the city. The day we met, he and Wang Chun Ling took the wrong bus, traveled to the opposite side of the city, and arrived more than an hour late.

We had met near Beijing University, a short taxi ride from the Summer Palace, a vast garden with lakes, beautiful bridges, halls, palaces, temples, and pavilions. I invited Wang Chun Ling and her husband on their first sightseeing trip in Beijing.

Wang Chun Ling took 60 pictures with her cell phone camera. Running around like a child, she jumped on her husband's back, skipped, and put her head on his lap. Wang Chun Ling was "in heaven," she said. "I like being a tourist," she told me.

THE GREAT FLOOD

In the summer of 1998, the Yangtze river saw its biggest flood in 40 years. The Great Flood shook China, and devastated the lives of millions living along the Yangtze. By September, when the Yangtze calmed and the waters subsided, thousands were dead, millions uprooted, and scores of villages destroyed. Pain and sorrow prevailed.

While the adults lived in constant fear of more flooding and more devastation, in the village of Ku Caoba, a sleepy hamlet of 50 or so families near the Yangtze in Hubei Province, a little girl and her friends were enjoying the temporary excitement, and the change in their ordinary lives. Only ten years old, Liu Xia had the time of her life. The flood had stopped normal life. For Liu Xia and her friends this meant a time for more childhood games and the excitement of living on the edge.

"My village is near a dam. Everyone thought that the dam would break and the flood would destroy our village." The flood had devastated other villages, and the residents of Ku Caoba stayed by the dam to make sure it was secure. "Everyone was so scared. My family spent many nights by the dam," Liu Xia recalled years later. This was Liu Xia's most memorable time in the 17 years that she had lived in Ku Caoba. "I lived a typical life. Not much happened in the village." The flood was the best time of her childhood.

The boredom of mundane village life ended when Liu Xia stepped onto the train for her long ride to Shenzhen in the summer of 2005. Life changed from that point on.

She had never been on a train before, never been away from home. The train was full of farmers, men and women in their thirties and older. Their skins wrinkled and reddened from exposure to the sun, the older passengers wore dusty worn-out shoes and Mao suits. Dressed in their best, and amazed at everything they encountered, young boys and girls, Liu Xia's age or older, squatted in the corridor, talked with their friends, told stories, laughed, and kept awake the tired farmers dozing off in their seats. For many hours, Liu Xia did not close her eyes. She sat by the window, staring at the landscape, the villages, and farms along the way, and at the masses of people who got in and out of the train at each stop.

"Before leaving home, I thought our villages were the only villages in China, and we were the only poor people. I learned this was not true when I took the train to Shenzhen. I saw many more villages, and a lot of poor people like my neighbors."

Arriving in the Luohu train station, a brand new and state-of-the-art station in the heart of Shenzhen, Liu Xia was surrounded by fancy, tall glass buildings, five-star hotels, shopping malls, bars, restaurants, massage parlors, hair salons, and McDonald's. Four-story brick homes were the tallest buildings she had seen back home. Never before had she been around so many people, young men and women from all over China, speaking dialects she could not understand. She saw beautiful tall Chinese girls, six feet tall and more, and girls with light skin, wearing tight jeans, or short skirts revealing their long and slender legs. Like everyone she knew, Liu Xia was short, and her skin not so light. "I saw tall Chinese for the first time." Liu Xia stared at these beauties with envy and admiration. This was a China unknown to her, and to her friends in the village. She was "awe stricken."

A job was awaiting Liu Xia upon arrival. Unlike many girls her age who worked in Shenzhen's subcontracting factories, Liu Xia joined the service sector. A classmate and friend of her older sister had opened a teahouse in Shenzhen not long before. She was to become a waitress at the teahouse, her sister had told her. Liu Xia was excited. After a short rest to recover from the journey, Liu Xia walked into the teahouse. She did not know the art of making and serving Chinese tea. "Working in the teahouse changed my life," Liu Xia told me.

15   At the train station in Beijing: returning to the village

*   *   *

The sweet scent of freshly brewed tea and the soothing sound of a harp pulled me away from the noisy world of vegetable shops, smelly restaurants, honking cars, and young women standing outside storefronts shouting into handheld megaphones and hustling passersby to their stores. I stopped and peeked through the window of the small, ordinary-looking teashop. Encouraged by the friendly face and the welcoming gesture of the woman behind the counter, I entered. I walked down a small passage and found myself in a large cave-like space furnished with plastic tree trunks as tables and benches. Green and red fluorescent lights lit the cave.

Clad in knee-length pink silk dresses with two butterflies embroidered on the front, half a dozen young waitresses greeted me. "Welcome to China," a short waitress with rosy cheeks and thick-rimmed glasses said in heavily accented English.

I chose a table far from the entrance. With a smile bordering on a giggle, the young waitress gave me the house's elaborate tea menu. I was discussing a choice of tea with my interpreter when the waitress returned with a small electric burner, a pot for boiling water, a tray with an elaborate set of small teacups and pots, and small airtight and compressed bags of tea. She pulled up a white plastic stool and sat across from me. Still smiling, she put the pot of water on the burner, turned the knob, and said, "I'll teach you the art of drinking Chinese tea." This was my first encounter with Liu Xia.

I watched attentively as Liu Xia poured the contents of one bag of tea into a small porcelain cup, added boiled water, covered the cup, and gently moved the cup clockwise while holding the cover with her right thumb.

"We will not drink this," she said. Liu Xia bathed three teacups in that first wash from the tea, added boiled water to the tealeaves for the second time, waited a few seconds, and poured the first round of drinkable tea.

I held my cup on the top with my thumb and two fingers, and my pinky straightened outward.

"No! Not this way. This is how women drink," Liu Xia protested.

"I'll show you the right way for men and women to hold a teacup."

I followed her instructions, held the cup around its hot base with my pinky and other fingers closed, and swallowed the tea in one sip.

"No!" she cried again.

"Not this way. This is how we drink wine. In China, we don't *drink* tea. We *taste* it," she said, now laughing loudly.

Patiently, Liu Xia taught me how to drink the tea in three small sips, and explained how it was a sign of respect and love to fill only 70 percent of the teacup. This was unlike the way the Chinese served wine, she told me.

"Chinese people *savor* their tea."

Drinking Chinese wine was a different story, she said. As I would learn soon in my frequent wine-drinking outings with Chinese friends, drinking *baijiu*, the smelly and unpleasant-tasting Chinese distilled alcoholic beverage known as white wine, had its own ritual. The small wine glass had to be filled to the top, and not drinking the wine in one sip was a sign of disrespect to the friend serving the wine. "Bottoms up," Liu Xia said in English, laughing. "This is how we drink wine in China. Do not confuse tea with wine!"

In the next couple of hours, Liu Xia boiled more water and filled the cups to the 70 percent limit. She opened a second bag of tea. "This is Korean green tea," the best in the house, she said. She closed her eyes, smelled the tea, and took a deep breath.

By now, I had mastered the art of drinking tea. Carefully holding my cup, I took small sips, and smelled the tea with each sip. "You are a fast learner," Liu Xia said.

*   *   *

Liu Xia had lived on a farm with her family for 17 years. As with most other farm girls growing up in the age of economic reform, her parents raised her to have a future different from their own. She would not be a farm girl for the rest of her life. Living in the village as a child, Liu Xia had never worked on the farm. Her hands were soft, her skin not reddened or roughened by exposure to the sun. She rarely took part in household chores. "I don't know how to cook," she told me, laughing.

She spent her free time playing with friends. Her favorite times were chasing animals, or having a picnic with her classmates, making a fire to bake potatoes, and fishing in the river near the village. "We used to breed chickens and ducks. When I was young we chased the animals around, ran after them, and played with them. These are my good memories from that time."

Raising a family of four, Liu Xia's parents had to work hard. They would get up very early in the morning and spend all day in the fields. "The harvest season was the hardest for them," Liu Xia recalled. Growing corn and cotton, the family earned 6000 yuan a year (less than $800) for most of Liu Xia's childhood. Liu Xia remembered her parents never having enough money to buy "northern region fruits"—apples and peaches. Eating apples was a special treat on birthdays, or during the Spring Festival.

Two bicycles and a small black-and-white television were the only luxury goods the family possessed. Their income changed radically, however, when they abandoned planting corn and cotton, and turned the land into an orange orchard. That was what the local government had encouraged them to do. "We have 400 orange trees," Liu Xia boasted.

Not long after the family entered the new business of growing oranges, Liu Xia's older sister joined the ranks of migrant workers. She was 18 and ready to begin a new life. Liu Xia's sister wanted to be an "independent woman," and there was only one place she could realize that dream. She said farewell to her family one day and took the train to Shenzhen. Days later, she was a receptionist at a medium-sized hotel in the city's Luohu district. She sent home her meager savings in the beginning of every month. By then, the family was earning more than 20,000 yuan a year. With that came a refrigerator, a color TV, a new bicycle, and many things that Liu Xia could not have dreamed of as a small child. That was the year 2000. Liu Xia was in heaven. Finally, in 2002, her family moved to a three-story brick house in the nearby town. They commuted to the orchard every morning and returned at night. All around them, neighbors razed their mud houses, replacing them with nicer brick homes.

"When my mother was a young girl, village homes were built with mud. They became brick houses in my time. Now, there are lots of two- or three-story buildings in my village," Liu Xia told me.

* * *

Liu Xia was not much of a student. In fact, she hated school. "I didn't like to study. I had stomach aches every day before going to school," she told me, laughing. Traumatized by the teachers, their demands for studying, and everything that school represented, Liu Xia dropped out of high school before the end of the first year. "I saw no future in staying in senior high. I hated getting up early in the morning and studying till late at night. I found that very boring. I had to walk to senior high in the nearby town. We had a bicycle, but I never learned to ride a bike—my father was scared that something would happen. I had to walk to and from the school, 25 minutes each way."

There were four senior high schools in the town, ranked and named by ascending numbers, from the best to the worst. "I attended Senior High 4, the worst," she said, and broke down in hysterical laughter. Teachers and schools in China were evaluated and ranked by the average score of each class. "I think my teachers were happy when I dropped out. I would have brought down the average of my class if I had stayed. Everyone was happy at the end."

Liu Xia dropped out of school at age 17. A month later, she was working in the teahouse.

* * *

Nearly a month after our first meeting, Liu Xia accompanied her sister and her two-year-old nephew home for her father's birthday. She called me the first day she was back in Shenzhen. "I missed you," she said in English. We met in a local restaurant near the teahouse that evening. She wore a light blue knee-length skirt, black blouse, and heels. Tucked back and tied in a knot, her hair gave her a more professional appearance than usual. Lui Xia was happy.

She sat beside me, took out her cell phone from her bag, and showed me pictures from home: her mother and sister, the rice paddies on the way to the village, the bridge over the river, the family's three-story brick home, and images of her nephew playing with the family dogs.

"The rice paddies are very beautiful," she said. "This is my dog," she said in English.

"It is the happiest time for my family any time I go home," she said. "They are very busy the rest of the time, planting trees, farming, spraying the trees with pesticides, fertilizing the land. They have a lot of work to do, but everything stops when I visit. We are all very happy."

Lui Xia stopped suddenly and stared at a photo.

"This is my mother," she said and gave me the cell phone.

"My mother is a typical Chinese woman. She gave my sister and me a lot of love."

"How about your father?" I asked.

"Father loved us too, but he had a bad temper at times. I think father is kind inside."

Liu Xia became quiet, played with the half-empty cup of coffee in front of her, and stared at the cell phone. "My father is very stubborn." She put down the phone.

"He would never admit to his mistakes." A long pause followed.

"My father is a male chauvinist. He made every decision at home. Sometimes he got drunk and hit my mother."

"Does he still hit your mother?"

"He has changed. At that time, he was young, and our economic conditions were not good. He acted irrationally sometimes. It is understandable." With the improvement in the family's finances, Liu Xia's father became more relaxed. There was no more fighting. "Except for rare occasions, he forgot his hitting hand, and became a loving husband."

"What would you do if your husband hit you?" I asked.

"It depends on whose fault it is. I may forgive him once or twice if it is my fault. Everyone makes mistakes. Compromise is the most important thing in saving a marriage."

"What if this gets repeated, and becomes a habit?"

"If the hitting continues," she paused, "I may leave for a while to give both of us time to think about the relationship. We will have to decide whether we should stay together or go our separate ways. Anyway, it is wrong for a man to hit a woman. A wife is someone to love, not to hit."

*   *   *

Liu Xia liked men, but she did not have a boyfriend. Discussing the subject made her giggle.

"What do you think of boys?" I asked one day.

"Boyfriend?" she said in English, laughing.

"Yes, I mean a boyfriend. What is your ideal boyfriend?"

"Someone to love me and protect me. I don't care about looks very much. I care about honesty and fidelity."

"Why don't you have a boyfriend now?"

"I am not ready. I have to change my job first. If I work in an office, I will be more confident. I will have higher standards when I look for a boyfriend. Men will also view me differently. Now people look down on me—I am just a waitress. The first thing I need to do is to learn computer skills."

The job at the teahouse had changed Liu Xia's life, she would repeat each time we met. It had taught her new skills, made her "open minded," showed her how to socialize, and introduced her to people she would have never met in the village. "I know I am not making a lot of money now. I don't care. I am becoming a different person, and that is what matters."

Liu Xia's parents and her older sister pressured her to save money. "How can I save?" With a salary of less than 1000 yuan, Liu Xia ran out of money days before the end of each month. She shared a "dormitory"—an apartment without kitchen paid for by her boss—with three other waitresses, and spent most of her money on food. "Even fast food is expensive. I spend 30 yuan a day just eating. I need money for telephone, bus rides, and clothes. But I am still happy."

She did not want to remain a waitress the rest of her life. Liu Xia dreamed of working in an office someday. "Before coming here, I had never met anyone working in an office. I did not know how they looked. I know it now, and I know I can be an office worker someday. I want to be a *white-collar* worker." For this, she had to learn to work with computers, her sister told her.

Learning computers while working in the teahouse did not seem possible. Many girls her age, and with computer skills, were entering Shenzhen every day. The market was getting tight. Lui Xia was losing her chances.

"Now I know how important it is to have other skills, like working with computers. I wish I had learned this at school. I was too lazy."

BEAN CURDS

One stage before the completion of making tofu, bean curds are cheap, and affordable even by the poorest of the poor. Yu Xinhong's father loved bean curds, she recalls. He would eat them with soy sauce. Sometimes, Yu Xinhong would notice her father sobbing while eating bean curds. Tears would run down his cheeks. She did not know why he was sobbing. She would say to her father, "This food is so delicious. Why are you crying? It would be even better if you added some sugar." Years later and away from home, Yu Xinhong understood the reason for what had puzzled her as a child—eating bean curds reminded her father of the old times, the poor times.

* * *

In a village not far from Liu Xia's, the little Yu Xinhong lived with her parents and two older brothers on a farm at the foot of the mountains. Two years apart in age, the two girls were childhood acquaintances. Their older siblings were good friends. Hard-working peasants, Lui Xia's mother and father knew nothing but the farmland and the monotonous and tedious work they had inherited from their parents and grandparents. That was not the case, however, with Yu Xinhong's family. Yu Xinhong's father was a schoolteacher, a man of books who had big plans for his little girl. No daughter of his was going to become a farmer, or drop out of school like the other girls in the village, he always told Yu Xinhong.

As a little girl, Yu Xinhong saw men in their late twenties or thirties leave the village for the city. They were among the first generation of migrant workers, recruited by new private enterprises in Shenzhen and nearby cities. Returning home in a few years with money saved from working in factories or on construction sites, they would build better houses for their family, resume their work on the farm, or start small businesses.

Those leaving the village before Yu Xinhong had one foot on the farm, another in the city. Floating between two worlds, they were farmers temporarily employed as urban workers. While in the city, they worked backbreaking jobs, and lived in overcrowded dormitories housing ten to twelve people in a room, or in ghettoes, sharing small spaces without kitchens and bathrooms. Work in the city was a means to a better life in the village. Wages were low, but a lot higher than they would have earned on the farm. For most migrants, this was a temporary arrangement, only helping a better life back in the village.

That was no longer the case by the time Yu Xinhong's brothers left for Shenzhen. Migration was now a one-way journey. Born during the years of reform, the children of farmers had an improved standard of living. Many attended school. Working in big cities introduced them to a new world of global culture and consumption. They cherished window shopping in malls in their spare time, occasional outings to McDonalds and KFC, visiting karaoke joints with friends, going to movies, dating freely, meeting foreigners, and feeling part of the *open* China.

Although most lived on the margins of this new China, they dreamed of a day when they would acquire all that their country supplied to the rest of the world. They did not know about farming, and detested life on the farm. In the opinion of these migrants, farm life belonged to the old China, the China of their parents. The city provided hope; farming did not. They did not intend to return. They were members of China's new working class, expecting to benefit from all the promises of the Chinese dream—most of all, a home, and a full and normal life in the city.

When they visited their villages after a few years of work in the city, the migrants would help others to leave, to become workers in China's sprawling manufacturing and service industries. Yu Xinhong's brothers left the village for Shenzhen when she was a teenager. She was excited, knowing her time would come soon. She had to finish high school before leaving home, her father insisted. She complied. Days after graduating from high school, she packed a small suitcase and boarded the train to Shenzhen.

*   *   *

I was shelling pumpkin seeds and drinking tea with Liu Xia one late afternoon when I noticed a petite waitress with high cheekbones and short hair pulled back and tied in the back surreptitiously staring at us. Passing by, she would timidly smile, pretend to be busy at a table near us, and eavesdrop.

The end of Liu Xia's twelve-hour shift was approaching and she was preparing to call it a day. "My friend will take care of you," Liu Xia said, and pointed at the girl with high cheekbones. That was the first time I had met Yu Xinhong. She sat elegantly beside me with her back straight and her knees crossed, and spoke in a calm voice.

*   *   *

Of all the people in her life, Yu Xinhong was most influenced by her father. Talking about him, she would become emotional and tearful. An elementary schoolteacher supporting a family of five, Yu Xinhong's father earned 100 yuan when she opened her eyes to this world in 1985. This was a sharp increase from his salary at the beginning of his teaching career in the 1970s. Still poor, the family could, however, afford more and better food when Yu Xinhong was a young girl. "We were not starving," she told me. However, life remained difficult during Yu Xinhong's childhood. "Both of my brothers attended school. Father could not support the family on his salary."

Yu Xinhong recalled her mother waking up early in the morning and working on the farm until sunset. At times, her brothers would wake with their mother and work in the fields before leaving for school. Yu Xinhong would remain in bed. "I was too young," she said. She stayed away from the farm even when she grew older.

The government had allotted the family four small plots of land in different parts of the village. A short walk from the house and on the slope of the mountain, the first plot was a rice paddy. Not owning any machinery, mother tilled the land by hand, Yu Xinhong recalled. "She had to go to the rice paddy every day to check the water level, and remove the wild grass."

The family owned three pigs, and had no trucks. Yu Xinhong's mother carried pig manure to the field to use as fertilizer. Single-handedly, she planted corn, wheat, beans, and potatoes on other plots. Occasionally, the family hired extra hands, neighbors who would work for money. That was a common practice during Yu Xinhong's childhood.

"When I was very young, we did not have a television. Most villagers did not. Only one family in our village had a small black-and-white television. I remember there was a popular joke among the villagers at that time: 'Do you have any electronic appliances in your home? Yes, we do, we have a flashlight.'" For the first time in our meetings, Yu Xinhong broke into laughter.

Many things had changed since those childhood years. Not long ago, Yu Xinhong's father's salary had jumped to 1100 yuan a month. Working in Shenzhen, brothers were sending money home. Yu Xinhong's family purchased a color TV and a refrigerator.

With more disposable income, Yu Xinhong's mother gave up the rice paddy, but took care of the remaining fields without needing help from others. There were no extra hands to hire even if she had needed help. Joining the massive army of migrant workers, all the young men and women from Yu Xinhong's village, and those in nearby villages, had left for Shenzhen and other big cities. Farmers her mother's age were not in any position to help others. Some needed help themselves.

*   *   *

Yu Xinhong's father taught at an elementary school in a village an hour's walk from their home. The school took only the first four grades. Father found commuting to and from the school every day a tiring task, so he stayed in a small room at the school during the week, and saw his family only at weekends. Yu Xinhong's birth made this arrangement too painful for him. He missed his little girl, and wished to spend more time with her. When Yu Xinhong reached school age, father persuaded his wife that he should take his little girl away, and he enrolled her in his school. The two shared a room and spent their free time talking, and reading schoolbooks and novels. "I like reading even now. I don't have any free time to read, but I will someday," Yu Xinhong told me.

When she graduated fourth grade, Yu Xinhong had to leave her father's school, return home, and enroll in another school in a faraway village. "That was when I began jumping tractors," she said, with a mischievous look on her face.

Yu Xinhong lived in a house on the mountain. Looking out from her living room window, she could see the road a few hundred feet below, curving and going up and down. There were no cars, only tractors and trucks on the road in those days, she recalled. With the sound of tractors driving down the road, she "would become like a boy," excited, ready to break her boredom. At times, she would wait by the road for tractors with other boys from the village. They would run after the tractors and climb onto them, always hoping not to be noticed by the driver.

"I remember once we climbed on a tractor. It was strange, the tractor was running when the driver turned around, got on the top, and threatened us with a thick rope. We were so scared. We jumped off and ran home without stopping on the way. He was not even chasing us."

When she turned eleven and started fifth grade in a village an hour's walk away, tractor-jumping was no longer a game but a necessity, as it shortened the journey to 20 minutes. Yu Xinhong could not pass up that opportunity, she told me.

She was badly injured from falling off a tractor once, and her father made her promise to stop doing it. She kept her promise for a while, then, tempted by the reduced journey, she resumed her habit until her oldest brother bought a used truck. "I would sit beside him and leave all the tractors behind. We were a lot faster."

Yu Xinhong's brother left the village for Guangdong three years later. He worked different jobs, and finally landed a good position in Shenzhen. Graduating the middle school, Yu Xinhong enrolled in a high school away from home. She remembered the day her father took her to register.

"Father gave me money and let me register and do everything by myself." Once all was arranged, father and daughter ate lunch in the school cafeteria and returned to the small hotel room where they were staying for the night. "The hotel was 20 yuan a night, and the meal 1.5 yuan," Yu Xinhong remembered. Yu Xinhong's father was quiet that day. They stayed in the room without talking. Next morning, he would be returning to the village, leaving his daughter behind in a strange city. The night was tense. He had tearful eyes, Yu Xinhong remembered. Before leaving in the morning, he gave Yu Xinhong a letter.

"I don't expect you to eat nice and expensive food, but make sure you eat enough. I don't expect you to wear nicer clothes, but make sure you are clothed," he wrote to his daughter. "I still keep that letter." Tears rolled down Yu Xinhong's face.

Because of her father's encouragement, and unlike many girls her age, Yu Xinhong remained in school and graduated from senior high with good grades. "Father wanted me to go out and get to know more about the outside world." To Yu Xinhong, the outside world included the West. Shenzhen was only a gateway to a bigger and better world, and working in the teahouse was a temporary and convenient step towards this exciting future. She was sure of that. "Even though I was born in a poor family, my father always taught me to be independent and have dreams."

*　　*　　*

A ritual emerged as we met more frequently in the teahouse. Arriving in the early afternoon, I would choose a quiet corner. Liu Xia would bring a big plate full of pumpkin seeds marinated in jasmine tea, and roasted. Large quantities of boiled peanuts would follow. "This one will make you feel calm," Liu Xia would say, preparing a mildly sweet-tasting Korean green tea. Yu Xinhong would run to the corner store and return with slices of watermelon, or exotic Chinese fruits. For hours, we would shell seeds, drink tea, joke, and share stories. Practicing English was Liu Xia's favorite, and Yu Xinhong would sit quietly and watch her clumsy attempts.

"Green tea is very healthy."

"I work in a teahouse," she would say, and break into a frenzy of laughter.

"Computer."

"Sit down, please."

"How are you?" was the first English sentence Liu Xia had learned in school. She had a technique for memorizing English words: she would remember a Chinese word with a similar pronunciation. "My friends and I used *San gen you* for thank you." She laughed.

It was during one of those English lessons when Yu Xinhong changed the subject abruptly, looked me straight in the eyes and asked, "Do you miss your home?"

"That is a difficult question. I don't feel I have a home. I was born in Iran, where I cannot return. There are many things that I miss about Iran."

"Why can't you return?"

I told the girls about Iranian politics, the 1979 revolution, Iran's war with Iraq, the persecution of intellectuals and workers by the government, the torture and the killings, and all the things that made my return impossible.

"Who do they torture and kill?" asked Liu Xia. For the first time in our meetings, she looked troubled.

"They kill anyone who dares to disagree."

"You must be a democrat! Is the government of Iran still the same?" she asked.

I explained the changes Iran experienced after the death of Ayatollah Khomeini, the short period of reform, and all that followed with the presidency of Mahmood Ahmadinejad.

"I had no idea about this. I cannot believe how cruel and violent the government of Iran is. I thought people were equal everywhere. I thought people in other countries had a situation similar to ours in China. Now I know they are different from China. We don't have any problems here."

Growing up, Liu Xia knew little about China, less about the rest of the world.

"I knew about the Forbidden City, and the Great Wall. I had seen them on television."

When her family bought a television, Liu Xia's father asked her to watch the news every evening, and learn more about the world. But Liu Xia found politics a waste of time. "I never cared for politics. I found it so boring." Images of the American war in Iraq, and the wars in Afghanistan, Sudan, and Somalia, upset her. War and destruction looked foreign and distant. "China is the best country. There is no war here. People don't kill each other," Liu Xia said. Yu Xinhong interrupted.

"I hope you stay in China. Make China your home. Home and family are very important to the Chinese. We have several festivals here that celebrate the family."

"Why do you care about Chinese people?" Liu Xia asked.

I patiently explained China's new role in the world and the significance of Chinese exports in America and elsewhere, and told Liu Xia how the Chinese workers had become a part of people's lives in other countries by producing clothes, TV sets, computers, and other things they used.

"Why would anyone buy Chinese products? Chinese goods are very low quality. I did not know about this. I think Japanese and Korean goods are better. I prefer them," she said. "Anyway, I don't make clothes or televisions. Why are you interested in me?" she laughed. "Don't worry, I will tell you everything about my life," she said after a short pause. Turning to my interpreter, Liu Xia asked, "What is the English word for humor?"

"You have a good sense of humor," she told me in a mixture of Chinese and English.

"How long will you stay in China?" Yu Xinhong interrupted again.

"I'll stay as long as it takes to finish my work. It takes time to get to know people. You need to build trust."

"I trust you. I will be happy to tell you my story. I feel very comfortable with you and think I can learn a lot from you."

*   *   *

We had been at the teahouse for hours one hot summer day. Evening customers were slowly appearing. This was Yu Xinhong's day off and we were preparing to leave for dinner at a Guangdong restaurant when, suddenly, she looked at me and said, "I think Western women are very attractive and sexy."

"Do you think Chinese women are beautiful?" she asked.

"I think American girls are most beautiful. I like the way they are, the way they dress, and their manners. I think they are who they are. They don't care much about what other people think. China is different. Women care about what others think," she said.

Earlier that afternoon, when my interpreter left us temporarily, Yu Xinhong came closer to me and whispered in accented English, "She is very beautiful." "She will be in America soon, studying for her PhD," I tried to say to the girls, and finally made them understand after many attempts. My interpreter was a tall and educated Chinese girl on her way to a university in America. She was breaking all boundaries, achieving what was unimaginable for most of the teahouse girls. Yu Xinhong admired her. "She is so beautiful," she said again.

As a child, Yu Xinhong had often thought about America and imagined herself in a big American city, living like an American. She had spent nights and days make-believing life in America. She would pretend she was walking in the streets of an imaginary American city, visiting stores with nice toys and clothes. It was a dream that would never come true, she thought. America was too far away. How could she ever get there? It would take her years to travel, she thought at one point. She could take a plane, she realized later. But tickets were so expensive. Impossible! She could never get to see America. Even living in Beijing or other cities in China seemed beyond her reach. Beijing was a city in fairytales and history books. It too was out of reach.

Years later, in Shenzhen, she met real-life American women, sat beside them, drank tea, and talked with them. She felt much closer to their world. They and their world were more tangible now. She liked touching their hair, she told me. For the first time in her life, she felt the feasibility of her dream when she saw the airplane ticket of a woman on her way back to Chicago. "For all those years, I had thought the airfare would be so high that I could not afford one, even if I worked hard all my life. Now I know that is not the case. I could pay the fare with hard work. I could do it," she said. "I know I can be there someday."

European and American women she met had told her about the success of Chinese restaurants and teahouses in the West. Others told her of the popularity of Chinese medicine. Chinese tea is very popular in the West, one had said. Yu Xinhong was determined to tap into that market. Many before her had made a good life in America. She told me of an uneducated village girl who became a famous singer, making a lot of money, and writing a book about her journey to success. "Have you read her book?" she asked. Yu Xinhong did not have a good voice, did not know about acting. "But I know the teahouse business. Yes, that's what I will do."

For now, she was unable to save a penny, let alone enough to pay for her ticket to America with her 800 yuan a month salary. She knew that was to change in the future. She would not remain a teahouse girl forever. Yu Xinhong had much bigger dreams. "I will leave this job soon. There is no room for growth in the teahouse. I have learned the craft and will use it in the future someday. For now, I have to experience other things."

I WILL BE MY OWN BOSS

When she moved to Shenzhen, for nearly a year Yu Xinhong worked in an export-processing assembly line and produced monitors and small personal computers shipped to faraway markets outside China. This was 2003. Her first salary was 282.8 yuan a month, $33 at the exchange rate of the time. "I think 282.8 was a lucky number because it had a double two and a double eight," she told me, laughing. Not working overtime, she did not receive any extra. She had to share a small and dirty dormitory room with eleven other girls. The food was bad. "I missed my mother's cooking." A month later, Yu Xinhong's salary increased to 450 yuan, a dramatic increase, she thought.

There were a lot of meetings during the day, she recalled. The company's boss was a young Taiwanese who was obsessed with discipline, obedience, and efficiency. Supervisors spent a lot of time training the workers. The organization in the factory was complex. Every department had its own, very strict, procedure.

She began her days joining hundreds of other girls, standing in perfect lines, saluting, shouting, and getting energized and prepared for the shop floor. Across Shenzhen in other factory towns millions of young workers participated in similar practices, copying military drills the Taiwanese bosses had brought back to China after the 1980s. Yu Xinhong did not mind the daily drills, the discipline, or the low wages.

At the beginning, the work was hard and tiring. After three months, the boss promoted her to team leader. For the first time in her life, Yu Xinhong was supervising a group of other women. She loved the responsibility and the status that came with the job. She could see herself moving higher and higher in the company. Not long after the promotion, Yu Xinhong applied for another, asking to work elsewhere in the factory. The boss refused, and she left the job the following week. She left not because of the difficulties of the job, but because she wanted "better and more challenging positions." "Although my wage was not that high, I learned a lot working there."

Over the next two years, Yu Xinhong moved between four factory jobs, lived in different dormitory rooms, some less crowded than others, and continued to search for a position that suited her education and dreams. "I had a high school degree. Most of the girls I worked with only finished junior high," she said. She was not cut out for assembly line work, Yu Xinhong believed.

* * *

One year after leaving home, Yu Xinhong met a man twelve years her senior. He was a security guard in a small factory. She had her first real boyfriend. "I needed someone to protect me," she said. The boyfriend was kind and respectful to her. Yu Xinhong's brother, however, protested. "He is too old for you," he told her, and demanded that she break up with him. To ensure his sister's separation from the older man, he ordered her to leave her job and return to the village.

Yu Xinhong acquiesced. She said farewell to her boyfriend, and returned to the place she thought she had left behind for good. "I cannot say no to my brother and father. They are the most important people in my life."

Yu Xinhong took a job at a copy center in a nearby town. She loved the warmth and the friendliness of the village, but life back home lacked the excitement and energy she had felt in Shenzhen. "Shenzhen is different from our village. We live on the mountains and have less connection with the rest of the world. We are isolated, but people are friendly and kind. People are cold in Shenzhen. Even the neighbors don't know each other. There are many lonely people here. But I still wanted to live in Shenzhen and make it my new home," she told me.

Yu Xinhong missed her life in Shenzhen. Working at the copy center was dull, the pay was low and the job was boring and uneventful. She did not meet new and exciting people, did not learn new skills. She felt trapped. "I was depressed." Her parents felt they had to do something to help. They talked between themselves, consulted with Yu Xinhong's older brother, and finally found the perfect answer—marriage.

Yu Xinhong was old enough to marry, they thought. She was smart and hard working. She deserved the best husband, and they finally found him after searching around and talking to others. He was only 23, the richest young man in their town, and son to millionaire parents who were the owners of a profitable tea factory. The young man took a liking to Yu Xinhong, finding her pretty, and a suitable candidate to be the mother of his future children.

Liking her and having a lot of money were not, however, sufficient criteria for a good husband, Yu Xinhong believed. In fact, despite her family's belief, Yu Xinhong was not ready to marry. "He was good in every way, young and responsible and from a good family. My family was very poor. His was rich. We were not the same," she told me. But the young man had problems, Yu Xinhong thought.

Managing his family's business, the boy lived in comfort, drove a nice car, and built himself a beautiful home. Every single girl in town was after him, Yu Xinhong said. "He had had many affairs. I think he had lost his belief in love—all he wanted was a wife." Yu Xinhong, however, was in search of true love, and a life of her own. She had bigger dreams than being a rich man's wife at such a young age.

Finally, after three months of dating, and making the preliminary arrangements for getting married, Yu Xinhong broke up with the wealthy young boy. "If I had married my fiancé, I would have stayed in that small town for the rest of my life. I wanted better things. Before leaving, I told my fiancé: 'Someday, I will be a boss. Maybe not a big boss, but a boss none the less. I dream of owning my own business, even if it is a small one.'"

The breakup was liberating, but it meant she had to start life all over again. Remaining at home was not an option. "I had to leave. I had to find a job somewhere, but I didn't know where to go." Yu Xinhong was lost. She had passed up a golden opportunity, a dream for many girls in her position. Now she had to prove herself, show her family that she made the right choice in refusing to marry the rich man. "They respected my decision—my father did not oppose me, but I knew he was disappointed. They were worried about me." She was worried too. Where could she go now? It was at this time of confusion that an old friend came to her rescue. "He was kind of my boyfriend in high school. I had not seen him for a while."

Three years earlier, the friend had left home to start a new life in the eastern province of Zhejiang. Within two years, he owned a small business, and enjoyed a comfortable life, he had told Yu Xinhong. "He asked me to go and work with him. I liked him and trusted him. I was very happy." Yu Xinhong packed her suitcase again and boarded a train to join her old friend. "I was scared and excited. I didn't know anyone there but him."

Yu Xinhong's friend was waiting for her when the train rolled into the station. She was happy to see a familiar face. The old friend showed Yu Xinhong around, treated her to a "very nice dinner," and took her to his apartment for the night. She would start work in a few days and find her own place, he told Yu Xinhong. "I was so happy I had a friend in this strange place." However, something was not quite right when she arrived at the apartment.

"I was very confused at first." The friend's apartment was spacious and luxurious. There were many girls, "beautiful girls," going in and out. "All of them claimed to be his girlfriend." The girls were all dressed in fashionable clothes. Yu Xinhong was bewildered. "My friend was very casual. The girls were nice. They would go to the bathroom and come out with lots of makeup."

The doorbell rang at one point. A man entered. "He talked about price with the girls." Yu Xinhong overheard the girls talk about being late for work. It was night-time and they were dressed up. "Where could they be working?" she asked herself. She struggled to reject her initial thoughts. "No, it can't be possible," she said to herself. The evidence, however, was too strong to deny.

Yu Xinhong had heard many stories about young village girls lured into prostitution in cities across China. She had met a few in Shenzhen. "Life in the village is very hard. A lot of girls run away from home to find a better life. Some get lucky, and others don't. Some are deceived at first. But the money is good. They get used to it and stay," she told me. Had her old friend asked her to come there to be a prostitute like the other girls? The thought was devastating to her. She wanted to cry, run, and disappear. She was smart, and aware of the situation. "I was not going to fall into this trap. I could have had easy money if I wanted to. I wanted something else for my life." When all the girls left the apartment, she found the courage to confront her friend. "You are so young. You have a long life ahead of you. Choose another job. Your life will improve gradually. You don't need to do this," Yu Xinhong told her friend.

That night, she sat on a corner and cried until she fell asleep. The next morning, she borrowed money from her friend, and took the next train back to her family home in the village. "I had nowhere else to go. I was very embarrassed."

*   *   *

Housing prices had more than doubled in Shenzhen since the beginning of 2006. New state-of-the-art office buildings, hotels, malls, and luxury condominiums were being erected everywhere. Bursting with economic activity—large and small export-processing factories, banks, insurance companies, hotels, and other lucrative service industries—Shenzhen ranked second in per capita income in China, slightly under Shanghai levels in 2006. Many had prospered in Shenzhen, making the city an icon and an example of what economic reforms could bring to the rest of China. Shenzhen had become the epicenter of the Chinese Dream, continuing to attract scores of migrants—talented and educated, and young villagers like Yu Xinhong. All of that was fueling a remarkably lucrative real estate market.

Cranes were seen everywhere in Shenzhen in 2007. Real estate agencies were mushrooming in every district of the city, sometimes two or three on a single block. Packed in small offices behind computer screen, uniformed young migrants were busy making rental and sales deals. "I make 3000 yuan a month," boasted the young realtor who found me my apartment in the Beautiful Rose Garden. This was three times higher than the average monthly income of a factory worker. My 20-something-year-old landlady, a migrant from the north and a realtor herself, had saved enough money to buy two apartments, he told me.

Watching the real estate bonanza in Shenzhen, and the quick money that many had made in short time, was making Yu Xinhong restless at the teahouse. She was wasting time, she thought. "I want to be a realtor. I know how to talk to people. I will be good at it," she would tell me. For Yu Xinhong, and the young migrants with a high school degree, becoming a realtor was a promising entry point into the world of money. She dreamed of buying a home in Shenzhen someday.

"I want to live in Shenzhen and buy a house and a car. This is a part of my dream. My life in this teahouse is too simple and easy. This is better than working in a factory, but it is not active enough for me and not good for my dreams."

Days after expressing her interest in becoming a realtor, Yu Xinhong left the teahouse. "I am a realtor," she said with excitement when she called me.

Yu Xinhong worked seven days a week, starting her days at seven in the morning, and finishing at eleven at night. The company had given her accommodation in a "dormitory," a four-bedroom apartment without a kitchen. Fifteen other employees of the company, her manager included, lived in the apartment. The company specialized in apartments in a wealthy district of Shenzhen. Yu Xinhong's clients were wealthy Chinese and foreigners, and educated and better-paid young migrants. She met "colorful" people, she told me.

Calling, and text messaging, I kept regular contact with Yu Xinhong and made plans to meet, many of which had to be canceled because of her demanding work schedule. With the help of a friend, a college graduate who spoke English, Yu Xinhong would send me text messages, greetings, and good wishes in English. At times, she would text message popular Chinese poems.

"I want to meet you when I have had an achievement in my new job, when I have already rented a place," she wrote once after canceling our plan for a meeting.

Three weeks into the job, she made a successful deal. Yu Xinhong had her first rental, and I was among the first people to get the good news in a text message.

"You have been an important influence in this process. Thank you for your encouragement," she wrote.

"I am not making a lot of money yet, but things will change. I am learning. Once I gain the experience I need, I am going to move to a bigger company. This is only the first step," she told me when we met to celebrate.

RED LANTERNS ON THE MOUNTAIN

After our last meeting in Beijing, Wang Chun Ling contacted me a number of times, each time with a new number. Then, suddenly, the calls stopped. I called the last number that I had from her. It was out of service. I called her husband. There was no answer. I tried Fan Xiu Qin, her friend from New Balance. The number was no longer in service. Had Wang Chun Ling left Beijing for Shenzhen? I called the number I had for her in Shenzhen. It was out of service. Every month or two, I tried all the numbers I had. Wang Chun Ling had disappeared. I often wondered if she returned to the village after the 2008 economic crisis, remained in Beijing with a new number, or moved to another city in China. She wanted to see the world, she had told me.

Getting a local SIM card and a cell phone was the first thing the young migrant workers did when they arrived in Shenzhen. The cell phone was the migrants' main link to their families back home, and the friends they would meet along the way. The link, however, was far from reliable. Losing cell phones was common. Migrants moved frequently, changing addresses and leaving no trace behind them. With each move came a new number.

I left China before the outbreak of the financial crisis. I tried to contact all the migrant workers I had met in my earlier visits when I was preparing to return to China after the world financial meltdown. Many had disappeared. Yu Xinhong was an exception. "I kept the same number hoping that you would come back and find me," she told me when we met one late afternoon in Longgang. "I thought about you often. I am so happy you are here. My life has changed a lot—I have so much to tell you," she said.

When I last saw Yu Xinhong she had just started her real estate career. "I am working hard. My job is exciting. I am meeting new people. I am not making much money yet, but I will soon. I will make you proud of me," she told me. In less than two years, Yu Xinhong was a savvy and successful broker working for a big developer in Shenzhen. With a record sale of a hundred apartments in ten months, she was "the number one broker" in her company. She had come a long way in a short time—she had saved "40,000 yuan," she told me.

Yu Xinhong had big dreams, and she was realizing them, one at a time, and fast. She had dreamed of buying an apartment in Shenzhen. By the end of the summer of 2009, she had saved enough to pay the down payment for her very first home. She had her eyes on a 350-square feet apartment in a new luxury housing development belonging to her company. She would pay 40,000 yuan first, and 1000 yuan every month for 30 years. "I would like to buy something bigger. But this is a good start. In two years, I will buy a bigger apartment and rent out this one."

* * *

I met Yu Xinhong at a restaurant in Longgang. She was wearing jeans and a white polo shirt. "This is my day off. I dress formally when I work," she said, and sat opposite me at a corner booth away from the noise and the crowd. "Tonight is my treat," she said, and insisted on paying when we left the restaurant.

Yu Xinhong spoke like a professional with years of experience and gave me a lecture about the real estate business in Shenzhen, square foot prices in different districts, and the competition among developers to find and keep potential buyers. "My job is not that difficult. They spend a lot of money on advertising. Customers contact me."

When she first joined the industry, Yu Xinhong was a "level three" broker helping landlords find tenants, and tenants find apartments. Yu Xinhong, however, had bigger ambitions. She wanted to sell, and sell apartments in new and expensive condominiums. "That's where you can excel," she said. Only two months after leaving the teahouse chance knocked on her door. A friend she had met recently talked about her to his boss, the head of the sales unit in a giant real estate firm. Days later, Yu Xinhong began working as a "level two," selling apartments in new developments. This was hard work. Competition was fierce, and making money was more difficult than she had imagined. Working long hours, she sold four units after many months. "I could not save any money. Shenzhen is very expensive. I spent everything I earned."

The new job did not make her rich, but it introduced her to more people, influential people with money and connections. A year after starting the job, a friend introduced Yu Xinhong to another developer who was building luxury condominiums in Longgang. Yu Xinhong left for Longgang. That was October 2008, the beginning of the great economic slump that devastated the world.

Except for a short period, the real estate market in Shenzhen continued to grow. Prices rose from 13,000 yuan to 18,000 yuan per square meter in central Shenzhen, and it was the same in Longgang. "Real estate here is a sunshine industry because of the coming World University Students Olympics in 2011. Everyone wants to buy in Longgang now. I am so happy I made the move and came here. Everything happened for me after that."

Yu Xinhong was a fast learner and had gained a good deal of knowledge about the business while working in Shenzhen. The contacts she had made proved useful in her new job. Her old clients brought their colleagues and friends with money to invest in Longgang's burgeoning housing market. "My clients were so grateful. The apartments I sold them doubled in price in some cases." Not long after starting with the new company, Yu Xinhong was earning 6000 yuan a month, an enviable income in China, especially for a village girl with only a high school degree. "I spend 2000 yuan a month and save the rest. I even send money to my family."

*   *   *

"I have a good life now, but still the most important thing for me is to find the right man. No matter how much money you earn, nothing can compare to that." Finding a husband was Yu Xinhong's other dream, and that was not an easy matter. She had to take a number of things into account. Her parents' happiness was top of the list.

With all her successes and her financial independence, Yu Xinhong continued to live under her family's influence. "I owe everything to my family. I would not have been here without my father and his teachings." Far away from home and her father, she considered his wishes in every important decision she made, especially when it came to choosing a life partner.

Finding the right man started with some basics, she told me. He should be around 35 years old. Of course, it would be better if he had a house and a car. Looks mattered, but Yu Xinhong was ready to sacrifice appearance for other qualities. "If you love someone, he will look like the most beautiful person in the world to you. I think it is all about destiny anyway. The right person may be very different from your expectations."

A high school diploma was sufficient for Yu Xinhong's future husband as long as he was knowledgeable and "had a good attitude towards work and life." Men without ambition and the desire to earn money did not attract her. "In China, we are happy as long as we have a family and enough money."

More important considerations surfaced once a man met all these requirements. Yu Xinhong and her chosen man had to have the same animal sign. "That is a must." Yu Xinhong is a snake, and would only marry a 35-year-old who preferably had a car and a house, and who was a snake. With all of these criteria met, the man had to pass the last hurdle. He should be from the same hometown or at least from a place near her hometown. This was a requirement of Yu Xinhong's parents.

"My parents can check my husband's family background if he is from the same area. That is very important to them. They can build a close relationship with my husband's family. We will be one big family," she said, stretching her arms to signal something big. She was giggling.

No one had yet met all these requirements. However, there was one suitor "under consideration." He was an operating manager of an express service company, and six years older than Yu Xinhong. The candidate was Yu Xinhong's client in Shenzhen. "I showed him so many places but he didn't like any of them. Finally, he felt guilty and treated me to lunch." That's how their "relationship" started. He seemed like a good man, but there were many drawbacks. His monthly income was 4000 yuan, less than Yu Xinhong's. That was the first drawback. The suitor also had a different animal sign. That was the second drawback. Nevertheless, she kept him around. They spoke on the phone, and text messaged. "I am very busy. I work a lot and cannot see him," she reasoned.

*   *   *

Yu Xinhong was in a permanent state of homesickness. "I would love for you to visit my home someday. It is very beautiful. The local people are so hospitable. Back home, instead of saying hello to people you say, 'Have you had lunch? Or breakfast?' That's all. We always invite others to eat with us," she said in our last meeting. A big and beautiful smile appeared on her small face. "Life back home is very simple. My parents go to bed at eight or nine in the evening, but in Shenzhen, I go to bed around midnight. In the village, we eat what we grow. The food is safe. If you want to eat something, you just go to the farm, and pick it yourself. That's not the case in Shenzhen. You have to have money to eat well. Now I eat anything I want. I have the money for it, but many others don't," she said. "I miss home. Home is still the best. I will go back when I get older and have enough money. I will go back to an easy life and a beautiful environment." Yu Xinhong remained silent and played with the food in the bowl before her. When she began talking again, it was all about the village and her childhood memories.

"A river runs down the mountain outside my village. My house is on the river's east bank. There are many wild fish in the river. They are delicious. After it rains, the mountain looks like it has just been washed. It is clean and fresh. It smells beautiful. The mountain is often covered by thick fog. Once the fog moves away, the mountain comes out and shows its beauty. You can see hill after hill, peak after peak. You realize that you are standing between many mountains.

"The most beautiful day is the eve of the Spring Festival. Late at night, every family in all the villages lights a lantern outside their home. From the opposite side of the mountain you see long lines of light. The whole mountain glitters. It is especially beautiful at night.

"The funniest thing during the Spring Festival is sliding in the snow. We turn over a wooden bench outside the house to make a slide, and go down the slope. This is the best time, very funny.

"Yellow flowers cover the mountains in October. Everything is yellow. Standing by my window, looking at the mountain range on the other side of the river, you see how everything gradually changes. The whole area changes from yellow in the fall to white in winter, and to green in spring. Gradually, you see the corn grow bigger and bigger. This gradual change is very beautiful."

A WHITE-COLLAR WORKER

"Do you remember Liu Xia?" Yu Xinhong asked abruptly during a meeting in August 2009. "We came from the same place, but she had a much better situation than me when she got here. She had a successful sister, a home, and a job waiting for her. But Liu Xia doesn't have any dreams. She is easily satisfied."

The last time I saw Liu Xia she was still working at the teahouse and sharing a small apartment with four other waitresses. The teahouse closed in fall 2007, and I lost touch with her. I tracked her down with Yu Xinhong's help. The two had remained friends and stayed in contact, but they had not seen each other for months. "Life is very busy in Shenzhen," Yu Xinhong told me.

Liu Xia returned home to spend time with her family after the closure of the teahouse. Despite all that she loved about home, she missed her life in Shenzhen. At home she was restless. After a few weeks she packed and took the train to Dongguan, a hectic, noisy, and overcrowded factory town a short bus ride from Shenzhen. By the time I reached Liu Xia, she had already left Dongguan for Longgang. "My sister needed me," she said on the phone. Liu Xia had begun working in her brother-in-law's business. She was helping her sister with the company's accounts.

In the summer of 2007, Liu Xia was a waitress dreaming of a job as an office worker, "a white-collar worker" as she put it. Two years later, she was working with computers, learning basic book-keeping. "I learned a lot in the teahouse, but what I do now has a future. This is mental work. Teahouse was manual work. Very different." Liu Xia was at last "a white-collar worker."

With this "mental work," Liu Xia's salary increased to 1500 yuan a month. She even saved from time to time. "Very little," she said, giggling.

With the money and the new job, Liu Xia was thinking of things she had never considered before. "I like your lifestyle. You travel a lot. That must be very nice," she said. Now, for the first time, she was dreaming of seeing the world. France was at the top of her list. "I would love to visit the Arc de Triomphe in Paris," she said. She had seen images of the arch on a Taiwanese TV travel show. "The show introduced a lot of places to me. I like this show. It makes me feel like I am traveling to those places. You should watch it as well."

*   *   *

Married to a Hong Kong man with a small business on the mainland, Liu Xia's sister had found herself a comfortable life. She had a four-year-old boy, and worked in her husband's business. She had married a man who was not from her province. Her family was, nevertheless, satisfied. Their daughter lived comfortably. More importantly, she visited home frequently. The family adored her little boy, and his pictures were on every wall in the house. Grandparents had bought him little trucks, cars, and all types of toys. Neighbors and relatives from other villages came to see the grandson when

Liu Xia's sister visited. "Isn't he beautiful?" Liu Xia said, showing me pictures of the boy on her cell phone.

Liu Xia's sister was a happy woman. She had a successful husband and a good marriage. Yu Xinhong, however, had other opinions. "Do you know about her husband?" she whispered one day. "He is very ugly." The husband was "older" and "repulsive looking," she said. "He has cancer." The Hong Kong man was lonely and ill. He needed someone to take care of him and his business, and Liu Xia's sister needed security. The marriage worked for both—he got attention and care, and she got financial security. He never visited his wife's hometown. Apart from Liu Xia, no one in the family had met the husband. Her parents did not complain, however, as long as they could see their grandson. The husband and wife seemed satisfied. "They both got something out of the marriage," Yu Xinhong said.

*   *   *

I met Liu Xia one sunny afternoon in a park in Longgang after she had finished her eight hours of work in her brother-in-law's company. A lot had changed in her life, even her appearance. Gone were the thick glasses. Her short hair was lightly permed, as was fashionable among many Chinese women.

I had met with Liu Xia with different interpreters in the past. My first interpreter, the tall and light-skinned woman on her way to the United States, was her favorite. "She was so beautiful," Liu Xia said, asking about her. I told Liu Xia that my interpreter would soon leave the U.S. for Hong Kong to marry her boyfriend, a classmate from her university years in Beijing. She was done with studying, and did not want to stay in the United States any longer. She wanted to be with the man she loved. "She is so lucky. She has found a good boyfriend. She will have a family and a good job," Liu Xia said, and looked unusually thoughtful. "I wish I could find someone," she said, and fell silent.

Liu Xia was "looking for the right man" while managing a long-distance relationship with someone she had met a year earlier in Dongguan. They were co-workers in the spa where Liu Xia worked before moving to Longgang. He was a "director," working in the same job since he had left his village in Hubei Province five years ago. He was Liu Xia's first and the only boyfriend.

In the beginning, Dongguan scared Liu Xia. She no longer had the comfort of working at her sister's friend's teahouse, and did not have her sister to look after her in times of need. The city was big, chaotic, and bustling with activity. Every day, thousands of girls like Liu Xia were arriving and taking the first steps on the journey to a future better than that of their parents and their neighbors back home. Many would fail. Liu Xia had heard about girls who were lured into prostitution. She would not fall that low, she was sure of that. Now she was more experienced than the first time she left her village. She had come this time to become a white-collar worker. Nothing could keep her from achieving that. She had to be watchful of people around her, she thought. A boyfriend would have eased her fears—she needed the protection of a man.

A month after starting her job at the spa, she found that protection. Liu Xia moved in with her boyfriend soon after. "We lived like a married couple."

She had reservations about the young man from Hubei, but she felt safe and happy. "He is fat," she said in English when I asked about the boyfriend's looks. Shorter than five feet, and 180 pounds, he was "genetically fat," she said. That was not a problem. Liu Xia could live with that. The boyfriend, however, had other, more serious faults.

He was "very childish and spent all his money on silly things." And that was not an easy thing to forgive. She needed a responsible man who thought about the future and proved his ability to take care of a wife and children. Her boyfriend was failing that test. Still other problems made planning for a long-term relationship unrealistic: Liu Xia and her boyfriend had different animal signs. Liu Xia was a dragon, and the boyfriend a snake. That was a serious hurdle.

"Animal signs are important," she told me. Liu Xia was set on finding a man with the same animal sign. To do otherwise was taboo. Even if *she* agreed to the marriage, her parents would not. They would fight it to the end. After all, not only did he have a different animal sign, he was also from another province. Liu Xia's parents had already given a daughter to a Hong Kong man. Losing one to a boy from Hubei was not going to be taken lightly. "I think I can convince them if I really want to marry him. I have to make a decision first. I am not sure he is the right man for me."

Liu Xia was 21 and determined to have a family by age 25. Time was running out, and getting married was a priority above earning more money or learning skills. "My husband can take care of me," she said. Her current boyfriend seemed incapable of that. "He hasn't grown up yet. I cannot depend on him."

*   *   *

Liu Xia left her boyfriend and her life in Dongguan because her sister needed a helping hand in the office. "I had no choice. Family comes first," she told me. She worked in the office during the day and spent many evenings with her four-year-old nephew. She considered herself lucky to see him so frequently. Being close to her sister and her nephew helped her fight the "unbearable homesickness" she felt at times.

Unlike her friend Yu Xinhong, Liu Xia was "not emotional," she told me. She laughed about everything. "I like to enjoy myself," or "I am silly," she would say. "I like to smile," she would say in English. "We can spend our days being happy, or sad. The choice is ours. I choose to be happy," she would say. "Life is short," she would say in English. That evening, however, for the first time, Liu Xia was melancholic, without her smile. "I worry about my parents. They are getting old," she said. In their early fifties, Liu Xia's parents were still strong and working on the farm. Unlike most others in the village, they had a health insurance policy for major problems, surgery, and hospitalization.

"My sister bought the policy for them for ten years. They would still have to pay 50 percent of the cost, but this is better than nothing."

"Your parents are young. Why are you worried?"

"Things happen suddenly. I am not with them. I cannot stop thinking about this."

Liu Xia's grandmother had died unexpectedly three years ago. She was 65, and healthy. "She went to bed one night and never woke up. I was in Shenzhen." Earlier in 2009, tragedy hit the family of a close friend and classmate of Liu Xia's sister. She was in Shenzhen at work when her mother informed her of her father's stroke. He was only 50, and has been in coma ever since.

"Being in Shenzhen is like living in a foreign country. You are so far away from home. You cannot react fast enough. My village is different." She remembered neighbors, playmates, and the security everyone felt in her village. For the first time in our meetings, Lui Xia was homesick.

"You know, there were a lot of orange trees in my hometown," Liu Xia said. "I remember when I was in elementary school. My friends and I would walk to school every day. When the oranges were ripe, we would climb the walls, and steal oranges from other people's orchards. We would eat some of them there, and fill our pockets with big juicy oranges and run to school. The owners would frequently come to my school and complain to the principal," she said.

"Do you remember the pictures of my family's orange grove?" she asked. The grove was no more, she told me. The local government had bought the land to clear it for an industrial park. "You cannot smell the oranges anymore."

Not long before selling the orange grove, Liu Xia's family had sold their two old dogs. "Do you remember them? I showed you their pictures." Getting rid of the dogs was not a decision the family made happily. "They had no choice," Liu Xia said. A car hit and injured one of the dogs, and despite the care and the attention Liu Xia's family gavehim, he continued to suffer. The other dog fell sick for no reason. "I think he became depressed," Liu Xia said. The dog did not move, and slept most of the day. Wishing to end their pain, the patents sold the dogs to a local butcher. "I remember them helping my parents during the orange harvest season. Those dogs were so smart. One would sit outside by the road, and the other would guard the oranges on the grove. Nobody could come near the oranges," she said.

Book III
The Accidental Capitalist

ZHAO GANG: THE DECLINING EXPORT-PROCESSING INDUSTRIES

A short taxi ride from the Li Family Village, Sunland Fine Chemical Sci. & Tech. was a 100,000 square feet yellow-tiled compound of production facilities, R&D labs and administrative offices, and workers' dormitories. The compound had a small courtyard with patches of green space, a couple of trees, and a basketball hoop. Surrounding Sunland were more factories, graffiti-covered factory walls, streets with broken asphalt and deep potholes, and garbage. Sunland produced crayon soaps, bubble bath, children's shampoo, and decorative bath products for one of the largest American retailers.

Except for a few workers resting and smoking cigarettes under the shade of the trees, or a couple of shirtless young men shooting hoops, the courtyard was quiet and uneventful most of the time. Factory girls ran between the plant and their dormitory rooms. A bored driver dusted the boss's car. It was a different story, however, during the final stages of preparing the shipment to the United States. The compound bustled with activity and the plant worked round the clock. Trucks went in and out of the courtyard, and young workers in blue uniforms ran back and forth between the buildings.

16   Zhao Gang at Anhui University

Putting in 16-hour workdays, Zhao Gang, the 42-year-old boss, roamed around and chatted with his workers, and remained in his office long past midnight. He would return to his private sleeping quarters by the dormitories, rest a few hours, and resume work in the early hours of the next day. Zhao Gang rarely saw his wife and his teenage daughter, who lived in a condominium in central Shenzhen. At normal times, the boss spent two nights a week with his family. At busy times, even one night was a luxury.

Some 500 young migrants labored long hours at Sunland during the peak season. They lived in the factory's modest dormitory rooms, dined in the canteen, and spent weeks without leaving the compound. Sunland's dormitory rooms had no television and no common space. The single basketball net in the courtyard was the only escape from monotonous work and boredom for the boys. Text messaging, listening to their cell phones' MP3s, or sleeping were common pastimes for the girls.

Occasionally, in low seasons, Zhao Gang organized tours of Shenzhen and its popular sightseeing attractions for his workers. "I give each a free bottle of water and free lunch," he told me. The workers were grateful. For many, this was the only chance to see Shenzhen and its beautiful parks, state-of-the-art government buildings, banks, and hotels.

*   *   *

Chance and the importance of friendship in Chinese culture brought me to Zhao Gang. The chain of events started in the United States days before I left for China. A Chinese acquaintance recommended me to a friend in Beijing. The friend, in turn, called her friends, and they called theirs. Days after arriving in China, I had my first meeting with Stanley Zhu, a manager in a Chinese trading company in a Special Economic Zone on the outskirts of Shenzhen. I told Stanley Zhu about my interest in writing the life stories of Chinese workers and capitalists. "My university classmate and friend, Mr. Zhao Gang, would be pleased to spend some time with you. His factory is very close to where you live. Zhao Gang is a typical Chinese with a strong sense of entrepreneurship," Stanley Zhu said.

Two days later, on a hot afternoon in late June, Zhao Gang sent his driver to take me to Sunland for our first meeting. He was standing outside his office on the third floor of the administration building when I arrived. Zhao Gang was tall and athletic. He was clad in a fake designer polo shirt—the uniform of nearly every factory owner or manager I met in China—tucked into a pair of blue trousers. With a big smile on his face and a strong handshake, Zhao Gang greeted me and led me to his office.

"Nice to meet you," he said in English. "Nice to meet you," he said each time we met. That was the extent of his spoken English. Like most Chinese in the world of business, Zhao Gang had an English name. His was Kevin. "I cannot remember foreign words. Sometimes clients call and ask for Kevin, and I say, 'Who is Kevin?' I cannot even remember my English name," he said. "I will tell you why I never learned English." While others in his position tried their best to learn a foreign language, Zhao Gang was content making jokes about his poor English. He told me the story of twelve-year-old Huang Shuai, an elementary school student on the outskirts of Beijing who became a national hero for opposing her teacher and daring to rebel during the Cultural Revolution.

The Cultural Revolution, at least in the first few months, encouraged young people to break taboos, and to question authority. Legend had it that, inspired by the spirit of the time, Huang Shuai challenged her teacher, wrote critical open letters to the *Beijing Review*, and did heroic things no one expected from a fifth-grader. Huang Shuai became a national sensation, "a rock star." Tales of her courage, some true, and others made up by fans, reached remote corners of China. Zhao Gang liked one popular story in particular.

A teacher once asked Huang Shuai to write a poem in English. "I am Chinese, and I do not need to learn English. I don't need the ABC to be a red vanguard," wrote the rebellious Huang Shuai instead. "This is why I never learned English. This little girl affected many Chinese people, including me. Otherwise, I could have talked to you in English," said Zhao Gang, laughing.

*　　*　　*

My first meeting with Zhao Gang lasted three hours. "I will do anything to help you, because my dear classmate introduced you to me," he said when we parted. Zhao Gang was soon my patron in China. When he found a free moment from his busy factory responsibilities, he searched through his address book and business cards for other entrepreneurs and anyone who could help me understand the complexities of China. "I want the Americans to have a better understanding of China,"he told me. "Fate brought us together. At first, I helped you because I felt responsible to my friend. Now I am helping you because I respect what you are doing. I want you to succeed," Zhao Gang told me after a few meetings. "I wish I could leave my job and travel with you. I envy you," he said later.

*　　*　　*

When I first met Zhao Gang, Sunland was a young company. He opened a drawer under his desk, took out a small photo album and a dozen or so laminated pictures, put them in front of me on a coffee table across his desk, and delivered a photo essay on the birth of a Chinese subcontracting company. Like a parent showing friends pictures of his newborn, Zhao Gang's eyes sparkled with excitement. "This is how Sunland was born," he said.

The first photo showed an empty factory and a courtyard with overgrown wild grass. The date was May 12, 2004, the very first day Zhao Gang and his partners signed the lease for the compound. Next was a picture of Zhao Gang on a balcony. He was gazing at the courtyard. "I am thinking about the unknown future." That was day two, May 13.

"We signed our first contract before we had any machinery or workers here," he said, holding a picture of a Japanese buyer working by candlelight in one of Sunland's rooms. "We did not even have electricity." That was May 14. The plant began operating at the end of May. Days later, the first shipment left Sunland for Japan. "We created a Longgang speed, beating the Shenzhen speed," Zhao Gang said, joking about how he broke the record in setting up a factory, producing, and shipping out the final product.

* * *

In the spring of 2004, two friends from earlier jobs in Shenzhen visited Zhao Gang. They had a business proposal, but no money. "They wanted me to put together and run a chemical factory." The friends were experienced and hard working, one with knowledge of technology, and the other with years of experience in chemical industry. They had a convincing proposal. "They even had a committed Japanese buyer waiting to sign a deal." All they needed was money. For that, they came to Zhao Gang. He was penniless but well connected.

At the time, Zhao Gang had no desire to change jobs. He was a vice-president at the Hospital Management Corporation in Hong Kong. He bought non-functioning hospitals on the mainland, found new management for them, and brought them to profitability. Life was good. He was comfortable. Zhao Gang turned down the offer. The friends insisted and, by April, they had him on board.

Zhao Gang had a sure source of money in mind—one Mr. Lue, who owned a lucrative business in Hong Kong. A classmate at Anhui University and a philosophy major like Zhao Gang, Mr. Lue had come to Shenzhen immediately after he graduated in 1993. He had become a developer, and had made an enviable amount of money in real estate. "He had always told me to call him if I needed help." The time had come at last, and Zhao Gang visited his classmate.

No questions asked, Mr. Lue agreed to help. "We value friendship in China. Mr. Lue put out the investment only because he trusted me. Some people cannot manage money, but they can get the money because of who they are. I am one of these people," he said, cracking up again.

With that, Zhao Gang joined the world of labor-intensive export-processing businesses in China. Seven months after opening the gates of the factory, Sunland doubled its initial working capital in profits. With only one buyer in Japan, Sunland's growth was much higher than the average in Shenzhen. By the end of 2004, an American customer was enlisted. And the Japanese buyer protested.

"My Japanese client actually did not want us to work with Americans. They were afraid that our standards would deteriorate and our workers would get used to producing lower-quality products," Zhao Gang told me. After many meeting and negotiations, Zhao Gang and his partners convinced the Japanese of their commitment to quality despite working with the Americans. "It is funny, we were a new company but the Americans trusted us because we had a Japanese client." Everyone in the business knew the Japanese as producers of high-quality products, Zhao Gang said. Sunland was a subcontracting firm producing for the meticulous Japanese. "That was a valuable asset for us."

The Japanese, however, remained concerned. To guarantee better product standards, they dispatched three inspectors and quality control experts to live in the factory compound all year long. That was not the case with the Americans. Occasionally, an inspector would visit the plant with a "to do and not to do" list. Sunland's American customer forbade its inspectors from accepting free meals and other gifts, or taking money from the boss. Most of its inspectors, however, disobeyed the orders. "The inspectors would actually ask for money if I didn't offer the bribe myself. I have to pay a bribe every time they send a quality control person."

"What if you don't give him the money?" I asked.

"He would disqualify the products. This is kind of a rule that everybody knows in China.

"What if there really is a problem?"

"He would write a report if the problem is really big. Otherwise, he would ignore it. That's how things work here."

Earlier that day, Zhao Gang had visited the Lee Wan hotel, one of the two five-star hotels in Longgang, to meet an inspector sent by his American customer. Driving to Sunland, Zhao Gang gave the inspector money in a sealed envelope. I started laughing when he told me the story.

"Why are you laughing?"

"I am laughing because of your honesty."

"I am doing what is a common practice. This is normal in China."

An hour after arriving at Sunland, the inspector visited Zhao Gang in his office. He returned the envelope. The problems were too serious to ignore.

"I gave him back the envelope. We are working to fix the problem now."

*   *   *

One especially hot day in August, Zhao Gang called to invite me to the factory. "Come to Sunland this evening if you are free. We will be here until very late. You can talk to the night shift workers." It was late in the evening and pouring down when I arrived at Sunland. Zhao Gang shouted from the window of his office. I joined him, and for a while we stood by the window and watched the workers go about their business under the torrential rain.

Protected by their hooded nylon ponchos, some ran between the plant and the administration building. Others loaded two large trucks parked with their backs to the building. Held by three men at each end, a long sheet of thick canvas connected the rear end of the truck to an open window on the second floor of the administration building. "Conveyer belt Sunland style," Zhao Gang said, laughing. Young workers slid boxes from the second floor to the truck. To protect the boxes from the rain, they used another layer of thick canvas as a cover. "They cannot stop even for a minute. We have to meet the deadline to avoid additional charges," Zhao Gang said.

Back on the second floor, young workers placed colorful packs of bubble bath and crayon soap in large boxes. A picture of Spiderman decorated the small blue packages of bubble bath trademarked by a company in Bloomfield, New Jersey. There was no sign of Zhao Gang's factory on any packages.

Across from the administration building another group of young men and women worked the night shift in the plant. It was one in the morning and I followed Zhao Gang for an inspection of the night shift. "Look at them. They are so pitiful," Zhao Gang said, pointing at the workers trimming bars of decorative soap with small knives. We were on a ramp inspecting the main floor. "They look like little ants from here. They work so hard every day. They are exploited by others." For the first time in our meetings Zhao Gang was talking about his workers and their welfare. He was somber.

"Do you feel sorry for them?" I asked.

"There is nothing I can do," he said, shrugging.

"I remember the first truck we loaded for Japan. My workers were moving up and down, carrying heavy boxes all night. I cried that night. But I stopped crying later. I became accustomed to it." Zhao Gang stared at his workers with a blank gaze.

"You can always pay them more. Isn't that what the workers want?" I asked.

"In a low-value-added factory like mine, profits only come from the exploitation of the worker and strict management. I cannot change that," he said. "I am not even good at this," he paused. "My wife tells me I am not a good entrepreneur. She says I worry too much about my workers. Maybe she is right."

This was a Wednesday night, one of the two nights in the week that Zhao Gang usually spent with his wife and 15-year-old daughter. "Tonight belongs to my family, but I don't feel good going home when I know they are working so late here. I cannot do much for them, but even me being around makes some of them happy. They can come and talk to me if they want to."

In my earlier visits I had seen workers come to Zhao Gang with their problems. "Just come directly to me if my lights are on," he told them. A few came every day, and a lot more in busier times. The foremen and supervisors on the factory floor discouraged the workers from complaining to Zhao Gang. "Actually, I am kind to the workers because I am the general manager. The foremen who work with them on a daily basis have to be harsh. I can afford to be kind; they cannot. Someone has to be harsh to make things run. A factory needs discipline. It would cease to exist otherwise." On occasion, he too could be harsh. He did what was common in factories across Shenzhen, Zhao Gang told me.

Only six months after Sunland's opening, Zhao Gang faced his first employee action. Workers demanded a modest wage hike. Zhao Gang was out of town on business. Unable to cope with the trouble, his partners requested his immediate return. "I am a good negotiator. The others were not," he told me. Negotiations began, and Zhao Gang found a peaceful way out of the crisis. Work resumed and all returned to the factory floor. Not long after, a second strike broke out.

"I had to use very harsh methods this time." Zhao Gang asked the striking workers to introduce their leaders to begin negotiations. Four leaders stepped forward. Next day, he fired all four. Work resumed immediately. That was the last strike in Sunland. "I had to do that. A factory needs continuity to be profitable. A more typical manager, a crueler manager, can definitely produce higher profits. I am not cruel, but I need discipline in the factory," Zhao Gang said.

"What are the things that a cruel manager would do?"

"He would close his eyes to the beating of the workers by the factory guards," he said. "Let me give you an example. People are always losing things in the dormitories. Sometimes the workers steal from one another. If the guards catch them, they give them a good beating. "

Why would the guards beat up the workers? What authority do they have? In America, the guards would call the police and hand over the culprit to the authorities. No beatings, I told Zhao Gang.

"Here, we hand the worker over to the police *after* giving him a good beating," he said, laughing.

* * *

Zhao Gang and I would meet at Sunland frequently. After long hours of discussing the factory, the Chinese economy, and the difficulties he and similar exporters were facing in China, we would talk about politics, and things that did not involve the business of Sunland. I would tell Zhao Gang about Iran, and my worries about my family and friends. In 2007, many saw a U.S. attack on Iran as being imminent. I would tell Zhao Gang of my recurring nightmares about the American bombing of my family home, the leveling and destruction of my old neighborhoods, and all the places I so cherished in my heart. These discussions always took Zhao Gang away from the mundane problems of Sunland. A different Zhao Gang would emerge. He would talk about his lost dreams, and the things he admired and respected in his life. "Do you think anyone would go to defend Iran as many people did during the Spanish Civil War?" he asked me once.

The Spanish Civil War inspired thousands of students, labor unionists, doctors and nurses, and ordinary men and women from around the world. They left their homes and loved ones to defend the young Spanish Republic against the attack by landowners, the Church, and the loyalists who had gathered around General Franco. Despite their sacrifices, the Republicans lost the war and Franco rose to power in October 1936. For Zhao Gang, however, the Spanish Civil War remained "a proud moment in human history."

Fighting for a cause always impressed Zhao Gang, he told me. As a boy, he had dreamed of wearing a soldier's uniform. He admired soldiers for their courage, and envied their status in society. They were heroes, ready to defend their country at all costs. The soldiers' uniform was "the most beautiful outfit. Wearing a soldier's hat was an honor," he thought.

Zhao Gang's dreams were shattered when doctors diagnosed him as nearsighted. He could not serve in the army. However, his admiration for the men in uniform remained. Years later, he listened to military music in his car. He knew by heart the lyrics of most of the songs, and sang along with passion. "Even now, I think the most suitable career for me is in the army. I think my personality and character fit the uniform the best. I am not a natural businessman."

Zhao Gang lost hope of helping his country in uniform, but he soon found a new dream. A government job, his elders told him, was a noble way to serve people and his country. In the China of Zhao Gang's youth, the government was the soul of the nation, a father to its people. Joining the government became Zhao Gang's driving ambition when he entered Anhui University as a freshman in the late 1980s. "We were always taught that the purpose of education and knowledge was to become a better person to help your family first, your country next, and the world in the end," he told me.

Choosing the right major was crucial. He ruled out math and sciences from the outset. They were difficult subjects that required devotion and long hours of studying. Zhao Gang was not one for hard subjects. All his childhood years he escaped from studying, and he was not going to change that now. After long deliberation, he opted for philosophy. That was an easier subject to study, and "had a good chance of getting me a job with the government."

It was during his years of studying philosophy that he learned about the sacrifices of the young idealists who fought in the Spanish Civil War. Philosophy introduced him to the writings of Karl Marx, and of Che Guevara, Zhao Gang's hero for many years to come. Reading about Che, Fidel Castro, and other revolutionaries inspired him to try to make the world a better place. Zhao Gang wanted to make a difference, to leave his mark on the world. "Look at me now. I became a capitalist instead," he told me. "But I still have these dreams."

"How can you still hold on to your old dreams as a capitalist?" I asked.

"There is a Russian proverb that says, 'When you are in a circle of wolves, you learn to sound like one.'"

"Have you become a wolf?"

"No! So far, I may only sound like a wolf. Maybe someday I will be one like the others," he laughed. A long gaze followed.

CHILD LABOUR

By the summer of 2007, the Western press had reported widely on the use of children in mines, brick plants, and export-processing factories in China. Horrifying images of children—some as young as eight—working in a slave-labor operation in the brick kilns of Shanxi Province had caused an uproar in China and around the world. Meeting Zhao Gang, I would frequently raise the question of child labor, and my concerns about the type of economy China was promoting. I would tell him of the reports in the Western media about the substandard working conditions in Chinese factories, and the common abuse of the workers, especially children, by their bosses. I would tell him about the history of child labor and anti-child-labor laws in America. I would lament about how the American and other foreign firms were using China to escape higher labor standards at home. Zhao Gang would listen, never questioning my thoughts.

Driving to central Shenzhen one afternoon to meet a manufacturer whose business the government had recently shut down on charges of corruption and bribery, Zhao Gang said, "I know you care about child labor a lot. Come to Sunland tomorrow and meet some of my new workers. You can hear their stories directly."

It was August, and Sunland had to ship out orders to the United States before the Christmas shopping season. "Everything has to be in America by October," Zhao Gang said. To finalize the orders, Zhao Gang had hired "high school students," through an agent, he told me. Hiring schoolchildren during the summer was an inexpensive solution to the labor shortages that managers of many factories around Sunland were facing in those days. "There was a time when the workers would be waiting outside the gate for days in a row, hoping to be hired," Zhao Gang told me. Now, factories had to find creative ways to recruit workers who stayed. The new workers were demanding more money, better dorms, hot water, and television in the common room, Zhao Gang said. Zhao Gang did not have television in his workers' dormitories. His rooms were small and overcrowded. But he paid his workers the minimum wage, and did not cheat them on overtime pay.

Cheating the workers and not paying them for overtime was common in many factories, especially those not monitored by large foreign firms. There were two ways to calculate workers' pay. Some received direct hourly wages, while others were paid piecework based on the quantity of output they produced. The technologist in the factory determined the hours of direct labor needed to produce a given quantity of output. "Let's say that it actually takes twelve hours to produce a hundred units of a product, but the technologist says it is only ten hours. Here the worker is cheated of two hours of work," Zhao Gang explained.

Inexperienced and without skills, the new recruits took a lot longer to produce the same output. Most did not know the difference between piecework rates and the hourly wage system. They were the prime victims of the piecework scheme. "I pay direct hourly wages to the new recruits. They are so innocent. Anyone can cheat them easily," Zhao Gang said.

Zhao Gang did not cheat his workers. However, like most other subcontracting exporters in China, he relied on the work of "high school kids" when he faced a temporary labor shortage. They were boys and girls from small towns and villages in Guangdong. Most came to Longgang for the "factory experience," and the meager money that came with it.

Zhao Gang paid four yuan an hour for each worker. The headhunter kept 1.5 yuan, and gave the workers 2.5 yuan, 30 cents an hour at the going exchange rate. "This is a low wage even by Chinese standards," Zhao Gang explained.

* * *

The air was stagnant and humid when I arrived at Sunland. Two dozen boys and girls were awaiting me in the courtyard. Some played with their cell phones. Hardly old enough to be in high school, some looked like frightened children away from home. "She must have used a fake ID card, lying about her age to get this job," my interpreter said about a small and scared-looking girl in the crowd.

"Mr. Behzad wants to know about your experiences as workers. Are you willing to tell him your stories?" Zhao Gang addressed the group.

"Yes!" the boys shouted. A round of loud applause followed.

I took my camera out of the knapsack and joined the young workers in a circle on the lawn. A short, thin boy asked permission to touch the camera. "Take my picture," I said, and posed. Another worker grabbed the camera from his hand, played with it, and passed it to others eagerly awaiting their chance to take a picture with a camera other than the ones in their cell phones. A boy in a blue T-shirt offered me a cigarette. I accepted, and took out a new pack of Marlboro Lights.

"Please smoke these," I said and put the pack on the ground in the middle of the circle.

"How do they taste?" asked a skeleton of a boy in white undershirt.

"Much milder than Chinese cigarettes," I said.

"How much do they cost?"

"I always thought American cigarettes were longer," a girl spoke for the first time. She took out a cigarette, held it in her small hand, examined it, and returned it to the pack. "I don't smoke," she said. A boy to my left passed around the pack of Marlboro.

"Do teenagers smoke in America?"

"A lot, sometimes," I said.

"Then I don't feel bad smoking. I always thought that only Chinese people smoked," he said. Laughter broke out.

I continued to puff and choke on the cheap Chinese cigarettes offered to me by every boy in the crowd. As soon as I was done with one, someone would take out a pack and offer me another. Another would light the cigarette, and greet me with a nod and a smile. We chain-smoked for the next two hours.

More boys and girls joined the circle, some squatting, others lying on the grass. Some moved back and forth, in and out of the circle. The girls giggled, and the boys smoked.

The arrival of a short woman in her late twenties brought a loud cheer from the crowd. "Present from the boss," she said, and put down a plastic crate full of small bottles of Coca-Cola. A five-year-old boy held on to the woman's skirt. Opening the bottles with an old opener tied to the crate with a long string, she offered me the first, and handed the rest to the cheerful crowd. Zhao Gang watched from the window of his office. He was smiling.

I was talking to the boys, smoking, and laughing when a short girl with penetrating eyes and a round freckled face arrived from the dormitory building and sat beside me. Hugging her legs, she stared at the ground. Other girls joined the circle and sat beside her. I introduced myself. The girl sitting by me smiled. Others giggled, and the boys shouted and wrestled.

"Do you miss America?" asked the boy in the blue T-shirt.

"Do you miss home?" I asked the girl sitting next to me.

She looked away and hid her tearful eyes with her small hand. "Don't ask that anymore. They are too young. The girls may cry," a boy protested. "Of course we miss home," he said after a pause, and offered me a cigarette.

"We are just not used to this. We have never worked before. We used to spend money without thinking. Now, we know earning money is not easy," a boy in a yellow T-shirt said. Everyone laughed.

"We came out to train ourselves. We wanted to check out the world outside our towns," said another, pulling the sleeve of the boy beside him, wrestling with him.

I was the first foreigner they had ever met. Many had watched American shows on television. They worshipped Arnold Schwarzenegger, and the women in *Sex and the City*. Did I live a life like the one they saw on television, one asked. I had come from an untouchable world, a world of dreams. "I will tell my family about you," said a small girl with short hair with bangs.

"Do you know Arnold?"

"Do you eat Chinese food in America?"

"Do you have a car?"

"Do you live in a dormitory?

"Do you work in a factory?" asked a tall boy in a buttoned-down blue shirt.

"Oh, great. So you will be our teacher when we come to America," he said when I told him that I was not a factory worker, but a college professor.

"Can I see what a dollar bill looks like? I never saw one before. I hear it is very different from ours," a boy spoke for the first time. A friend hit him on the head. They laughed. I apologized for not having a dollar bill. "Don't forget to bring one next time," said the boy.

"How much does it cost from here to America?" asked a girl on my right.

"One thousand dollars, one way," I said.

"One thousand dollars!" shouted everyone. They soon converted the fare to yuan, talked among themselves, debated, turned towards me, and debated more.

"Eight thousand yuan," a boy said with awe. Others disputed.

"Seven thousand!"

"Seven thousand and six hundred!"

"Nine thousand!"

"We can never save that much money," said the girl who had asked the question.

"What would you buy if you did save any money?" I interrupted.

"I would buy a cell phone."

"I want to buy a computer."

"I want to go to college."

"I want to go to America. I have a cousin there," said a boy in a red T-shirt, and told me his cousin's name. "Do you know him?" He was disappointed to find out that I did not know his cousin. "America is a big country," I said.

"Is America beautiful?"

"How many people live in America?"

"We have a lot more in China."

"Is New York the biggest city in the world?"

"Goodbye," said a boy in English and remained with the rest of the crowd.

"That's all the English he knows," said his friend.

"Do they grow rice in America?"

"We grow the best rice."

"What do you think I should do in the future?"

"I want to be a doctor. Do you think I can?"

"Do you like Chinese movies?"

"Do you like Jackie Chan?"

Questions came from every corner, even from the girls who had sat quietly on the side and watched the boys engage with the American.

"Do you chat in QQ?" asked a girl. The most popular chat engine in China, QQ attracted millions of young Chinese. They chatted long hours, and found new friends, lovers, husbands, and wives. Everyone had a QQ account.

"I chat with entrepreneurs and ask them about their experiences," said a boy who looked older than most.

"How do you find them? Do you know them before you chat with them?"

"No, I search for them online."

"How can they be willing to chat with you if they don't even know you?"

"I am not a bad person. I don't want to commit a crime. I am not a killer or a robber, just a student who wants to learn how they started their business. I will have my own business one day too."

*   *   *

We had been together for more than two hours, and some had begun drifting, moving around. To keep their attention, I suggested a walk outside the factory. They shouted and clapped. Girls adjusted their clothes, boys collected their cigarette packs. All jumped to their feet.

"We are ready," they said.

Followed by 20 or so boys and girls, I left the factory and entered the deserted area outside. It was pitch-dark. Breaking the deadly quiet of the night with their youthful laughter and shouting, they walked in groups of three or four, girls holding hands, boys playfully harassing their friends, pushing them, and pulling their shirts.

"We never come out of the factory," said one.

"Do you like this?" I asked.

"Yes," they shouted in unison.

We were in a deserted street surrounded only by factories and walls with barbed wire.

"What did you do when you were my age?" asked the QQ boy, walking by my side.

I was telling him about my youth in Iran when the flashing headlights of a car behind us broke the darkness of the night. A large white van came to a full stop beside us. I gathered everyone to the sidewalk.

We were asked to return to the compound by the agent's representative in the factory.

"We are responsible for these children. The streets here are not safe. We don't want anything to happen to anyone," the representative said.

"I don't want to go back," said the shy girl and stood beside me.

"I am bored. I don't like this job. We have nothing here. I miss my family," she said and walked with me back to the factory.

"I don't want to be a factory worker all my life," she whispered, then said goodbye and walked to the dormitory building.

THE ANCESTOR'S TOMB

From our first meeting, Zhao Gang had talked about the need for me to visit rural China, live in peasants' homes, and get a glimpse of their lives. I would tell him about the progress in my work, the people I had met, and my findings in Shenzhen. "Behzad, Shenzhen is not all of China. It does not represent the experience of most Chinese," he would say. However, concerned about me traveling alone in China's hinterland, he would warn me of the problems I might face. "I am worried about you interviewing people in villages. A foreigner asking questions and talking to people may raise unnecessary suspicion. You need a local accompanying you."

In December 2007, Zhao Gang made a plan for me to follow him to his ancestral village for a taste of China's rural life. This was also a chance for me to meet his family and friends. "It is our custom in China to hold memorial ceremonies for our ancestors during the winter solstice. I will go to my father's village to repair my ancestors' graves with my brother and relatives," Zhao Gang said. He invited me to join him for the memorial ceremony. I accepted, and flew to Hefei in the morning of December 16. He was already at work in the village.

Hefei airport was small and old, and had a modest waiting room. A handful of poorly dressed and provincial-looking Chinese awaited the arrival of friends and family. A greeting team of four adults and an infant welcomed me with smiling faces.

"My nephew will pick you up at the airport in Hefei," Zhao Gang had told me before leaving for the village. Zhao Gang did not have a nephew in China. His only nephew, his sister's son, was studying at the State University of New York, Buffalo. I would soon meet many more of Zhao Gang's "nephews" and

17   Old farmer in Anhui Province

"brothers," members of the larger Zhao family, distant relatives who lived in Zhao's ancestral village.

The "nephew" leading the greeting entourage was 22-year-old Zhao Xiang. Thin, average height, and dressed in a blue suit, a navy blue V-neck, and a blue shirt, Zhao Xiang was a peasant in a city outfit. He approached me with a gleeful smile. Following him were his short, and round-faced older sister and her husband, and their ten-month-old boy, hidden inside multiple layers of fleece and blankets. A friend had accompanied the family to drive us to the village in his car. We used sign language, bowed, and smiled, and proceeded to the car for the two-hour drive to the village.

I jumped in the back seat behind the driver and next to Zhao Xiang, his sister, and her child. A long debate about the direction to the village ensued. Unable to participate, I looked out the window and gazed at the changing landscape. It was cold and misty. We were soon in China's vast and open hinterland, passing impoverished towns and villages and vegetable farms. Narrow, bumpy, and winding dirt roads followed better-paved highways. "Roads in China's heartland are not the same as those in America, or the highways in Shenzhen and Beijing," Zhao Gang had warned me, apologizing in advance for any possible discomfort I would experience during the short journey.

The boy remained asleep the whole trip. The driver chain-smoked. I said a few words in English, and they responded in Chinese. We looked at each other and smiled. After two hours of driving, we left the main road and turned onto a dirt road with wide and deep mud-filled holes, and big bumps. I rolled down the window and took in the fresh and cold air. We had arrived at Kao Shan Xiang, Zhao Gang's ancestral village.

We passed a newly built white-painted three-story brick home with balconies on each floor, and entered a constellation of decrepit mud houses with falling roofs, homes made of unpainted and bare cinderblocks, and ruins of older houses. A man in a Mao suit mixed gravel, cement, and water in the middle of the road. A barking dog chased our car. A small child with a runny nose and dirty face squatted on the side of the road. The car stopped in the open area in front of a brick house.

Clad in a long hooded down jacket, a tall and slender woman with shoulder-length dark brown hair approached the car. "Welcome. I am Zhao Yan, Zhao Gang's sister," she said in English, and shook my hand. A short-haired, round woman took slow steps towards the car. She was old and smiling. A black scarf with white and yellow flower patterns covered her neck. She wore an aged waist-length red jacket, and dust-covered black pants. The deep wrinkles on her face betrayed the many long years that had passed since she was young and beautiful. "This is my mother, Liu Xiuyun," said Zhao Yan. I bowed to Liu Xiuyun. More family members and neighbors arrived.

Standing behind Liu Xiuyun and wearing a dirty yellow fleece jacket over an old orange turtleneck, a ten-year-old boy stared at my arm. His skin dry and chapped, and his nose running, he was shivering. "Say hello," Zhao Yan said to the boy. "This is my nephew, Zhao Hang." I patted Zhao Hang on the head. "What is this?" the boy asked, and touched the hair on my arm. Laughter broke out. The boy had never encountered a man with hair anywhere on his body other than his head. Entertained by this discovery, he pulled my hair, patted my arm, and pulled again. "*Amao,*" hairy, he shouted, laughing. "*Amao, amao, amao,*" he repeated. After months in China, the ten-year-old Zhao Hang had given me a Chinese name! "Hairy," everyone called me in the village.

"Let me take you to Zhao Gang," Zhao Yan interrupted Zhao Hang's mischievous game, and we walked towards the plains and the hills outside the village. Eleven-year-old old Ya Quin, with rosy cheeks and short straight hair, tagged along. *"Amao,"* shouted Ya Quin and Zhao Hang, jumping in mud puddles, splashing, and laughing. A stray dog joined the chorus.

The village was behind us, and ahead was a vast open field. The air was clean, and the weather biting cold. An uneven dirt road cut through the greenery, winding, going up and down the hills, narrowing and widening, falling abruptly. Occasionally, small three-wheelers passed us by. And, from afar, I saw Zhao Gang and other men breaking ground, moving dirt, and repairing a tomb. "Come, *amao*," shouted Zhao Hang, holding my hand and running off to the field.

Shovels in their hands, cigarettes hanging from their lips, ten men, young and old, all with the last name of Zhao, toiled by the tomb of the"great-grand-father." Clad in an old turtleneck tucked into dust-covered black pants, the four-feet-tall and chain-smoking Zhao Mingshu shook my hand and offered me a cigarette. "My brother," Zhao Gang said. A farmer in his fifties, Zhao Mingshu was my host in the village.

18   Repairing Zhao Gang's ancestor's tomb

An old gravestone stood vertically in front of a twelve-square-foot rect-angular-shaped box filled with dirt and bordered by a four-foot-tall cement wall. The men removed the overgrown weeds and replaced the old soil with new earth they had dug out in nearby fields. They patted the dirt with their shovels in rhythmic motions, and created a nicely curved dome. It was time for a short break. Everyone but Zhao Gang lit a cigarette. Some squatted, some stretched, and others gazed at the faraway hills. They were now ready for the final stage of the ritual.

Zhao Mingshu took a stack of fake paper money, confetti, and firecrackers from a bag in a small truck. Two men spread the papers around the gravestone. "We are ready," said Zhao Mingshu. Lighters in their hands, the men lit the firecrackers, one at a time. The sound of small explosions broke the silence of the vast plain. Pieces of burnt paper flew in the air. Standing in a line away from the tomb, the men watched the spectacle and smoked more cigarettes.

Zhao Mingshu placed stacks of fake money and confetti by the tomb. A young Zhao lit the first stack. Red, yellow, and purple flames swept through the stack. Thick smoke covered the area. Piece by piece, layer by layer, the paper money caught fire. Coughing men covered their faces with dirty kerchiefs. "Burning paper money brings prosperity and good fortunes to the deceased in the afterlife," Zhao Gang told me.

It was getting dark. The men had completed the repairs and performed the ritual with success. It was time for the evening festivity.

*   *   *

Zhao Mingshu was better off than many of his neighbors. He had a relatively spacious and well-kept one-bedroom brick house. Colorful rice bags filled with dried corn and potatoes filled one corner of the living room. A tall ladder, a washing machine, agricultural tools, hot-water flasks, and plastic containers were lined up against the walls. A small wood stove stood in the middle near the entrance to the house. The house's door opened to the living room. It was wide open all day, even in cold winter weather. Zhao Mingshu had recently built a two-room extension some 20 feet behind the main house. "This is the guesthouse," Zhao Gang said.

A bucket in a small hole in the shrubs was the Zhao family's outhouse, some 30 feet away by a dried creek. Piles of toilet paper and pieces of newspaper (used as toilet paper) lay in and around the bucket used for human waste. The bucket's contents served as fertilizer in the small vegetable garden behind the house.

The family fetched water from a well at the front of the house. A large kitchen outside the main house operated for most of the day. Using a wood-burning oven, Zhao Mingshu's wife, Zheng Qin, prepared the daily meals for the household. An appetizing aroma of garlic and Chinese herbs mixed with the smell of burning wood filled the air when she was at work in the kitchen.

Ample food and wine followed the hard day of work. We sat around an aged wooden table in the living room. Zhao Gang opened two bottles of *baijiu*. Zheng Qin placed a large pot of beef, carrots, and potatoes, and smaller dishes of pork, chicken, and vegetables cooked with garlic and ginger, on the table.

Wearing a blue apron with two red apples embroidered in the front, and holding a bowl of rice and two chopsticks in her hand, Zheng Qin stood to the side by the table. She would fill up her bowl with pieces of meat and vegetables, move in and out of the room, bring clean bowls and more food, and take care of her guests for the next couple of hours.

Individual and group toasts continued throughout dinner. A guest from afar, I was toasted more frequently than others were. "You can hold your drink," they would tell me with nods of acceptance. A thick layer of cigarette smoke hung low in the air. After nearly two hours of eating and drinking, Zheng

19   Zheng Qin

Qin cleared the table and served everyone green tea in clear plastic cups. All remained at the table, and a long session of chain-smoking and talking started.

I had come to the village without an interpreter. Zhao Gang spoke little English. Others spoke none. But we had the help of modern technology in this old village in central China: we had Google Translator. Equipped with mobile Wi-Fi, my laptop served as an efficient interpreter. Zhao Gang and eight members of his extended family sat around the dining table, chain-smoked, and told family stories, and the tales of life in the village in times long gone.

Zhao Gang took out a notepad and drew pictures when words and the computer translations failed to help. Zhao Hang ran in and out of the room. Ya Quin sat with the adults and listened to their stories of war and revolution. "*Amao,*" she would say, and add more hot water to my green tea. Visitors arrived. Visitors left. And the storytelling persisted. Still smiling, Zheng Qin stared at my laptop.

With men yawning, and children rubbing their tired eyes, it was time to end the festivities and prepare for another day of work on the ancestral tombs. Zheng Qin boiled water on the wood-burning stove and filled up a shallow plastic container. We were to soak our feet in hot water, and dry them with towels held ready by Zheng Qin. A guest of honor, I had the first wash. Waiting their turn, other used the same water after me. I retired to the guestroom behind the brick house. My bed was comfortable, and the sheets were white and shining. The cover was thick, clean, and colorful.

I woke up early next morning to the sound of roosters and barking dogs. When I opened my eyes, I saw a smiling Ya Quin standing by my bed and offering me a peeled orange. Ya Quin spoke with excitement, and without pause. She made shapes with her small hands, and made every effort to tell me a story. I sat on the bed trying to make sense of her sign language. Frustrated by my failure to understand, she grabbed my hand and walked out of the room. Ya Quin dragged me across the courtyard to a small stable two doors away from the house. "Stay here," she told me with her hand gestures, and entered the room.

Ya Quin returned holding a beautiful brown puppy even smaller than her hand. Ya Quin's dog had given birth to four puppies a day earlier, and she wanted to share her excitement with her foreign guest. Ya Quin giggled and I peeked through the open door. A tired dog was resting beside her puppies.

* * *

War and revolution swept across China in the early years of the twentieth century, and landlordism faced its final years. Zhao Gang's great-grandfather, a nobleman and landlord in the village of Kao Shan Xiang, lost his fortune not to the uprising of his peasants, but to his children's drunkenness and decadence. An influential man with widespread respect, Zhao Gang's great-grandfather owned vast farmlands, and collected tribute from his many peasants. Legend had it that the wealthy nobleman was fair-minded, and that, unlike other big landlords of his time, "He treated his peasants with kindness, and was liked by most people." It was a different story, however, with two of his sons, the older brothers of Zhao Gang's grandfather.

Wealth and power brought them uncontrollable hunger for gambling and an unending lust for concubines. Drunk, drowned in the ecstasy of opium, and addicted to gambling, they lost the family's wealth and its vast lands to rival landlords in the area. Many paid a price for their excesses and wasteful lifestyles. As they lost money in gambling and in the pursuit of their lusts, their peasants fell into even deeper despair. Forced to work longer hours, they kept less of the fruits of their labors. As time passed, even the dreadful condition of the peasants could not save the family. By the end of the 1920s, the brothers had lost all the family fortune. Once powerful people with servants and peasants, they became paupers, vagabonds scorned and ridiculed by others.

Disgraced and humiliated, Zhao Gang's grandfather left his ancestral home, and took his wife and two sons to the land of their old rival. He joined the ranks of landless peasants in China. The son of the great nobleman became a tenant farmer. Zhao Gang's father, Zhao Zeng Ting, was only seven.

Zhao Zeng Ting spent his childhood and youth working on other people's land, took care of their cattle, and endured what his family's peasants and their families had endured for many long years before his birth. All that, however, changed one fateful afternoon in the summer of 1947. Exhausted from the backbreaking work that began before sunrise, Zhao Zeng Ting lay down on a patch of grass. He fell asleep. Heavy blows on his head and stomach, and the angry words of a foreman, ended his momentary peace. The beatings continued as he rose to his feet and stumbled away like a grazing beast.

In 1947, a bloody civil war between the communists and the nationalists engulfed China. The Communist Party promised an end to landlordism, and poor peasants were joining the communists in rising numbers. The young Zhao Zeng Ting knew of others his age or younger who had taken sides and joined the communist army. For many months now, he too had contemplated escaping his misery, and joining the men and women who were fighting and dying on his behalf. He had wavered, always remaining on the farm, and enduring more beatings. The beating that afternoon, however, pushed the young peasant over the edge. Zhao Zeng Ting took stock of his situation. He was not going to remain a tenant farmer for the rest of his life, he decided.

He packed a small bag and walked away from the village and farm. He said farewell to his village and the life he so detested, and became a communist warrior. Zhao Zeng Ting remained a devout communist until he died of bronchitis in 1995.

*   *   *

Zhao Zeng Ting fought with astonishing zeal and devotion. A good fighter, respected by other soldiers and admired by his commanders, he was soon promoted to *jie fang zhan zheng*, a low-ranking officer. After the victory of the Communist Party in 1949, his commander sent Zhao Zeng Ting to the Military Cadre School to train to be an officer proper. "Father was a very bad student in the military academy," Zhao Gang told me. Unable to attend school as a child, Zhao Zeng Ting was slow at learning. "I must take after my father. I was never good in school. I hated studying," Zhao Gang said, laughing.

While depressed and trying to face his shortfalls as a student, Zhao Zeng Ting discovered a new passion that changed his life. "My father played excellent basketball at a time when very few even knew about the game," Zhao Gang said. Over six feet tall, and athletic, Zhao Zeng Ting gave basketball his best, excelling the way he excelled in the People's Liberation Army during the war. Zhao Zeng Ting became a professional player in the army's provincial basketball team when he graduated from the academy. "My father's classmates became officers or government officials. They became influential people." Hu Kui Feng, a loyal friend and a classmate, became the mayor in a small county in Anhui Province.

The mayor had an old housemaid, a good woman with loving children who would visit occasionally, and take their mother home for national festivals, birthdays, and other family affairs. It was during one such visit that for the first time the mayor laid eyes on the maid's beautiful daughter. The young woman was stunning, the mayor thought.

"Is your daughter married?" the good mayor inquired of the mother. The beautiful girl was available, her mother said.

"In that case, let me be a matchmaker for your daughter," the mayor said. "Let me introduce her to a wonderful man, my comrade in arms," he said, and arranged a meeting in his house. This was how the young basketball player met his future wife. Dressed in his best, Zhao Zeng Ting came to meet the maid's daughter, the petite and beautiful Liu Xiuyun. She was as beautiful as the mayor had described her. He was in love at first sight. She was not.

"Mother was not very happy with my father because he did not have any schooling."

Liu Xiuyun was fond of reading. She was an educated girl from Fan Chant County near Wu Lake, and had attended nursing school. Although she was not very happy, Liu Xiuyun accepted the young soldier as her future husband because the matchmaker was none other than the mayor. "There was no way for her to refuse the offer," Zhao Gang said. Liu Xiuyun returned to her county and the young couple dated for two years. They wrote letters and met occasionally.

Writing letters, however, proved to be an ordeal, a problem that the beautiful Liu Xiuyun had to solve one way or another. Zhao Zeng Ting was not accustomed to writing. He wrote in embarrassing handwriting, the handwriting of a man without proper education. Embarrassed by the primitiveness of his handwriting, Liu Xiuyun would not show his letters to friends and family. "She cared about what people said."

After months of contemplation and agony, Liu Xiuyun found a solution. "Each time she wrote to him, mother included a self-addressed envelope for my father to use." The young lovers finally married in 1952, and moved to Hefei, the capital of Anhui. Liu Xiuyun began work in a steel mill.

*   *   *

Liu Xiuyun was among the first generation of steelworkers in communist China. A proud communist working to build a new society, she would volunteer for the most arduous tasks. Revolution had removed the old gender boundaries. Chinese were making history, and Liu Xiuyun was proud of participating. Unlike most other young men and women in the mill, Liu Xiuyun was also educated. She had talents that she could use to further the revolution. Volunteering during her free time, Liu Xiuyun became a journalist for the steel mill's newspaper. She was a good writer with a great deal of communist zeal. "Mother even saw Chairman Mao three times when he visited the mill. You don't know what that meant to her. She still talks about that,' Zhao Gang recalled.

In 1958, during the Great Leap Forward, China started a national movement to increase steel production and surpass America in 15 years. The government instructed villages to produce their own steel. Local furnaces were set up everywhere, and farmers gave all their metal products to the village communes. Local self-sufficiency in steel production became a national priority. Liu Xiuyun was proud to be a steelworker during this period. "Exceed America, Surpass England," Liu Xiuyun and others chanted in the mill. Revolutionary enthusiasm was so high in those early years that factories had to lock their gates to keep out workers who wanted to work even at night, Liu Xiuyun told Zhao Gang. "Imagine something like that these days," Zhao Gang said.

Liu Xiuyun was later transferred to a mine in Tonling. She was a mother of two at the time, and left for Tonling with Zhao Gang's older brother and sister. Liu Xiuyun and Zhao Zeng Ting were separated for the first time after their marriage. Soon after, Zhao Zeng Ting was dispatched to Lujiang. He became a bank employee and continued to play basketball. In no time, his fame as a master basketball player had reached every corner in the province.

After many attempts, Liu Xiuyun succeeded in obtaining a transfer to Lujiang. She became a hotel receptionist and joined her husband in an apartment in the small housing complex provided by the bank's work unit. A year later, Zhao Gang was born. Not long after, Zhao Zeng Ting was promoted as director of the bank. He remained with the bank until his retirement.

LUJIANG

Zhao Gang opened his eyes to this world at the beginning of the turbulent years of the Cultural Revolution. The Cultural Revolution was Mao's last theatrical act, and the last attempt to put his stamp on a revolution that had gone astray. The 1949 revolution abolished landlordism in rural areas and private property in the cities. It brought education and basic healthcare to remote places, and improved the lives of millions. The revolution gave Chinese people self-esteem. However, by 1966, many promises of the revolution remained unfulfilled. The new system had failed to end inequality between cities and villages, factory workers and peasants, technical workers and ordinary laborers, permanent workers and those with temporary status. Above all, although the revolution had eliminated the propertied classes, it had produced a new elite and a growing bureaucracy with all the privileges and power of the overthrown classes. It had created new masters of the people. The Cultural Revolution was Mao's desperate attempt to "save the revolution" by calling on the youth and the Chinese workers to "dare to rebel" against their new masters.

The youth and the workers heeded the call. They rebelled. They formed Red Guards and fought Communist Party bosses, and their new masters in workplaces and schools. As the fighting continued, competing factions emerged among the rebels. Red Guards fought other Red Guards. An orgy of political accusation, distrust, bickering, and violence erupted throughout the country. The emboldened youth and workers were marching forward, establishing their independent power, taking revenge, and defying the power of the party. The genie was out of the bottle. Beijing lost control of the situation. The monopoly rule of the Communist Party and its Central Committee was in serious danger. By encouraging the Chinese to rebel, Mao had undermined his own rule. To regain control, he called upon the People's Liberation Army. The PLA restored order, persecuting those who dared to rebel.

Thousands had died during the PLA crackdown and through random violence, by the time the Cultural Revolution officially ended in 1976. The Cultural Revolution rarely spared anyone, and the trauma of its senseless violence lasted for seven years after Mao's death. Parents told tales of the horrors to their children. Brothers and sisters told of their own hardships to their younger siblings.

*   *   *

Zhao Gang was a child during those chaotic years. Unlike his elders, he had pleasant memories of the Cultural Revolution. "The Cultural Revolution might have been a disaster for others, but my memories of those years are very positive. I had fun," he told me. "Maybe many people suffered during those years, but I had an easy and comfortable life," he said, laughing.

Zhao Gang was born in a "typical Chinese revolutionary family." He was the son of a soldier, a low-ranking communist officer. Zhao Gang's mother was once a star worker in a mill. Zhao Gang was from a perfect family with a "good class background." During the Cultural Revolution, working-class families, those with a good class background, were respected and praised as symbols of the new China. They were the hope of the future, the foundation of a new society that was to be built on the ashes of centuries of superstition, prejudice, and injustice. "Thirty or forty years ago, a family like mine was regarded highly in the society. It is very different now. But during the Cultural Revolution we were the envy of the country."

While Zhao Gang enjoyed the special status of his good family, he also found the Cultural Revolution a blessing in ways not imagined by its masterminds. Even as a child, Zhao Gang had disliked studying. The prevalent anti-intellectual and anti-educational atmosphere of the years of the Cultural Revolution suited him well. There were never any pressures to study. Students seldom attended classes. Even some of the teachers did not teach on regular basis, Zhao Gang recalled. "We played all the time and no one complained. That was the best part of the Cultural Revolution."

The Cultural Revolution unleashed an anti-intellectual crusade. Young students were encouraged to ridicule and scorn teachers and school principals "with bad class background." Students his age paraded their teachers in the streets, made them kneel, spat on them, and beat them without mercy. To save themselves from this humiliation and abuse, many committed suicide. To defy teachers was a revolutionary act. School attendance was irregular, studying unimportant. "It may be hard for you to imagine, but, at that time, people were not proud of studying. Good students were not those who studied hard. Good students were good revolutionaries. We called those who studied a lot *Xiao Mianyang*, little sheep."

While Zhao Gang played with friends and classmates, his parents and neighbors marched in the streets and chanted slogans. He saw street battles and scuffles, and heard men and women making proclamations that he did not understand. "People shouted and danced in the streets," he recalled. All of this confused the little Zhao Gang. "There were two opposite sides in the streets—the supporters of Chairman Mao, and the others," he realized after a while. "I was not interested in any side. I just wanted to play." Zhao Gang's father was on Chairman Mao's side. However, "he was very kind to the other side. He would try to protect them as much as possible," he recalled.

Zhao Zeng Ting was a communist, and a Red Guard. He was on high ground during the Cultural Revolution because he did not have money and power as a young man. Taking part in rallies and marches with his wife, he would come home late every night wearing a "bamboo helmet," and carrying "a white stick with both ends painted red." To make his boy happy, Zhao Zeng Ting even made a toy stick for Zhao Gang. "My parents used their sticks to fight. My stick was only used for fun."

Zhao Gang recalled the tribunal of one Wan Gun, the director of the bank, and Zhao Zeng Ting's superior during his first years in Lujiang. "Beat Wan Gan," he remembered people shouting. "They were not hitting him, but shouting slogans." Using his own body, Zhao Gang showed me how Wan Gun's hands were tied behind him. A placard was hung around his neck, and he was forced to kneel with his head down. "Later, Wan Gan's son became one of my best friends, because my father was very moderate and did not let others beat his father."

"Were you not scared of these fights and the violence as a child?" I asked.

"Never! I was from a revolutionary family, and I was just having fun. The fun ended when I was forced to study."

*   *   *

A devastating earthquake struck Tangshan, a city 95 miles south of Beijing, and 5000 miles away from Zhao Gang's home, at 3.42 a.m. on July 28, 1976. More than one million people were asleep in the area. They were unaware of the catastrophe that was awaiting them. The quake-monitoring centers had not anticipated the calamity. Animals in the affected area were giving all the usual warning signs of the coming tragedy the day before the earthquake— chickens ran around excitedly and refused to eat, mice and yellow weasels looked for places to hide, and goldfish jumped out of their bowls, the locals recalled. The quake lasted 14–16 seconds and took a quarter of a million lives, according to official accounts. It became the second worst earthquake disaster in recorded history, and one of the deadliest natural disasters of the twentieth century.

Many hours after the tragedy, Beijing was not even aware of what had struck the country. Unequipped, riddled with power struggles, and dealing with Mao Zedong lying on his deathbed in a hospital in Beijing, the authorities reacted too late. Once the dust settled, Beijing went into panic mode.

Beijing ordered all work units in the area to build new shelters if they had land, or to demolish one of their buildings and replace that with a shelter if they did not. It ordered residents to stay in shelters in anticipation of another tragedy. Another earthquake was imminent, the authorities believed. "The earthquake was really devastating. It shocked the whole nation. Everyone was scared of the possibility of another one. The quake destroyed a whole city. People built quake-proof shelters," Zhao Gang recalled years later. He was only ten at the time. While the adults lived in fear and anxiety, the ordeal brought unusual excitement and joy to Zhao Gang and his friends.

Following the order from Beijing, Zhao Gang's father's work unit built a shelter for its employees and their families. "I was so happy the first day in the shelter. There was no school, and we played all day long." Thinking another quake was on its way, Zhao Gang returned home to check if he had left anything valuable behind. "The most valuable thing was my ping-pong racket. That was *my* treasure. I grabbed it and took it to the shelter." Everyone waited nervously. "I made my own quake monitor—I put a number of books on the top of each other, and waited to see if they moved. I was watching the pile so carefully." But the earthquake did not seem to be coming.

While the country waited anxiously for another natural disaster, a different type of tragedy shook China. The state-run radio station announced the death of Chairman Mao. He was 82 years old. "Till this day, I remember the exact day Chairman Mao died. It happened on September 9, 1976." A mourning frenzy swept throughout the country. Old and young, even children, mourned the death of the Chairman. "Old women were crying themselves to death. People believed the sky was going to collapse," Zhao Gang recalled.

Meanwhile the perceived threat of another quake remained. Zhao Gang's hometown, Lujiang, was on a fault line. Hoping to save their youngest from possible catastrophe, Zhao Gang's parents sent him away to his grandmother's home by the Chang Jian river. "After half a year, there was still no earthquake and I went back home," he said, laughing. Zhao Gang's friends and neighbors in the bank's housing complex were impatiently awaiting his return, he said. "We had lost months of playing. We needed to work hard to catch up," he said, and broke down laughing.

*   *   *

For the past 40 years, Liu Xiuyun had lived in the same two-story complex built by her husband's work unit. "We wanted to move mother to a better and newer place after father died, but she decided to stay. She knows all the neighbors here. This is home," Zhao Gang said.

The housing complex was once a middle-class residential unit and a symbol of the promises of the Communist Revolution. With the start of reforms in the 1980s, this and similar units became a part of the past that the new China wished to forget. Liu Xiuyun's home was facing its slow demise when I visited in December 2007. The exterior cried out for new paint, new plaster, and repairs of all kind. Years of exposure to rain and pollution had darkened the compound's walls. The chipped plaster, the falling bricks, the broken cement, and everything about the compound smelled of decay and old age.

A narrow, dark, dirty passage connected the street to a small courtyard paved with broken cement, and enclosed by a rectangle of two-story apartment buildings. A twisting stairway connected the courtyard to the apartments. "*Amao,*" Liu Xiuyun cried through the window of her apartment. I crossed the courtyard and took the old stairway up to her home, a two-bedroom apartment with bare floors and furniture that Liu Xiuyun and her husband bought when they moved to Lujiang. A small dining table was placed against the wall by the entrance. Liu Xiuyun offered me a seat, and fetched a plastic bag full of sesame candy from the kitchen. "I made them myself," she said. I took one, then another. She put a fistful in my hands. "For later," she said.

Looking out the window that faced the courtyard, Liu Xiuyun pointed to the roof of the row opposite her home and said, "When Zhao Gang was young he played on the roof with others children. I was worried to death." Zhao Gang smiled. "I had the best years of my life in this apartment," he said. I followed Liu Xiuyun to the room across the entrance. A photo frame with a picture of a man in his fifties stood on the wall. "My husband," Liu Xiuyun said.

Communism, friendship, sports, wine, and cigarettes were Zhao Zeng Ting's passions in life. He remained loyal to communism to the last day of his life. Communism had saved him from his humiliating and torturous life as a peasant. It had given him respect. He was a well-known athlete in his county and beyond, a basketball coach, and a man with many friends and admirers. When he died in 1995, the family buried him in the hills on the outskirts of Lujiang. Zhao Zeng Ting's funeral was a spectacle, Zhao Gang recalled. Fans from places far beyond Lujiang came to pay their respects. "They came to say farewell to a basketball star," Zhao Gang said.

Zhao Zeng Ting died in 1995 after a long and agonizing battle with illness. Years of chain-smoking and heavy drinking finally took their toll. Frail and visibly in pain, he continued to smoke and drink rice wine at lunch and dinner. "My father had a slogan, 'No Smoking, No Drinking, No Life,'" Zhao Gang told me, laughing loudly. As Zhao Zeng Ting's health deteriorated, and his family's finances become dire, he became angry and agitated, frequently quarreling with Liu Xiuyun. "I watched him destroy his body with smoking. I decided not to ever smoke, and not to drink in excess," Zhao Gang said.

* * *

Zhao Gang was not a good drinker. One or two shots of *baijiu* made his eyes bloodshot, and his face and neck red and blotchy. Nevertheless, he would continue to drink. "I cannot let you drink alone. In China, drinking is not for its own sake. You drink for friends. We have a saying in China, 'Damage your body, but do not damage your friendship.'" Zhao Gang had learned this from his father. "You drink yourself to death for your friends," he told me.

Zhao Zeng Ting's death left a void in Liu Xiuyun's life. Retired and without her husband, Liu Xiuyun lived alone. She spent her days cooking, and painting flowers and landscapes. "This is for you, *amao*," she said, giving me a painting of colorful flowers from a batch of 50 or so rolled canvases. "Painting keeps her busy," Zhao Gang said. Nevertheless, Liu Xiuyun missed her husband. "He was a good man," she said, and invited me to join her for his memorial.

It was a beautiful and sunny day. Liu Xiuyun carried a small basket of food, a bottle of *baijiu*, paper money, and firecrackers. I followed Liu Xiuyun, her boys, and her daughter-in-law searching for Zhao Zeng Ting's tomb on a hill covered with dense brushwood and trees. Liu Xiuyun moved briskly, climbing up a steep hill, and holding on to tree branches and trunks. The sound of bursting firecrackers told of others paying their respects to their dead. Moving left and right, and up and down, Liu Xiuyun spotted the tomb. "There," she shouted. We followed her.

Gently touching the tombstone, Liu Xiuyun said prayers, bowed, and offered her deceased husband food and wine. Following Zhao Gang, Zhao Ming, and his wife, I bowed and prayed for the dead soldier. "This means a lot to my family and me," Zhao Gang said. "Thank you for paying your respects to my husband," Liu Xiuyun said and held my hand.

✳   ✳   ✳

Zhao Gang's visits to Lujiang were special occasions for his old friends to escape the boredom of life in a provincial Chinese town. For Zhao Gang, going back to Lujiang was a chance "to escape the troubles of managing a factory," even if it was for a short time. There was no vacation better than returning home. Zhao Gang cherished the long dinners with old friends, and late-hour singing in local karaoke joints. This time around, Zhao Gang's visit was even more special. He had come home with a guest from afar. Entertaining me was a collective project.

Zhao Gang's friends were from all walks of life. They were teachers and accountants, and successful men of business. They were classmates from kindergarten or elementary school. Some had attended university and returned to their provincial lives in their birthplace. The drastic changes in China had passed them by. Except for rare cases, most earned low incomes, and struggled to make the ends meet. An entrepreneur in Shenzhen, Zhao Gang had a special place among them. He was a role model.

"How much do you think a teacher makes here?" a 40-year-old high school friend asked. "I earn 2000 yuan a month. I have a university degree, and 20 years of teaching experience," she lamented. Wearing an old sweater with a hole in one sleeve, another high school friend, a thin, balding man of average height, spoke of the difficulties of managing his life after years of teaching.

Wuhong, a charming and petite 42-year-old classmate from kindergarten, returned home after graduating university, married, and began work in a local hospital. "You saw a rich farmer today. This is not how most farmers live in China," she told me the day we visited a large duck farm in the outskirts of Lujiang. "Most of us are not happy. Actually, we are miserable. We are only just surviving," she said.

China was preparing for the 2008 Olympics when I visited Lujiang. As with everywhere else in this vast country, talking about the Olympics was a favorite pastime. Hosting the games brought pride to a people who had felt isolated for many long years. "Beijing is too far away and too expensive. We have no chance to take part in the Olympics. But you can. I hope you can enjoy the games," Wuhong told me. "You are lucky to be able to see the world," she said.

* * *

Our meals were colorful and long, with multiple dishes of special local vegetables, rare birds, and other animals.

"This bird is only found in hills around here," Zhao Gang would say.

"Try this. Have you ever had porcupine?"

"No, don't eat that. That's dog meat."

As always, there were many individual and group toasts. "To friendship between China and Iran," a round-faced friend toasted during a long lunch. "We will stand behind Iran if America attacks," said another.

Singing in a karaoke bar followed dinner every night. We would sit on long sofas in front a large TV screen, drink cola or juice, watch video clips of famous singers—the audio part would include only the music, not the voice—and listen to friends sing from the heart.

"This is for you," Zhao Gang would say to me, holding the microphone in one hand, moving the other hand to the music, and singing a song about friendship.

"To our guest," another friend would say, singing amidst clapping by the others.

Soldier songs were Zhao Gang's favorite. Marching soldiers and heroic scenes appeared on the screen with each song.

"This is a Chinese opera for you," Wuhong said, standing in a corner, singing while making beautiful and delicate movements with her hands.

There were solos, duets, and group singing. Warm ovations followed every performance.

"He has the best voice," a friend said about Zhao Gang.

"He is a good artist," said another.

"I have never seen you so energized and happy," I told Zhao Gang.

"This is the real me. I rediscover myself when I come home, and when I sing with friends in a karaoke joint," he said.

LEAVING FOR SHENZHEN

By the time Zhao Gang was in middle school, he "had built a reputation as a bad student," he told me. Studying English was, in particular, a nightmare for the young Zhao Gang. His reluctance to learn English became a problem in middle school. The school director was also Zhao Gang's English teacher. He did all he could to punish Zhao Gang for his lack of interest in school, and in his subject.

There were two choices for students at the end of middle school: ending their education, or taking the entrance exam for senior high. Zhao Gang's teacher suggested that he stop with a middle school degree. "Don't waste your time. You will not pass. Get a job in a factory. You will be happier."

The suggestion angered Zhao Gang, and gave him the motivation to fight back. Determined to prove his teacher wrong, Zhao Gang enrolled for the exam. But he was too fond of playing to study. Others in his school studied day and night—he did not.

Exam day arrived. He returned home after taking the test, feeling defeated, and imagining his teacher laughing at his failure. Zhao Gang lay down in bed, closed his eyes, and saw himself along thousands of other workers in a large factory. The idea frightened him, he told me years later. He waited for the results impatiently. He knew his chances of passing were low. Factory work was his future, he told himself. Zhao Gang was in disbelief when he heard the results. "I passed the exam without studying. Other students who studied hard failed. I scored three points above the passing grade." Zhao Gang entered one of the best and oldest schools in his town. "Even though I was not that good, my high school was the best in Lujiang. I was the worst student in the best school. Something to be proud of," he said, laughing.

In those days, Zhao Gang recalled, only students from the village studied hard. "The city kids always fell behind those from the villages." The village kids were poor. Some did not wear socks even in winter, and others did not wash for days, Zhao Gang recalled. "But they were good students, and most of them entered university." They buried themselves in their books, and spent all their free time studying to win a university place. That was the only way they could have escaped the limits of rural life in those days. A university degree brought closer the possibility of finding a job in the city, obtaining a city *hukou*, and leaving the village for good. Zhao Gang did not have these pressures. "I was already in the city, and if everything else failed, there was always the bank. I knew I could get a job at my father's bank."

A job at the bank was always a good opportunity, Zhao Gang thought. To test his luck, Zhao Gang took the exam for securing a position while still in high school. He scored the highest, and "almost became a bank employee." However, he changed his mind before graduating from high school. Like most of his friends, Zhao Gang chose to go to university. Entering university was a battle most students could not win in those days. Zhao Gang had to pass a national university entrance exam. For a student who despised studying, passing the exam was "like trying to climb Mount Everest without preparation," he told me years later at Sunland.

While other students devoted themselves to their books in high school, Zhao Gang played sports. He was tall, athletically built, and strong. Following in his father's footsteps, Zhao Gang played basketball, and moved from one sport to another. "I mastered most." At age 16, he represented Lujiang in a province-wide football tournament. "I was among the first generation of football players in China." In 1982, when only a few families in China had a TV set at home, Zhao Gang was watching the World Cup on television. "Football was not a Chinese game. We could not even buy the shoes and the ball, not even in the capital of Anhui."

Zhao Gang spent most of his time playing, but he passed every year without any effort. "I was very lucky in high school," he said. His luck, however, ended the first time he took the university entrance exam. "I scored 100 points lower than the passing grade." His classmates who had passed the exam would return home during their breaks, and tell Zhao Gang about the good life at university. "You can go home as late as you want, play sports, and have fun," they would say. Zhao Gang wanted to go to university even more now. However, being accepted was "like millions of people trying to cross a very narrow bridge," Zhao Gang said. He had to pass the exam at all costs, even if it was only for the good times his friends had told him about, he thought.

Entering university was now Zhao Gang's life project. After months of "really studying," Zhao Gang failed for the second time. The third year was harder. Despite his love of sports, he devoted his time to his books, read sciences and other subjects, and passed the exam at the end of the third year. "I got the passing grade, not a point above, not a point below." With that score, however, he could attend only a mediocre university. "I was allowed to enter a university and become a prison warden." He was disgraced.

"Good luck had abandoned me for the first time in my life, I thought. I had studied for the exam, but failed to enter a good university." He had refused to

20   With an old farmer

be a factory worker in the past. Now he refused to become a prison warden. Zhao Gang declined his seat at the university. A fourth attempt was awaiting him. This time around, he chose not to study for the exam. "I began dancing, and learning to play chess."

Meanwhile, he attended classes to prepare for the exam. "I sat in the back, hid from the teacher, and slept most of the time. I played chess with classmates when I was awake." Despite this, Zhao Gang passed the exam at his fourth try, scoring 15 points above the passing grade. "I did not even go to see if I had passed when the scores were announced. My mother did. She was so excited—I could not believe it when she told me the news. I remember asking her to double check that she had looked up the right person. I rushed to school to check the results myself. There it was: I was accepted to the best university in Anhui Province, despite being one of the worst students. My good luck was still with me after all."

*   *   *

His four years at university were the happiest years of Zhao Gang's life, he recalled. "I felt like a butterfly breaking free, flying away." After 15 years of studying, he had finally entered university. That alone was a lifetime's achievement for most people. There were other things, however, that made university life memorable for Zhao Gang.

Unlike hard sciences, philosophy did not require much studying in China in those days. "The professors did not push us to study hard. They did not care one way or another. I could play as much football as I wanted, No one controlled the time I spent playing," he said, and turned on his laptop to show me a digitized album of old photos from university.

"This is me in the volleyball team," he said, relating how he became a captain and brought pride to his university by leading the team to victory in the regional games.

"That is when I played the guitar," he said about a picture of a good-looking young man holding an acoustic guitar. "I was a lot more handsome then," he said, laughing.

"And this is a picture of my love." He was a sophomore when he fell in love at first sight with the beautiful Luo Qiong, an English major "chased by many boys" across the university. "The most important thing in the university years for me was meeting my wife," Zhao Gang said with a big smile on his face, and showed me old pictures of a smiling Luo Qiong. Petite, with a charming face, and named "after a beautiful flower," Luo Qiong was a classic Chinese beauty.

"I am a late bloomer," Zhao Gang said. He "did not know anything about girls" before meeting Luo Qiong. Many girls were interested in him even in the middle school, he recalled. "I was handsome and good at sports, but I was also very shy." Girls intimidated him. Some followed him around in middle school, even more in high school. Zhao Gang would find girls waiting for him on the way to school. "I was scared," he said. "I reported those girls to my school principal."

All that changed when he entered university. His shyness was gone, and he was no longer scared. Zhao Gang was ready to meet girls. However, he had another serious problem. "Like my father, I had a bad handwriting. I missed many chances to meet girls because of that." Living in overcrowded and separate dormitories, before the days of the Internet, text messaging, or even regular phones, writing and exchanging notes was an important means of communication between boys and girls. Embarrassed by his handwriting, Zhao Gang lost many opportunities to date, he told me. "I have two weaknesses— one my English, the other my handwriting. Sometimes I cannot read my own writing."

* * *

When graduation arrived at last, Zhao Gang had to face a serious challenge like most Chinese in his position. He was ready to make a difference and fulfill his dream of changing the world. His future career and the place of work, however, were to be determined by school administrators, and based on his grades. He had no say in that.

Four years of playing sports and music and courting the love of his life came to haunt Zhao Gang. He had had the time of his life, but he had also graduated with low grades. Good jobs were out of the question. Zhao Gang knew there were some openings for government positions that were available to his class, and that working for the government was one of the best ways to help his country. "At that time, government jobs were given only to bookworms. I was not one of them." He pleaded with his professors, telling them he was confident of his ability to do a better job than those with higher grades. The professors refused to accept his pleas. "Except for sports, you didn't do well in anything in the past four years," one professor said.

There were other challenges and fears. What if he and his love were dispatched to different places? After all, his parents had lived and worked in different cities before reuniting in Lujiang. Was he to face the same destiny? He dreaded being separated from Luo Quiong. "But I struck lucky once again," he said.

Zhao Gang and Luo Qiong were assigned to Chuzhou, a small town in eastern Anhui, and "the hometown of Zhu Yuanzhang, the founding emperor of the Ming Dynasty." The young lovers were relieved. Zhao Gang was to teach modern Chinese history and political science at a small technical school, and Luo Qiong was to be an office employee in a factory. The jobs were far from attractive, but they had no choice. The university administration had already transferred Zhao Gang's records to the school.

Zhao Gang was stuck. He and Luo Qiong left for Chuzhou in September 1991. "Instead of changing the country and the world, I was to be teaching in a small school," he said.

*   *   *

Zhao Gang left his suitcase at the train station in Chuzhou and walked straight to the school to meet the principal. "Where is your luggage?" the principal asked. He offered to send a vehicle to fetch the suitcase. Zhao Gang waited an hour for a car or a taxi sent by the principal. No one came. He waited longer, and no one showed. He was preparing to leave when he saw a tricycle wagon coming towards him. The principal was pedaling. "OK, take this to the station and get your luggage," he said. "A warm welcome," Zhao Gang said, laughing.

*   *   *

Zhao Gang began his career with a salary of 100 yuan a month and shared a room with three others in the teachers' dormitory. After a year in the job, he married Luo Qiong, and the young couple moved to a private room in the dormitory. "That was our first home."

The principal was kind, but old and conservative, Zhao Gang recalled. Having a boyfriend or girlfriend was taboo, not allowed for the students. There were strange rules even for the teachers. "There had to be a chaperone in the room when a girlfriend visited."

The job was not challenging. To keep himself excited, Zhao Gang continued to play the guitar, and took up singing. He was soon the most popular teacher among the students and his peers. The Chinese rock and roll singer Cui Jian was Zhao Gang's favorite. "Once, I sang a Cui Jian song at one of the school parties. The principal was very upset—he did not think that was worthy of a schoolteacher. Many looked down on rock and roll in those days."

Now, even singing and playing the guitar were not sufficient to keep Zhao Gang content. China was changing. By 1992, it was well into its new experiment with export-led capitalism. Zhao Gang knew of people from Anhui University who had gone to Shenzhen and joined the world of business. Some had made a fortune and others a comfortable life for themselves and their families. Zhao Gang was trapped in a small room with his beloved wife.

Unhappy with his job, at the end of the first year, Zhao Gang took a short trip to Shenzhen, hoping to get a chance in the world of business. He found no one interested in hiring someone with a philosophy degree. "Not only did I not change the world, I could not even succeed in changing my job." Returning to the school in two weeks, he resigned himself to making a happy life with his wife in Chuzhou. A year later, Luo Qiong gave birth to their daughter, Zhao Sijia. The family remained in the small dormitory room for the next seven years. Zhao Gang's salary increased to 1000 yuan a month.

*   *   *

While a university student, Zhao Gang had read a statement by a Soviet writer that remained with him for many years. "If you are not proud of your job, make your job proud of you," the writer had said. Zhao Gang decided to make his job proud of him. "I worked so hard." The principal was impressed. To reward Zhao Gang's commitment to the school and his job, he promoted him to director of admissions.

The 1990s saw the beginning of radical changes in China. While privatizing many State-Owned Enterprises, the government was pressuring other public enterprises, including schools, to find ways to achieve financial self-sufficiency. For the first time since its founding, Zhao Gang's school had to find a way to pay for its expenses. The principal was desperate to find ways to raise money and appease the authorities. His job depended on his success in this business. After months of planning, he found a brilliant way. He had a business plan, and Zhao Gang was the man to inject life into the plan. He was sure of Zhao Gang's abilities—and above all, he trusted the young teacher.

The plan was simple. China was starting to catch on to computer mania, and government employees of all levels were encouraged to learn to work with computers. The principal saw a captive market in this small town. Besides educating the school's regular students, he planned to create a special private school to teach computer skills to public employees. He released Zhao Gang from his teaching responsibilities at the school, and put him in charge of running the new enterprise. At last, Zhao Gang entered the world of business, although as an underpaid schoolteacher. There was, however, one problem. Zhao Gang's school had no computers, and could not afford to buy them. "I had to find creative ways to get access to computers." After days of thinking, Zhao Gang had a brilliant idea.

He knew of unused VIP rooms with many computers in Chuzhou's Stock Exchange. Not having much activity in those days, the Stock Exchange was often empty. It had no visitors. To make some money, the management of the Exchange often rented the main floor to local businesses. Zhao Gang had gone to "flea markets" at the Stock Exchange, buying jeans and shirts.

Set up for big clients with money, the VIP rooms had "nice computers," sitting unused most of the time. Why not hold classes in these rooms, Zhao Gang thought. There would be no need to buy computers. He only had to convince the management of the Stock Exchange. That was not difficult. "I told the director that my classes would bring more attention to the Stock Exchange." The director gave Zhao Gang unlimited access.

Soon, middle-aged government employees eager to join the modern world by mastering these magic boxes filled the VIP rooms. Zhao Gang was enjoying rising fame. Everyone came to him to learn the magic, the key to the new world. Local and national TV stations interviewed Zhao Gang, praising him as a model of entrepreneurship. "This was a proud time in my life." His fame traveled before him, and when he returned to Shenzhen for the second time in 1999, many recognized him from those TV interviews.

ARISE, YOU PRISONERS OF STARVATION

Signs of an impending global economic crisis could be seen everywhere by late 2007. Like all export-processing factories in Longgang, Sunland relied on contracts from foreign buyers. A drop in demand had dire consequences. Zhao Gang had, however, more immediate worries. His difficulties preceded the global economic crisis—he had "a Sunland Crisis." The 2008 crash only aggravated a decline already in the making. "I am trying to keep my head above the waters," he would tell me in early 2008.

Zhao Gang's troubles were the consequence of the Chinese government's new economic strategy. China was slowly closing in on low-end export industries like Sunland. The government was pulling the rug out from under the feet of industries that were once the engine of China's enviable success in the world market. For nearly 30 years the government had used its muscle and resources to help industries that were unbeatable because of their low production costs. Sunland's entry into the world of export-processing industries was at the tail end of a strategy whose time had run out. Sunland's successes were short lived. The Communist Party was nurturing other industries for twenty-first-century China. The country was marching into the second phase of its globalization and industrial triumph.

Meanwhile, for the first time since the start of economic reforms, the government was eyeing the domestic market. It was trying to build an economy that produced TV sets, stereo systems, clothing, furniture, and all the other usual Chinese exports for the 1.3 billion people living across this vast country. China was on the road to a strong domestic market, and a higher level of competition in the exports market. Zhao Gang's Sunland had little chance of remaining a success story in these conditions.

The "Sunland crisis" was symptomatic of the crisis of low-wage export-based capitalism in China. Chinese low-wage labor-intensive exports capitalism was on its deathbed. "My world is turning upside down," Zhao Gang would tell me. Everything that helped Sunland achieve its enviable success was now reversing.

* * *

The rising cost of labor was one of Zhao Gang's main problems in 2007. While China officially retained the old *hukou* system, the central authorities allowed the greatest migration in the world and supplied the country's budding export industries with millions of low-wage workers. By 2007 the seemingly unlimited supply of labor had ended, and wages were rising. For the first time since the reforms the government was supporting higher wages and better labor standards for its migrant workers. A sea change was occurring in China.

Longgang's minimum wage increased from 420 yuan in 2004, to 750 yuan a month in 2007. More increases came in 2008 and 2009. Meanwhile, the government was deliberating on policies that would actively discourage labor-intensive exports such as garments, clothing, electronics, furniture, and toys.

Zhao Gang entered the world of business when the low-value added export-processing industries that had brought China to economic prominence and breathed life into the Chinese economy faced a life-threatening crisis. They had served their historic purpose. Their time was over. Zhao Gang was among the last entrepreneurs who, for a few short years, made a small fortune. Sunland performed remarkably well in its first two years. It made its operating capital in profits six months after beginning production. Its 2004 profits were 15 percent, much higher than the industry average of 5–10percent, and above the rates in other industries.

In the heyday of China's low-end exports bonanza, producers like Zhao Gang had the advantage of tax refunds and subsidies, and cost-reducing policies that helped them beat the odds and advance in a short time. They had an inexhaustible supply of very cheap labor that kept flowing from faraway villages and small towns, knocking on their gates (literarily knocking) and begging for jobs.

Sunland was among the last Chinese subcontracting firms to benefit from this. But the company was also the face of a part of China that had outlived its usefulness. It represented an image that China now wished to dispel. Low-wage capitalism and low-end exports had made China the envy of the world. Thirty years after its birth, it had now become a *stigma*.

In 2007 the government lowered, and in some cases eliminated, export tax refunds for the export-processing industries. It reduced the average tax refund from 13 percent to 5 percent in Zhao Gang's industry. "The tax refunds were a big part of my profits," Zhao Gang said. The refunds allowed Sunland and other low-end subcontractors to accept the very low prices demanded by their foreign buyers, particularly the Americans.

Increased wages and the cut in tax refunds were, however, only a part of Zhao Gang's difficulties. "The Americans" were the main problem, Zhao Gang told me one day at a restaurant by the Beautiful Rose Garden. He took out a pen from his bag, jotted numbers on the place mat in front of him, and patiently explained how "Washington" was hurting his business and many others in China. That had to do with the exchange rates.

When Sunland started business in 2004, each dollar exchanged for 8.5 yuan. Zhao Gang had no worries about sudden changes in exchange rates and their destabilizing effect on his business. For a number of years, the Chinese government had guaranteed the same exchange rate by intervening in the foreign exchange market. It was an easy operation. When the yuan rose in value, the Chinese central bank sold millions of yuan and bought dollars in return. The bank repeated this frequently enough to avoid the slightest increase and fluctuations in the price of yuan.

The policy paid off. It worked well for Zhao Gang and other subcontractors who were paid in dollars by their foreign buyers. The American buyers signed agreements with Chinese subcontractors like Sunland for the delivery of a specific volume of the product at prices fixed and paid in dollars. Zhao Gang received 8.5 yuan for every dollar he earned from sales in the United States.

The earnings allowed him to pay his workers and cover other costs in yuan, and retain a good profit.

While Zhao Gang was happy with the fixed exchange rate of 8.5 yuan to the dollar, American policymakers were complaining that China was stealing American jobs by keeping an undervalued yuan. The current exchange rate made Chinese goods "artificially" more competitive and hurt American exports, they said. The real exchange rate, many argued in the United States, should be close to five yuan to a dollar. At five yuan, American exports would become cheaper and more competitive in China. The reverse would happen to Chinese exports. Washington pressured Beijing to stop intervening in the market and allow the yuan to increase against the dollar.

The Chinese resisted. Their exchange rate policy was a part of the national industrialization strategy of helping their low-cost exporters—they would not relinquish the policy until the time was right. And in July 2005, the Chinese believed the time had finally arrived for a change. Beijing started a gradual and successive revaluation of the yuan. It allowed it to rise. By the end of 2007, the dollar exchanged for 7.5 yuan. Zhao Gang earned 12 percent fewer yuan for every dollar he received from his American sales. Months later, the dollar sold for 6.8 yuan and a big part of Zhao Gang's revenues disappeared.

The yuan revaluation failed to put a dent in the soaring American deficit with China, but it hurt Zhao Gang and thousands of other Chinese exporters and their workers. Zhao Gang paid his workers in yuan, bought raw material in yuan. "All my costs are also going up. I pay more for raw materials and energy. And I am getting fewer yuan for every dollar I earn from the Americans now. I have less money to spend," he told me. The Chinese government was slowly chipping away the exchange rate subsidy it had given exporters like Zhao Gang. China was marching ahead with new high-tech industries that did not rely on this type of subsidy.

To make matters worse, Zhao Gang and other exporters like him were under constant pressure from their foreign buyers, especially the Americans, to lower their prices. China was becoming "too expensive," the Americans told their subcontractors. China was no longer the only game in town. With an equally large population, and low wages, India was becoming a formidable competitor. Everyone talked about India, Vietnam, Cambodia, and other low-wage countries waiting to join the game China had helped create some years ago.

Fearing the loss of business to India, many subcontractors were folding under pressure from their buyers. They were agreeing to produce at unprofitably lower prices. A crazy competition had infected the export industry. Pitted against one another by the buyers, the Chinese competed with each other, and the Indians, the Africans, or other real or imaginary producers. A true race to the bottom engulfed China's export-processing industries.

The buyers got the low prices they demanded, but something and someone had to pay the price. "In the end, the workers paid for all of this," Zhao Gang said. They bore the brunt of the problem through harsher working conditions, nonpayment or delayed payment of their wages, and other forms of abuse, especially in smaller factories. "In a low-value-added factory like ours, profits only come from the exploitation of the worker, and strict management," Zhao Gang had told me.

As if squeezing more labor out of their employees were not enough, subcontractors cut corners, and used lower-quality and cheaper materials to restore profitability. Hundreds of small and large factories, all producing the same or similar products, competed fiercely for American contracts. Enduring lower revenues, they compensated by using lower-quality material to survive. "When you buy plastic, you can choose from two types: one that is good for the environment, and one that is harmful," Zhao Gang said. "Of course you choose the cheaper one. And when the inspector visits the factory, you bribe him to keep his mouth shut."

*   *   *

The collapse of Lehman Brothers in September 2008 and the economic crisis that followed dealt a heavy blow to Sunland and other exporters in China. Many factories in Longgang closed down, leaving 20 million migrant workers without work and with no place to sleep. Zhao Gang fired 80 percent of his workers. "The financial crisis had a serious effect on China. The impact has been greater for the companies that depend on exports. Mine has been very hard hit," he wrote to me.

Sunland's future was in jeopardy, and Zhao Gang was contemplating a radical change in the company's work. The signals from the government that export-processing enterprises like Sunland had no future in the emerging high-tech China were everywhere. Zhao Gang was frantically searching for a way out. "I am now thinking about shifting to the domestic market. I went to Shanghai to look at the possibilities. It will not be easy," he wrote in an email.

Desperate to make some fast money to save Sunland, Zhao Gang invested a big part of his personal savings in the stock market in early 2008. The financial crisis wiped out more than half of his investment. To make matters worse, Sunland's Japanese client set up a factory in Longgang. Zhao Gang lost his most reliable buyer. "My most important partner left Sunland after the Spring Festival. We are losing everything. Without a stroke of good luck, or some good new clients, it will be very difficult to continue. The future does not look promising. I may have to leave Sunland by May," he wrote in early 2009.

Accompanied by a 50-something-year-old Japanese woman who owned a small shoe factory in Longgang, Zhao Gang traveled to Japan to look for new clients in March. "I have to do my best." The trip did not bring any results. He made a few contacts but nobody wanted to make a commitment, he told me. "Of course, I'll keep trying with all my strength. Although I've been defeated, I'll start afresh."

*   *   *

The global economic crisis was a shock to China's export-based economy. For Zhao Gang and many like him, it also proved to be a temporary blessing.

The sudden drop in China's exports forced Beijing to temporarily revise some aspects of its policies towards the weakened export-processing industries. The tax refunds so crucial to Sunland and similar exports were reestablished. "We could not have survived without it," Zhao Gang told me when we met in summer 2009.

Furthermore, soon after the outbreak of the crisis, the Chinese government put in place an aggressive stimulus package. It tapped into its accumulated savings from years of trade surplus with the United States and the rest of the world, and prevented the economy's collapse despite the dramatic decline in foreign demand. "We followed what Roosevelt did during the Great Depression. And it worked. Look at all the construction work around us. This is the same everywhere in China," Zhao Gang told me.

I had not been in Longgang for more than a year. The district had a new face. There were new high-rise commercial and residential buildings everywhere. A metro connecting Longgang to central Shenzhen was making aggressive leaps towards completion. Preparing for the World Student Games in 2011, the local government was building state-of-the-art sports facilities in Longgang. The construction frenzy that preceded the Beijing Olympic Games in 2008 had now come to Longgang, only on a smaller scale. Restaurants and shops were, once again, full of eager customers. There was no sign of crisis in Shenzhen. The government had defeated the beast.

Despite all this improvement, Sunland was hurting. Its sales and number of employees remained far below 2006 and 2007 levels. Zhao Gang was desperately seeking new markets. "I have to find a way to get into the domestic market," he repeated. Entering the local Chinese market was, however, even harder than penetrating the world market, he told me. All his efforts in 2008 and 2009 had failed. "We are not known here. I need a lot of money for advertising. Competition is fierce. It is hard," he lamented.

*   *   *

To get his mind off Sunland and its troubles, Zhao Gang had found a new hobby using old Chinese fortune-telling methods to predict the future. "He is getting really good at it," Yue Haitao said, and gave me four old Chinese coins in a small kangaroo-skin bag to take to Zhao Gang. "These are very rare coins. Zhao Gang knows how to use them to tell people's fortunes," he said.

I met Zhao Gang and his family in our favorite Anhui Province restaurant in Shenzhen. His eyes sparkled with excitement when I gave him the coins. He reached for his bag, untied a red velvet cloth and showed me an intricate board with many lines, numbers, and Chinese characters. "This is my new toy," he said. "During my meetings with foreign clients, I take out my board when they turn on their laptops. 'That's my laptop,' I tell them," he said, laughing. Luo Qiong was embarrassed. "Don't say that. Behzad will believe you," she protested. "He can never be serious," she said.

Problems with business had created visible tensions between Zhao Gang and his family. Luo Qiong was increasingly frustrated with Zhao Gang's long hours of work at the factory. "Zhao Gang is not a good businessman. He is weak," she said. "There is a saying in China: some people cannot be a general, others cannot manage their money. At this point, I cannot manage money, and I cannot be a good businessman, or a general," Zhao Gang said, laughing. "It doesn't matter. I was never prepared to be a businessman. Where I am today is only by chance. I don't think managing a factory is the best way to realize my human potential. I am in it now and I have to survive. There is no going back."

Although he maintained his usual sense of humor and joked frequently in the middle of serious conversations, Zhao Gang was slowly growing somber. Sunland was consuming his vibrant energy. He was changing, turning into a person he did not like. "I watched my ideals and my life taken by a world so foreign to everything I once stood for. But even that is not working now. I am not making it," he told me. Still playing with his board, Zhao Gang reminisced about growing up in a different China when there were "no class differences and people were happy if they had meat once a week." He recalled a time when "living a simple life was an honor, and having a patch on your sleeves was considered beautiful. People felt ashamed wearing beautiful clothes. We called them capitalists, because we were all members of the proletariat."

"Do you regret the loss of those simple days?" I asked Zhao Gang. "I know this is the trend towards development. These changes are inevitable," he said. "We gained a lot after we opened up to the world. We have many things we could not have even imagined having before. But we are not happy. We have lost our happiness," he said, and fell silent. Zhao Gang took out a pen and jotted a few words on the large white paper tablecloth. He turned to me and said, "This is the formula for happiness." The numerator of the fraction was what people already had, and the denominator was what they wished to have. "The denominator always increases at a faster rate. That is the problem with China now," he said. "People always compare themselves with others. We want what other people have. When people don't have a house they want to get one. Then they want a bigger house, and a house on the seaside. There is no end. They are never happy with what they have."

Economic reform and the changes that followed were unsettling to many. The old China was disappearing, and the new was transient and fast changing. Dizzied by a changing world beyond their comprehension, many took refuge in religion to find answers to their dilemmas and everyday problems. Others pursued an unending lust for money. As time passed, Zhao Gang became more attracted to religion and spirituality. "For years they taught us atheism. Now the Chinese need religion, any type of religion," he told me. "Now in China, people will do anything to make more money. There is no limit. The loss of religion took three things from the Chinese: being thankful, repenting, and cherishing what we have. Maybe the fear of God will stop people from doing certain harmful things."

*   *   *

Torrential rain was falling, and I accepted Zhao Gang's offer to drive me to my hotel, the last time we met. Zhao Gang played a CD of special music, military songs, and other favorites he had downloaded from the Internet. Turning to him, I asked, "You once told me that you dreamed of changing the world when you were younger. What is your dream now?" "Returning to 2007. Going back to how Sunland was in 2007. That is my dream now," he said and turned up the volume of the CD player. It was playing *The Internationale*.

> *Arise, you prisoners of starvation!*
> *Arise, you wretched of the earth!*
> *For justice thunders condemnation:*
> *A better world's in birth!*
> *No more tradition's chains shall bind us,*
> *Arise you slaves, no more in thrall!*
> *The earth shall rise on new foundations:*
> *We have been nought, we shall be all!*
> *'Tis the final conflict,*
> *Let each stand in his place.*
> *The international soviet*
> *Shall be the human race.*
> *'Tis the final conflict,*
> *Let each stand in his place.*
> *The international working class*
> *Shall be the human race*
> *Shall be the human race.*

Book IV
A Man for All Seasons

YUE HAITAO: SAVING THE WORLD IN THE NEW CHINA

Zhao Gang was a teacher in a small town before he moved to Shenzhen in the fall of 1999. He had once tried his chances in Shenzhen in 1992 and failed. He was going to succeed this time around, he told his wife in 1999. All he needed was a good contact. To make plans for his future, and on his way to Shenzhen, Zhao Gang visited his sister in Beijing. She was an accountant and married to an economist working in a major Chinese bank.

It happened that Zhao Gang's brother-in-law knew of a Yue Haitao, the boss of a Shenzhen-based medical equipment company, who was also visiting Beijing on a business trip. "This may be your ticket to Shenzhen," the brother-in-law told Zhao Gang, and arranged a job interview with Yue Haitao. Zhao Gang was nervous. "What could I have offered the company? I had no business experience," Zhao Gang told me years later. Zhao Gang's brother-in-law had found a solution. "You are a computer expert," he told Zhao Gang.

While teaching, Zhao Gang had taught himself computer skills, and for a short time, he even gave computer training to government employees. That is all he knew about computers. "I was anything but an expert." Nevertheless, Zhao Gang impressed Yue Haitao. "He hired me as his assistant and computer engineer in charge of all of the computers in the company." Zhao Gang was thrilled, but frightened.

Running Yue Haitao's computers was a challenge that gave him repeated nightmares. "I had to get through it, or at least find a way to cover up my ineptness." He had an idea that proved brilliant. Zhao Gang had made a few friends "who were good with computers," he said. He would bring his friends to the company after working hours whenever there were any problems with a computer at his job. They would fix the computer and there would be no signs of any technical problems when the office opened the next morning. "Mr. Yue still doesn't know that I was not 'an expert,'" Zhao Gang told me.

Yue Haitao left the company and Shenzhen in less than two years. In the short period they worked together, however, a deep relationship developed between the two men. Zhao Gang would not make any important decision without first consulting with Yue Haitao even long after the boss left for Beijing. Yue Haitao was his mentor in the world of business, and in life. Like a disciple mesmerized by an elder guru, Zhao Gang watched Yue Haitao, learned from him, and praised him.

21   Yue Haitao

When he was a young university student dreaming of changing the world, Zhao Gang worshipped Che Guevara. Now, many years later, as a businessman struggling to survive in a fiercely competitive market, Zhao Gang had a new hero, Yue Haitao, "a first-class Chinese entrepreneur, and a legendary man." Many people had influenced Zhao Gang in his 42 years of life, "but no one like Mr. Yue." Yue Haitao was a man for all seasons, an example to follow in "the way of work, dressing, eating, lifestyle after work, and writing skills." Yue Haitao was an exemplary man. "You have to spend a lot of time with Mr. Yue if you want to understand China," Zhao Gang told me.

*   *   *

I met Yue Haitao in his office in Beijing one mild September afternoon.

Filled with carefully selected old chairs, tables, vases, paintings, and calligraphy, the small office resembled the showroom of a fancy antique shop on Madison Avenue. He had handpicked every piece in his numerous business trips and vacations around the world. "I bought this cup in Malaysia," he said, serving me tea in a beautiful porcelain cup. He sat behind his small antique desk, lit a long fat cigar, leaned back, took a deep puff, and said, "I have been eagerly awaiting your arrival from Shenzhen."

In his mid-fifties, Yue Haitao looked older than his age. He was tall, averagely built, and light skinned. His neatly trimmed white beard gave him a distinguished look. A French beret and a cashmere scarf loosely wrapped around his neck were his signature clothes in fall and winter. Expensive leather sandals, high-quality linen pants, and Bermuda shirts were his favorite outfit in the summer.

He smoked expensive cigars, and drank expensive French wine. Red was his favorite. He worked twelve hours or more on most days. His day would not be complete without meeting friends, drinking wine, and smoking cigars. "I would be unhappy if any of the three were missing," he told me. "You will drink a lot of red wine with Mr. Yue. He has very good taste," Zhao Gang told me before I left for Beijing.

In the weeks that followed, Yue Haitao would invite me to expensive restaurants and five-star hotels to show me "a taste of Chinese hospitality," and the Chinese world I had not experienced in Longgang. "You need your money for your travels," he would say, refusing my occasional attempts to pay for our outings. "You are a guest in China."

He carried a stylish and expensive brown leather briefcase and a fine brown leather case for his after-dinner cigars. Yue Haitao had a special shiny silver tube for the very long and fat cigar he occasionally smoked after his meals. "Tiffany," he said, showing me "Tiffany and Co." engraved on the tube. A diabetic with high blood pressure and high cholesterol, he injected himself with insulin before his meals, and took daily pills that he carried in a beautiful silver box.

*   *   *

A number of young college graduates worked as my interpreters in Beijing. To most, spending time with a man of Yue Haitao's stature, and dining in places far beyond their reach, was the experience of a lifetime. "He looks like an artist," said the young man who accompanied me during my first meetings with Yue Haitao. "He looks like a distinguished philosopher," said another. "I would never have had a chance to meet someone like him," said another, thanking me for the opportunity. "He is like a patient teacher," a 25-year-old unemployed college graduate commented. Seeing her inability to fully understand and translate his words, Yue Haitao would search for alternative ways of explaining himself, repeating, pausing, and changing. "I will miss him very much when your work is finished," she told me.

There were those whom Yue Haitao intimidated. He was a living symbol of a part of China that many feared and envied. Always punctual, Yue Haitao was late for one of our meetings one afternoon in late September. Wishing to know whether I had misunderstood the place we were to meet, I asked my interpreter—a graduate student, and one of three children in a low-income family—to call him. The phone conversation was short. My interpreter blushed. "What happened?" I asked. He was quiet.

"What time will you be here?" he had asked Yue Haitao.

"You are in no position to ask me this question," Yue Haitao had replied.

The short conversation reinforced what my interpreter thought of himself, and his position in the new China. Educated and smart, with relative fluency in English, he lost his confidence, and his ability to be an effective interpreter.

Like a schoolboy awaiting punishment by the schoolmaster, he sat across from Yue Haitao, did not look him in the eye, and did not ask questions even when he failed to understand the subject of the interview. "I will tell you later. Let's just go on," he would say nervously when I found his translation confusing. Much of my interview with Yue Haitao that day had to be repeated later.

It took many long meetings before my interpreter lost his fear of Yue Haitao, and before he could smile and enjoy the good restaurants and cafés and the food he could never buy on his personal income. Interpreting for me one last time in a Starbucks in central Beijing, he was exceptionally relaxed, even charming. Graduating in a few months, he had begun searching the market for possible jobs. Like most students graduating in Beijing, he wished to remain in the capital, get a corporate job, and escape the low salary and boredom of his hometown. That was not an easy task. Working in Beijing required a local *hukou*. More than 200,000 university students graduated from schools in Beijing in 2007, and only a few could obtain a *hukou* for Beijing. To get one, my interpreter had to be sponsored by an employer—and for that, he needed a *guanxi*, a connection.

That night, the connection he so badly wanted came to him. Shaking his hand to say goodbye, Yue Haitao gave him his business card. "Call me if you need anything," he said. The young interpreter was astounded, but he refused to call and ask for help. "I will never do that," he told me. "People like me never get a chance to meet someone like Mr. Yue in real life. I am only here because of you. I am grateful for that. But I will try to find a job on my own. I will stay in my world and Mr. Yue in his. That's how things are in China."

*   *   *

I met Yue Haitao on the evening of October 15, 2007. Earlier that day, nearly 2000 delegates had assembled in the Great Hall of the People in Beijing for the opening ceremony of the 17th National Congress of the Communist Party of China (CPC). Delegates from across China had come to Beijing to approve President Hu Jintao's call for creating "development with a human face," narrowing China's growing income gap, and "building a harmonious society." China had changed from an egalitarian but poor society to one of the most unequal countries in the world in less than three decades.

At the time of the Beijing meeting, the average income of the top 10 percent of the population was eleven times that of the poorest 10 percent. The lowest 20 percent earned only 4.7 percent of China's income; the richest 20 percent accounted for more than half. The inequality was still rising, and China was experiencing alarming discontent. Government agencies reported 74,000 protests involving 3.76 million people in 2004. "Public order disturbances" reached 87,000 in 2005, ten times more than in 1993. Unlike the 1989 Tiananmen Square protest by middle-class students, those daring to challenge the authorities now were the workers and peasants.

Across the country, millions of migrant worked ten to twelve hours a day. They barely earned $100–150 a month. Fewer than 5 percent received a full or partial pension, and fewer than 3 percent enjoyed unemployment insurance. Despite the massive wealth the country had amassed, nearly a quarter of the households lived in under five square meters per person, and many had no sanitation facilities. More than 800 million Chinese farmers survived on an annual per capita income of less than $550. They lived in mud houses, or brick homes without tap water and heating, and lacked access to healthcare and other basic needs. Such was the situation of millions of Chinese in October 2007. The leaders were worried. I wanted to know Yue Haitao's opinion.

Sitting opposite him and sipping my coffee, I told Yue Haitao of the alarming inequalities in China. How was the Communist Party planning to change this? I lamented about the factory dormitories and the inability of migrant workers to ever buy even a small apartment, and their difficulties in keeping a family on the incomes that prevailed in China's export-processing factories. He took out a second cigar. Rings of smoke filled the air around us as he lit up.

"What you describe are necessities of development. Take America in the early years of this young nation. Thousands of Indians were killed. That was necessary for what America is today. It was the same during the civil war. Without the civil war, the 200 years of prosperity and democracy would not have been possible. But many lives were sacrificed during the war."

In his usual calm manner, Yue Haitao explained how the inequality and poverty experienced by many were necessary sacrifices for a better future for all Chinese. Chairman Mao wanted to make everyone rich at the same time, he told me. That was not practical in a poor country like China. Deng Xiaoping changed Mao Zedong's idea. He allowed some people to become rich first. In Mao Zedong's period, everybody had a job. Everyone made little money and had a low standard of living. With Deng Xiaoping, many lost their jobs, but the pressure also made everyone else work harder. Yue Haitao repeated the party line on the merits of Deng Xiaoping's pragmatism and the follies of Mao's idealism.

"Pressure is the driving force behind development," Yue Haitao said. "Imagine if there were no wolves or lions to chase the deer. The deer would degenerate. Human societies are the same. They are governed by Darwin's law of the survival of the fittest." The most diligent people maintain a steady place in society. Others have to be eliminated, Yue Haitao said. China followed this "law of nature" in order to develop after the death of Mao Zedong. "That was how America became the most powerful country in the world." China was only following in America's footsteps.

"What about the lives of the people who were sacrificed for this development?" I asked about the millions, like Hufang and her husband,who had lost everything when China privatized or shut down its State-Owned Enterprises.

"You cannot keep your eyes on just a few poor individuals." He paused, took a sip of his coffee, looked me in the eye, and said, "No society can progress without sacrifice. In China, the interest of the group or the country comes before any personal interest. It is natural here to sacrifice your own interest for the country. An old Chinese saying goes 'A general's success comes with the price of ten thousand soldiers' lives.' We cannot achieve success without sacrifice," he said calmly.

"Development is war. You cannot win without sacrifice."

*   *   *

In the eighteenth century, England gained the title "factory of the world" by producing high-quality and low-price textiles that brought all competitors to extinction. It captured the world market with the most advanced technology available at the time. Two centuries later, China was the sweatshop of the world. It was a dump, a haven for large Western corporations to practice what had been banned in their home countries. China was the land of eighteenth-century wages and labor standards in the twenty-first century. Its industries produced low-quality exports and hazardous consumer products. They were mass polluters.

By the end of the twentieth century, the Chinese low-wage model had trapped the country in conditions that were proving increasingly difficult to escape. It was threatening China's hard-gained social stability. Chinese leaders, seeking a way out, were planning for a new China, if necessary by sacrificing those who were the backbone of its earlier successes. Hoping to change the country's image as the producer of cheap and low-end products for others, the government was pouring resources into R&D for green production. It was supporting a new generation of visionary entrepreneurs who would make China a leader in clean energy production and green capitalism. Yue Haitao was among those visionary Chinese. In 2007, Yue Haitao was marching triumphantly into the new high-tech China. He was shaping China's future.

In the 1950s, Mao instructed the country to work hard and surpass the United States in steel production. The effort failed. Some 40 years later, Beijing was planning to outdo the West in green capitalism. This time, it was going to succeed. Yue Haitao was a proud participant in this new effort. He was making history.

In 2007, Yue Haitao was chairman of the Group Board of Supervisors of the Everthriving Investment Management Group, a mega holding company with controlling shares in energy and chemical industry, mineral exploitation, transportation of liquefied natural gas, the civilian applications of China's military technology, green technologies, and logistics transport. "We even do television production and entertainment," Yue Haitao boasted. He had his eyes on the future, a China that would be on a par with the great powers of the world, and not just "an exporter of socks and jeans."

*   *   *

"I am a corporate vagabond," Yue Haitao told me in the VIP room of a restaurant near his Beijing office. For the past 20 years, he had set up many ambitious and high-end ventures, helping them get off the ground, and leaving for another venture when the businesses were solidly on their feet. "Mission accomplished," he said. The waiter brought a bottle of chilled domestic wine. Yue Haitao took a cigar out of his shiny Tiffany cigar holder, cut the end, lit it with a match, and said, "Five years. That is all I spend on any business. This is my habit. I see my main job as to help the company grow. After that, I let professional managers do the management. My originality and sense of mission can play no role at that point. That's the time to leave."

Yue Haitao had no training in business before he arrived in Shenzhen in 1989. "Three things helped me succeed in the past 20 years," he said, taking a sip of wine. "First: I never cared about how much time I spent on a project." A long pause followed. "Second: I never cared about the working environment." He took a deep puff. "And third: I never cared for money. Not caring about time, the working environment, or money, that's my motto, and that's what I ask of my employees." He paused again, looked me in the eye, and spelled out *Gong Si Li Yi Gao Yu Yi Qie,* "The Company's Interest Above Everything Else."

*   *   *

In 2007, Yue Haitao and a team of computer engineers and software designers were busy working on a revolutionary project. "We are driven by a sense of mission," he said. "Our mission is to save lives and change the world." He leaned back in his chair and took a long puff.

The Chinese government had granted Everthriving Investment the right to develop civilian applications of its Baidou Satellite Navigation System. This was a big achievement. The government granted permission to use the Baidou to seven enterprises. Only three were operating in 2007, Yue Haitao said. Everthriving Investment was one among them. Yue Haitao had the good fortune of knowing important people in places that mattered. Access to government proved instrumental in getting the lucrative contract.

"We are confident that we can promote the development of the world through our teamwork," he told me. Yue Haitao patiently explained the work he and his team were carrying out to make the military satellite system useful "to ordinary people."

China was still a young revolutionary country when it began research on developing satellite navigation and positioning technologies. The turbulent years of the Cultural Revolution halted the research. With Mao's death and the beginning of economic reform, the research restarted with a new zeal. By 2007, China had launched five satellites. Beijing wished to obtain the ability to compete with the American Global Positioning System (GPS) with its own Baidou. The Baidou satellite system was developed primarily for military and defense purposes. The Chinese authorities were, however, increasingly interested in the system's possible civilian uses. Baidou was to become a Chinese GPS, serving 1.4 billion people, and more.

Yue Haitao could not have been more proud. He was involved in a grand project. "We are the first company in China allowed by the government to explore these possibilities." Sounding like a prophet preaching his holy text, or an alchemist in possession of new ways to save the world, Yue Haitao told me about his visions and his products. "I want to save peoples' lives," he said again, and explained how each of his new products helped save life.

"Product one!" he said, and explained Everthriving Investment's work on developing a monitoring and positioning device to be installed in large trailers transporting hazardous chemicals. Using the Baidou satellite, a center would monitor the movement of the trailer at all times. "There are many advantages to this," Yue Haitao said. The center would send firefighters and medical teams in the case of accidents. "Imagine how many lives we can save by our quick response." Yue Haitao, however, envisioned other important uses of the device—counterterrorism and national security. "We can prevent tragedies like 9/11," he told me.

"Product two!" he said and lit a cigar. By now, Yue Haitao was animated and excited. His enthusiasm increased as I asked questions. I was intrigued by his connections and his vision. "This is a real lifesaver. There is a saying in Buddhism, 'The benefits of saving a life are far more than building a seven-story pagoda,'" he said.

Yue Haitao's second project was *his* idea, he told me. It had the potential "to bring some real changes to people's lives in China, and the world." The idea was simple: it was an application of the Baidou system to monitor people's bodies for cases of sudden health failure. "All you have to do is to wear a device around your wrists. Just like a watch."

The wristband would monitor the person's heart rate, blood pressure, blood sugar, and pulse. It would send an instant message to a dispatching center after the readings reached a set target level, or in case of a sudden heart failure. The center would immediately contact the nearest hospital in the network of hospitals and health centers across the country. "We can react immediately, regardless of where the person is. Imagine how many lives we can save this way." Everthriving Investment was to provide hospitalization insurance to its clients. "This is a complete system."

Yue Haitao's first client was to be the People's Liberation Army (PLA), he told me. There were similar devices available in the U.S. For the military and the government in China, the American devices were of no use. "I can use GPS for other customers, but not for the army. Many of our generals are getting old. They will be wearing my device. We cannot let the Americans or others know about the whereabouts of our military leaders. For them, GPS doesn't work. Only Baidou."

Everthriving Investment would get most of the orders from the government. "This is like Lockheed," he said. The government contracts would make the product more acceptable to the public, "the ultimate clients," he said. "This has to do with the ability to manipulate the market. We won't need a lot of money to begin this work because of my relationship with the government. This is the special situation of China."

"Now, here is my other project," he said. In 2007, China ranked number two, only behind the United States, in the emission of carbon dioxide (CO^2).

"We will beat the U.S. in this if nothing is done," he said, laughing. "The situation is getting out of hand. The government is under a lot of pressure. This is where we can help," Yue Haitao told me. Yue Haitao's team was developing a device to install in every high chimney in the whole country to detect the amount of CO_2 and sulfur dioxide (SO_2) emissions. "We are the only enterprise in China to work on this mission. We will set the critical amount of CO_2 accepted by international community and our country. Our device will tell us if the CO_2 reaches the critical amount anywhere."

"Who would pay for this, the government, corporations, or the individual consumers?" I asked.

"Your question is the key to environmental protection management in China. This is the sticking point." He paused. The Chinese government could not afford to pay for this device for every car, he said. The government was responsible only for making corporations pay for it. "This is the ultimate question about environmental policy," he said. Yue Haitao had had meetings with high-ranking government officials to get the right policy passed for his device. The government had tacitly agreed. However, there was opposition to the project. "Large corporations," he said. "They don't want this to pass. But we are pressing hard. We cannot continue our old practices. We have no option."

LEAVING QINGDAO

Most Chinese know Qingdao for its famous beer, Tsingtao. The brewery's century old history mirrors the political and economic turbulence that China endured for much of the twentieth century. Founded by the Germans in 1903, the brewery fell into the hands of the Japanese between the two world wars. The Kuomintang nationalist government took over the brewery in 1945. The communists made it a State-Owned Enterprise after the revolution, and finally privatized it in 1993. And, in all these years of war and economic transformation, the beer that came out of the brewery maintained its popularity and high quality. Tsingtao is the beer that sooths the soul of the rich and the poor, the worker and the peasant, and those in the high towers of the new China.

*   *   *

Surrounded by water and the beautiful Laoshan mountain (the home of the immortals), Qingdao is located southeast of Beijing on the shores of the Yellow Sea. Qingdao's red tile roofs, colonial architecture, and beautiful beaches bring tourists from China and across the world to this old city. When Yue Haitao opened his eyes to this world in a rich quarter of the city in 1951, Qingdao and its people were haunted by the memory of civil war and revolution. Yue Haitao's family was at the center of it all, his father told him later. "My life story is a reflection of Chinese politics," he told me one afternoon in the beer garden of the Kempinski Hotel Paulaner Brauhaus. Sipping his freshly brewed dark German beer, and puffing on his cigar, he reminisced.

A protestant merchant owning many shops and homes, and large areas of land, Yue Haitao's grandfather, his father's father, was a well-known and respected member of the gentry in Qingdao. He was a descendant of Yue Fei, a national hero from the days of the Southern Song Dynasty. As the commander of the Song Forces, Yue Fei had fought a successful war against the neighboring Jin Dynasty after it had overrun the northern half of the area under Song rule. He was a self-educated man, a patriot, and a warrior who restored Song's rule in much of the lost territory.

Legend had it that Yue Fei once defeated an army of half a million with only 800 soldiers. A plot against him by his enemies caused his imprisonment and execution in 1141, the story goes. Centuries after Yue Fei's death, Yue Haitao's grandfather told his son, Yue Zhenhong, stories about the great general's heroism and sacrifices for his country. Family history and the teachings of his father turned the young Yue Zhenhong into a rebel, a warrior ready to make sacrifices for his people. He wished to be another Yue Fei. The opportunity to help his country came when he enrolled at Beijing Furen, an American Catholic university. When a youth cell of the Communist Party approached him to join, he agreed without hesitation. Soon, Yue Zhenhong was in the PLA and fighting the Kuomintang in the country's bloody civil war.

Educated and intelligent, and a proven communist, the young Yue Zhenhong was promoted to a commander during the war. And when a large number of Kuomintang soldiers and warships were preparing to leave the port of Qingdao on their retreat to Taiwan, the Communist Party dispatched Yue Zhenhong to his hometown to lead a special delegation to negotiate the surrender of the fleeing forces. The negotiations failed. With thousands of soldiers and the fleeing civilians on board, the ships left for Taiwan. The landowners, bureaucrats, capitalists, and many wealthy locals left the city for good. Among them were Yue Zhenhong's relatives.

Qingdao fell into the hands of the Communist Party and its fighters. Holding a red flag and leading a group of PLA soldiers, Yue Zhenhong returned home victorious and euphoric. He and his soldiers were the new heroes of Qingdao, loved and respected by those who had remained behind. The young male warriors of the PLA were celebrities, greeted by strangers in the streets. "They were embraced by women many years their junior," Yue Haitao said.

*   *   *

As one of its first revolutionary acts, the new government quickly moved against the old customs that governed the relationship between men and women. Under a new marriage law, women enjoyed equal rights with men and freely chose their partners. The Marriage Law of 1950 prohibited arranged marriages and child betrothals. It gave women the right to divorce their husbands. Widows could remarry. The party broke old taboos. "This was as important as the revolution against the Kuomintang," Yue Haitao told me.

Forced into unwanted marriages, many women used the new law to divorce their husbands in Qingdao. Even men broke free of arranged marriages. A new era of sexual freedom started. Many Communist Party cadres and PLA officers had passionate romances. They divorced their wives and began new families. Yue Zhenhong was among them.

Still a boy, Yue Zhenhong was engaged to a child his age, the daughter of another prominent family in Qingdao. As he grew older, Yue Zhenhong detested the thought of spending the rest of his life with his future wife. He wanted to fall in love, marry for love. But that was not possible. His future was predetermined. While he obeyed his family's decision and married a girl he did not love, he looked for every opportunity to escape his dreadful life. Revolution and war gave him the sought-after chance. Soon after marrying, Yue Zhenhong left for Beijing, and later joined the war. Revolution was a blessing from the sky.

After the communist victory, Yue Zhenhong returned as a commander and the secretary-general of the Communist Youth League in Qingdao, Yue Haitao told me. The young communist was in charge of the art troupes in the city, and it was in his new job that Yue Zhenhong found true love. She was 17 and Yue Zhenhong in his late twenties.

Yue Zhenhong met the glamorous Shan Ying, a dancer and singer, and the daughter of a wealthy Catholic family. For seven generations before her, many in Shan Ying's family had been herbalist doctors, practicing old Chinese medicine. Shan Ying's relatives on both sides of the family were feudal lords. Together, they owned half of the wealth and property in Gaomi County in Shandong, Yue Haitao told me. Wealth and family fortune made Shang Ying untouchable by many in Qingdao. Her beauty, however, made her desired by all. Shan Ying "was a well-known beauty," Yue Haitao said.

Of all the worthy young men in Qingdao, it was Yue Zhenhong, the communist commander, who succeeded in stealing Shang Ying's heart. A passionate romance started between them. Engulfed in the ecstasy of victory and love, Yue Zhenhong divorced his wife. He was no longer bound to the archaic customs that had ruled pre-revolution China. Yue Zhenhong was a free man. A year after returning to Qingdao, he married the young dancer, who was already pregnant with Yue Haitao.

A respected Communist Party cadre in Qingdao, Yue Zhenhong did not wish his wife to remain a dancer and singer. He did not want her to be the talk of the town, chased by men. Shan Ying had to leave behind her artistic past, he told her. Shan Ying agreed. She left the dance troupe and joined the Communist Party. The beautiful dancer became a librarian.

Soon after Yue Haitao's birth, another member of his family dared to challenge the ancient custom and taboo. Arranged to marry as a child, Yue Haitao's grandmother, his mother's mother, stood up to her husband, packed her belongings, slammed the door, and left her home of more than 30 years. She was in her late fifties. Feeling empowered by the new marriage law, she freed herself of an unwanted relationship and joined the scores of women across China who dared to imagine a new life.

Freed from her husband, she devoted the next few years of her life raising Yue Haitao, while her daughter and son-in-law were busy building a new society. "I did not see much of my parents in those days. I thought my grandmother was my mother until age five," Yue Haitao told me.

* * *

By 1955, the Communist Party had started the transfer of cadres with a broader knowledge of the country, its culture, and its economy to high positions in key institutions in Beijing. Yue Haitao's father was assigned to a post in the People's Bank of China. The five-year-old Yue Haitao left his grandmother's home for a new life in Beijing. Not long after arriving in Beijing, Yue Haitao's father was to undertake a special assignment to London. Yue Zhenhong had packed and was ready to leave when he was arrested and charged with "illegal transactions." The authorities barred him from leaving the country. "My father received disciplinary punishment from the party," Yue Haitao said.

Although the Communist Party nationalized all the large banks, factories, and enterprises when it seized power, a noticeable part of the economy remained capitalist. Unable to complete the socialization of the economy immediately after victory, the new government left alone thousands of privately owned businesses, shops, handicrafts enterprises, and industrial and trading companies. In some cases, they even encouraged the private sector to expand, creating natural opportunities for profiteering and speculative activities for many Chinese. The new opportunities to make quick money were not ignored by members and cadres of the Communist Party, and they joined others in profiting from the chaos of the early years of the revolution. Yue Zhenhong was among these enterprising cadres.

Worried about the consequences of these activities, in 1951, the Communist Party waged a series of campaigns against the remnants of the old classes and the "bourgeois mentality" among the cadres. The "three anti" campaign attacked corruption, waste, and bureaucracy; the "five anti" campaign targeted bribery of government workers, tax evasion, state property theft, cheating on government contracts, and stealing economic information for private speculation.

"The whole story was complicated. In short, my father was born into a capitalist family. A capitalist persuaded him to raise money for him to start a new business. This was legal at the time. It was before the 'three anti,' and the 'five anti' campaigns. My father didn't break the law. But somebody informed on him," Yue Haitao said.

The disciplinary action did not last long, and Yue Zhenhong resumed his post in the bank. Life proceeded without difficulty. Yue Haitao lived the privileged life of the son of a cadre family. He had money, comfort, entertainment, and good food "even during the Great Leap Forward. Many people died of hunger, but we had enough food," he recalled years later.

Yue Haitao's family was unaffected by the Great Leap Forward, but they could not escape Mao's next great national movement, the Cultural Revolution. He was in his last year of middle school when the Cultural Revolution shook the country in 1966.

For the second time in a decade, Yue Zhenhong and Shan Ying were subjected to the "revolutionary anger of the masses." This time around, however, they were punished for the sins of their parents. Both Yue Zhenhong and Shan Ying had a "bad class background." They were the children of propertied classes before the revolution. That was now a crime. They had to be cleansed of their class background and reformed.

With the advent of the Cultural Revolution, China was preparing for the spiritual cleansing of hundreds of thousands of its cadres of different ranks. In rural areas across the country, many May Seventh Cadre Schools were set up for the long-term re-education of the Communist Party cadres. High-ranking officials—among them Deng Xiaoping—and their families, and middle- and lower-level cadres with a "bad class background," were "sent down" to these schools for ideological training, and learning through manual labor. The schools were designed to bring the corrupt leaders closer to the masses and fight the endemic bureaucracy that Mao believed was destroying the revolution.

Yue Zhenhong and his wife moved to a May Seventh Cadre School in 1969. For the next seven years, he worked as a cook in the communal kitchen and fed other cadres. "My father became a very good cook," Yue Haitao told me.

*   *   *

In December 1968, when the youth in the United States, Europe, and many countries in the world were revolting against the political establishment and demanding a world more responsive to their dreams, Yue Haitao and 17 million other young Chinese were dispatched to villages across the country to live and work with peasant families and receive social and physical training for building socialism. Yue Haitao had just finished middle school when he headed to Datong, a poor village in Shanxi Province.

The young Chinese worked the land, tended the pigs and the farm animals, and lived a life that most grew to detest. Many did not recover from the agony of these lost years. Others succeeded in finishing their education upon returning home, attending university and slowly achieving normality in their lives. For Yue Haitao, however, the "lost years" were the years of "great learning."

Unaccustomed to hard manual labor, Yue Haitao worked alongside the peasants from sunrise to sunset, ate peasant food, and faced the same ups and downs experienced in the village. And he cherished every day of the years he spent in the village. "I came out of the Cultural Revolution a stronger person," he told me.

He was the child of a wealthy cadre family with no understanding of peasants and their lives. "They were the majority of the Chinese people, but

I knew nothing about them. I had never seen one, or talked to one." Datong introduced Yue Haitao to the "plain and simple lives of China's peasantry." It opened his eyes to the hidden China, the China that was foreign to him and to the children of other cadre families. The adults he knew were people of power and influence. He did not know anything about the lives of urban workers, let alone peasants and village life. Datong was extremely poor, Yue Haitao recalled. The land was largely infertile and dry. "Wheat could grow only as tall as a chopstick." There was never enough food. "We had little water to drink and none to bathe with. Winters were unbearably cold."

Instead of resenting his circumstances, Yue Haitao embraced them and felt exhilarated and reborn. "My body and mind began developing at that time," he told me. He worked long hours and did things he had never imagined doing in Beijing. Yue Haitao was changing every day. "I was becoming a different person. I liked what was happening to my body." He was growing, developing muscles, and "becoming a man." And it was not only his body, but also his mind that was transforming. Everything was a lesson, and every day an education that he would not forget. "I was influenced by the simplicity of the peasants' minds and lives." The peasants' hard lives helped Yue Haitao learn to cope with the difficulties he experienced in later years. "I think that period paved the foundation for my future. My whole life changed. I owe my wisdom and my strong body to that period. My mind was becoming stronger every day. Although life was tough, I was very happy."

Yue Haitao worked with zeal and enthusiasm and became a model laborer. "I achieved the highest work-point among the sent-down students and the villagers." He was number one worker in the Yanbei, with its 13 counties and one city. "I made every possible effort to excel. I worked as hard as four strong men. There were 1380 people in the village and my performance was the best." The villagers liked him, respected his energy and enthusiasm, and asked him not to return to Beijing. "Stay in the village and marry a girl," they told him. He was proud of the friendship he had developed with the peasants and their families.

Many students, mainly "fat women" with little chance of finding a husband, married local village men. They stayed in the village even after the Cultural Revolution. Yue Haitao, however, *had* to return to Beijing. "I had left behind the love of my life," he said.

RUNNING TO DIE

When China was swept by political violence, and the boys and girls Yue Haitao's age battled each other, denounced their elders, rebelled, and moved from province to province, and village to village, he was burning in the flames of love. He was in a world different from that of others. His love was innocent; it was "platonic," he told me many years later.

He was 14, and she 11. She was gentle like fresh roses, shy like the weeping willow, and "slender with Japanese features." She was the younger sister of Yue Haitao's best friend. They had spoken few words, and met only in the presence of family members and the elders. She was the daughter of a family "with warlord background." Maybe the prejudice against her family, and the angry politics of the time, would keep them apart for ever, he thought. But he loved her none the less. "She was the perfect girl for my heart," Yue Haitao said some 40 years later. He would remain faithful, wait for the right time to be with her. Until then, however, his love was a secret he would not share with anyone, not even with the girl he so worshiped. "My love was divine, holy. It was kind of sacred. I kept it in my heart."

In his solitude, Yue Haitao dreamed of graduating high school, enrolling in university, finding a respectable position, and marrying his love. He would fight every obstacle, he thought. But his plans came to an abrupt end when he finished middle school. He had to leave Beijing and his love for the village in Shanxi Province. He said farewell to Beijing, and carried his secret feelings to the village. Separation was unbearable. He tried to forget by working hard, immersing himself in village life, and studying in his limited free time. Between his chores, studies, and socializing with the villagers, Yue Haitao always drifted back to Beijing, always dreaming of her. "I would think about her and about our future together every day of the years I spent in the village. I thought about her when I was awake and dreamed of her when I was asleep."

Yue Haitao imagined her beside him, strolling aimlessly in the streets of the country's tormented capital, gazing at her, greeting the passersby, and laughing at each other's jokes. But he did not walk by her side, hold her hand, touch her tender body, or steal a kiss from her in the dark of the night.

* * *

Before the Cultural Revolution, Chinese students entered universities by participating in a standardized national entrance examination. To Mao, the practice favored the children of the old privileged classes and China's new bureaucracy. In 1966, he abolished the university entrance exam at the outset of the Cultural Revolution. Affected by student radicalism and the turmoil of the early years of the Cultural Revolution, universities practically shut down until 1969. When classes resumed, universities selected students from the ranks of workers, peasants, and soldiers, and on the basis of recommendation from their supervisors. Each province, district, city, factory, and rural commune received a quota of applicants to fill. University officials carried out the final selection through elaborate interviews.

In 1973, entrance exams were temporarily resumed on a trial basis for one year. Yue Haitao took part in the competition. A model worker, he had an exceptional letter of recommendation from the party boss in his village. He was among the "worker, peasant, soldier students" chosen to enter institutions of higher education.

"You know I did not attend high school. I took the entrance exam with many high school graduates. They were three or four years older than me." While in the village, Yue Haitao studied various subjects and prepared for the exam. "I studied when I was not working or thinking about my love," he told me. The exam, however, was more difficult than he had anticipated. He failed math, physics, and chemistry, but scored "the highest in the country" in Chinese language.

A recently founded foreign language university in eastern Beijing, the Beijing International Studies University (Erwai), did not have math and science requirements. The university instead focused on students with an aptitude for languages. Yue Haitao was relieved when Erwai selected him to study Spanish.

*   *   *

Before he began his university studies in fall 1974, Yue Haitao lived in the home of his love for six months. "My parents were still in the May Seventh Cadre School. I didn't have anywhere to live. My friend took me in." For the first time, Yue Haitao lived with the girl of his dreams under the same roof. He was tormented, yet full of ecstasy. He felt the presence of his love, every day, and at all times. "I still had to keep a distance. That was torturous. We had both grown older. She was a beautiful young woman, more beautiful than ever, and I loved her even more than before."

He lived in her family home, and loved her secretly. "Those short few months were heavenly but painful." Burning inside, "I dared not speak to her. In my heart, she was almost sacred. Such words of human love would have been blasphemy," he told me.

More than ever, Yue Haitao was determined to win his love's heart. He had to prepare. He had waited so long. In four years he would graduate from university, get a good job as an interpreter with the government, make a home, and marry her, he thought. Meanwhile, he would continue to keep his love a secret, he vowed to himself.

As time passed, Yue Haitao's behavior around his love became increasingly "abnormal." He would stumble, lose his ability to speak coherently, withdraw, and gaze at her. Watching his behavior around his sister, his best friend sensed Yue Haitao's intense passion for his sister. It was *he* who finally broke the secret and told his sister about Yue Haitao's feelings.

"I dared not talk to her. Everything I did perhaps cried aloud about my love. But I could not say it, not to her." When the secret was revealed, Yue Haitao was in the third year of his university studies. "I would have been ready in two years." But it was already too late, he would find out. His years of silence proved costly. While Yue Haitao hesitated and dreamed about the girl he loved, she fell in love with a classmate from middle school. She was committed, taken by another man. Yue Haitao had lost his chance. "Why did he not say anything for all these years?" she asked her brother in disbelief. "I love him like a brother," she said. Yue Haitao's world was shattered.

He withdrew from life, drowning in the maddening sorrow of lost love. At times, he would wander in Beijing, walk aimlessly, and try to forget his torment. What had he done to deserve this? He was young, strong, honest, and loved by many. What would all of this mean without her? Should he persist, beg for her love? But she was already in love with another man. How could he disturb the life that she had planned for herself? She might have loved him before, but her boyfriend may be a better choice for her. How could he ask her to leave him? Was it a mistake to keep his love a secret? Why did he wait so long? He had no answers.

There was no more hope. He had lost her, and there was no return. "She had already been with another man for six years. They must have known each other well. I realized he was a more suitable match for her. To express my love and pursue her would have created difficulties for her. I did not wish that for her. I loved her too much—I could not have caused her any discomfort."

After weeks of agony and pain, Yue Haitao found peace. He found an honorable solution to the first crisis of his life. "I had to step aside," Yue Haitao, told me. He chose to sacrifice himself for the happiness of the woman he loved.

"This type of love is unique to eastern people, especially the Chinese and the Japanese," Yue Haitao told me. "In the West, men fight to win the heart of their beloved as a trophy. They fight to the end. A Westerner would think of sacrificing happiness for the sake of love as total failure. But to the Chinese, this type of sacrifice is the sign of ultimate love. It is what we consider success."

Yue Haitao's love was selfless. He loved the beautiful young woman more than he loved himself, he told me. "Sacrifice is the highest form of love." He had chosen to step aside, and free his beloved from the agony he would have caused her. However, he could not continue to live without her. The pain of separation was too overwhelming, the trauma too unbearable. He could not escape the sorrow of estrangement. Life without her was meaningless. He felt trapped.

"I took an extreme step. I decided to kill myself in a dramatic way." Unable to live with the pain, he had to end his life. "I believe love is more important than life," he told me. "But I did not want her to ever know that I committed suicide because of her. I did not want her to ever feel guilty." His death had to be natural. It had to appear unfortunate, but not premeditated. Yue Haitao devised a perfect plan. "I decided to run myself to death."

Yue Haitao was a marathon runner, and had won many races. A year earlier, he had won third place in the marathon among university students in Beijing. Without preparing himself, Yue Haitao enlisted for a marathon at Beijing University of Science and Technology (called the College of Iron and Steel at the time). He knew that running in a marathon required intensive physical and mental preparation. As an athlete, he was aware of the challenge ahead, but he was far from being prepared. Now, unlike his earlier contests, he welcomed his lack of preparation. He would use all his strength and his mental energy to focus not on finishing among the first, but on perishing before the finishing line. "Dying was victory."

He had read in scientific magazines that, entrapped in a pen by humans, a male deer would run in circles to his death. The deer would use his physical strength to end his life. Yue Haitao decided to follow the death of the entrapped deer. He would exhaust his strength and die. His death would be natural. No one would suspect premeditation, a suicide. His beloved would continue to live a good life, not feeling guilty, carrying the burden of his death.

This was a 25-lap marathon, 2.4 miles each. Starting strong, he ran the first ten laps without difficulty. As his strength diminished, and his body began aching, he continued with determination. After five more laps, he nearly collapsed, regained momentum, and continued. He was now short of breath. The pain was excruciating. He was dizzy, mentally numbed, no longer able to hear the cheering crowd, or sense the presence of others running besides him. He fell to the ground and lost consciousness. This was the 24th lap. Unconscious and immobile, he had "an out of body experience."

"My soul left my body. I stood up and turned around. I saw my body still lying down with doctors trying to help, bringing me to my feet. A long and dark tunnel appeared in front of me. I walked into the tunnel." In that tunnel, Yue Haitao saw his life before him, scene by scene, on large video screens on each side of the tunnel. "The images began from the present. I was on the ground and surrounded by spectators and doctors. The last images were from my childhood. This was amazing. I felt like I was watching a movie about my life."

The tunnel ended with images of Yue Haitao when he was only 18 months old. Everything was suddenly bright. "I felt very comfortable. I thought I was in heaven." When he woke up, blood was oozing from his nose. The doctor told him that he saw in him a very strong will to live. "What gave you such a strong will?" the doctor asked. "I told the doctor that I fought hard to live perhaps because, at that very moment, I remembered that I had not even kissed a girl in my life. It was not my time to die. I could have have left this world without that experience."

Days later, Yue Haitao told his father about the images he had seen. He asked his father about his childhood. "I could not have had any recollection of my life at the age of one and a half. Yet I had seen things in my dream and I wanted to know if they were true." Yue Haitao's father confirmed what he had seen in the tunnel. "I was shocked."

"I had prepared to commit suicide in a heroic and tragic way, but I didn't die." His survival in the marathon was a message. He had to fight his sorrow and continue despite the loss of his love.

TAKING SIDES

By the time Yue Haitao began his studies at Erwai, the Communist Party of China was divided between two warring factions: a "left-wing" faction led by Jiang Qing, Chairman Mao's wife, and the Gang of Four; and a "right-wing" faction around Premier Zhou Enlai, Deng Xiaoping and other party leaders. Erwai was founded two years before the outset of the Cultural Revolution. Party leaders, particularly Zhou Enlai, promoted Erwai and supported it to become a training ground for young experts in foreign languages and international affairs. In 1974 Erwai was a battleground between the followers of different tendencies within the Communist Party. The two factions had a visible presence among students and the faculty. The university, however, was a stronghold of the Gang of Four, Yue Haitao recalled.

On January 8, 1976, Premier Zhou Enlai died of cancer at age 87. Four months later, in early April, and in preparation for the ancient Qing Ming Festival, the national day the Chinese mourned their dead, thousands of Beijing residents marched to Tiananmen Square, placing paper wreaths at the Monument of People's Heroes to pay homage to the late premier. Hundreds of thousands arrived from schools, universities, factories, and government offices on April 4. They came with wreaths, handwritten poems, and wall posters criticizing Jiang Qing. They came to eulogize Premier Zhou Enlai. Their wall posters and wreaths covered the largest public square in the world by the end of the day, Yue Haitao recalled.

"Before that day, participants in the rallies were only students from universities around Beijing. On April 4, workers, government employees, and ordinary people joined the students in Tiananmen Square. I was there among them. The overall mood was one of sadness. Soon anger replaced sadness. People were chanting, shouting. A crackdown began. Soldiers attacked the protesters with tear gas and batons, but no one was shot. The army did not fire into the crowd. They only used their batons."

Threatened by the development, the new premier, Hua Guofeng, ordered the municipal authorities to clear the square overnight. The next day, on April 5, a large crowd returned to protest against the obvious disrespect to the premier. Violence erupted. Many were injured, and more imprisoned. The Politburo declared the April 5 demonstration counterrevolutionary. However, the day became a symbol of struggle for rights; it became immortalized as the "April Fifth Movement."

By April 6, there were no signs of the earlier protests at the square. But the Tiananmen Square poems found their place in China's modern history through a brave effort by students and faculty at Erwai. With Bai Xiaolang, one of Yue Haitao's professors and a fierce opponent of the Gang of Four, as editor, students at Erwai compiled over one thousand of these protest poems in a four-volume underground mimeographed anthology, *The Tiananmen Poetry Anthology*. A witch hunt began for those behind the publication. The factional battle at Erwai increased. More students were drawn to politics. "I was also against the left-wing policies of the Gang of Four. I made a political stand," Yue Haitao said.

Having gained the upper hand at the university and in its administration, the followers of the Gang of Four assaulted their opponents physically. The supporters of the late premier became the target of exclusion in the allocation of work and housing, or recommendation for good jobs after graduation. Before these events, Yue Haitao had applied to become a member of the Communist Party. After April 4, he publicly took back his application. "I did not want anything to do with the party, and I made that known to everyone." The authorities and the school administration could not but notice. Not being a card-carrying member of the party was common. The Communist Party was always an exclusive club, and millions of Chinese never applied for membership. Others were denied entry for various reasons. Rescinding an existing application was, however, a different matter. Yue Haitao had crossed the line.

A year later, graduating from university, Yue Haitao expected a job as a translator for the foreign affairs office, a job overseas, or at a higher-up position in China. Instead, he was assigned as a Spanish teacher at a middle school in Beijing. "I had sided with the wrong group," he told me.

*   *   *

Recovery from the marathon and his defeat in love proved more difficult than Yue Haitao had imagined. Life was unbearable. He was helpless and had lost all hope when a classmate at Erwai came to his aid. She stayed at his side at all times and helped him stand on his feet and begin a new life. She was "a strong-minded girl" with an excellent performance in school. Their relationship began as simple friendship. Soon, they were inseparable; he found comfort in his new friend's company and her soothing words. "She was a good listener," and Yue Haitao needed just that. She eased his pain and helped him forget. "She was the closest person to me, consoling me, and spending time with me when I was down and drowned in sorrow."

As the political divisions at Erwai widened and Yue Haitao became more interested in politics and the democracy movement, so did his classmate and friend. During those times, she was a comrade accompanying him "every way, and in every activity." Like most men and women her age, she too had spent time in rural China. She was a "sent down kid" like Yue Haitao. And she knew well that her friendship with Yue Haitao, given his political views, could cost her dearly. She might be sent down, a second time now, as punishment. Nevertheless, she accepted the risk, for she was a loyal friend, and she had fallen in love. "She loved me in every way."

Yue Haitao felt responsible for his friend. He was not, and could not be, in love. He had not gotten over the slender girl with Japanese features. In spite of that, Yue Haitao vowed to stay at her side for the rest of his life. Not long after, he married his university classmate. "There were also some practical reasons for our marriage. We could get a bigger apartment from the government in Beijing."

At last, for the first time in his life, Yue Haitao made love to a woman. He was 28 years old, and delighted to have survived to see this day.

Six months after getting married, Yue Haitao's wife was accepted for graduate studies in Portugal as a part of the first group of students officially dispatched to study abroad. In those years, authorities did not allow married couples without children to leave the country together: "They feared we would apply for asylum and not return." Yue Haitao stayed behind. Two years later, returning home after finishing her studies, Yue Haitao's wife was dispatched as an official translator to Cape Verde in west Africa. She remained there until 2008. "If not for my opposition to the Gang of Four, I would have also been assigned to the Bureau of Foreign Languages. Politics separated my path from my wife's," Yue Haitao told me.

When we met in 2007, Yue Haitao was a married man without a wife. "I live alone and don't have any children," was one of the very first things he told me. Nearly three decades after their marriage, they lived thousands of miles apart, she in Africa, and he in China. "This was not a marriage of love. She had been so kind to me. My marriage to her was a kind of payback," he told me.

"Why did you not divorce and marry someone else?" I asked.

"I didn't want to hurt her and break her heart," he said. "I do not regret anything in my life. Only, if I had a second chance, I would hope for more luck in love," he said, and took a long puff from his cigar.

*   *   *

Teaching at a middle school was not what Yue Haitao had imagined when he began his university studies. Despite his cadre family background, the young Yue Haitao could not escape the unexciting life of teaching Spanish to uninterested 14-year-olds. Yue Haitao's parents made every attempt to help their son get another assignment in a job with a better future. They asked for help and letters of recommendation from higher-up party officials, but all efforts failed. "They badly needed teachers in those days," he recalled. Yue Haitao could not remain a teacher for the rest of his life, however. He needed change, excitement, and a way out of his mundane life. In 1978, he enrolled at Beijing Normal University for a degree in Chinese language. He taught three days a week to fulfill his obligations, and attended classes on his free days. Despite the difficulties he faced, Yue Haitao graduated in 1982. "I have two degrees: one in Spanish, and the other in Chinese." The second degree in Chinese became his passport to freedom.

*   *   *

In 1984, the *Beijing Review*, one of the most prestigious magazines in China, and the first government-controlled magazine published in foreign languages, was hiring reporters and translators fluent in Chinese and other languages, including Spanish. Yue Haitao was a perfect match. "My Spanish was never so great, but my Chinese was perfect," he told me. Yue Haitao took the entrance exam with great confidence. He passed. He had crossed the first hurdle to achieving the new exciting life he was longing for all these years. However, a more challenging obstacle remained. Yue Haitao still needed permission to leave his post at the middle school. Once again, his parents approached their influential party friends, and finally he received a *tiaozi*, a brief and informal note from a high-level supervisor that allowed him to leave. This was 1984, and he could not have known the changes that his new job would bring to his life.

The Beijing Review hired Yue Haitao as a translator, but promoted him to journalist in six months. A year later, he was assistant managing editor. He was on his way to being managing editor of the *Beijing Review*, one of the most respected media jobs in China, when the protests in Tiananmen Square changed the course of his life. This was spring 1989.

The Tiananmen Square protests and the massacre that followed on June 4, 1989 changed the lives of millions of Chinese: the protesters, and those who stayed away from the square in those turbulent days. The protests became a turning point in China's contemporary history, and a wakeup call for the Communist Party's leadership in the midst of the economic reorganization of the country. While the Communist Party allowed public discussion of the Great Leap Forward and the Cultural Revolution—teachers taught their students about these, albeit in a distorted way—the 1989 protests and what followed were removed from the official narrative of Chinese history.

The next generation of Chinese grew up not knowing about the protests and the government response. Worried about repercussions, their parents, some of them veterans of the student movement, kept silent. Discussing the 1989 events in Tiananmen Square became taboo. In a world of make-believe, many Chinese continued with their lives, pretending and forcing themselves to forget. Many did forget. Even the protesters forgot their days of youthful idealism. Graduating from the university, thousands joined the ranks of the new entrepreneurial class. They made a fortune from China's opening up to the rest of the world, bought luxury condominiums and foreign cars, and silently benefited from the continuing political repression that helped transform China into a stable and prosperous country. Some whispered about the heroism of the youth and the workers, and the shocking violence of the government. Yue Haitao, however, did not whisper. He was not afraid to tell me about the events that changed his life.

*   *   *

The protests began in early summer, when thousands poured into Tiananmen Square to mourn the death of Hu Yaobang, a champion of market reforms, and a former head of the Youth League and general secretary of the CPC. A libertarian Marxist of sorts, and drawn to individual and political freedoms common in the West, Hu Yaobang had become an inspiration among the intelligentsia and the youth in China. Following Mao's death, Hu played an instrumental role in rehabilitating the intellectuals and other victims of the party's anti-rightist campaigns. Hu's efforts to expose and curb corruption among the children of top party cadres angered Deng Xiaoping and other Communist Party bosses, but he was a hero to millions of intellectuals and ordinary people in China.

In January 1987, Hu Yaobang was forced to resign from his post because of his failure to crack down on earlier pro-democracy protests. Accused of siding with the liberal intellectuals plotting against the Communist Party and the revolution, Hu was removed from power after a long career that had begun when he was a teenage supporter of Mao Zedong and the revolution. The party forced Hu Yaobang to accept responsibility for the student protests of 1986–87. He was blamed for failing to fight bourgeois liberalization.

Hu's death was an excuse to bring to the square a restless youth who were willing to push the limits of officially endorsed reforms. The protests started as a spontaneous act by a group of graduate students from the Party History Department at the People's University on the night of April 15. Despite the ban by the government, some 100,000 students and residents of Beijing stood solemnly in the square for Hu's official funeral on May 22. More than a million lined the route of the funeral procession. Less than two weeks later, 300,000 people poured into the square on the seventieth anniversary of the May Fourth Movement—an act of defiance that started with protests by students in Beijing on May 4, 1919, and later led to a broad national movement that radicalized the face of Chinese politics, and resulted in the birth of the Communist Party two years later.

For the next 30 days, thousands of students and others occupied Tiananmen Square. Their number reached a million on May 21, despite the declaration of martial law by the Communist Party. What frightened the authorities and led to the eventual crackdown was the diversity and spontaneous nature of the protests, which united men and women from Beijing to the remotest parts of China. The Tiananmen Square protesters were free of the usual factional fights. No one controlled them, or used them to oust others from power. This was a theater organized by the people themselves. Even more frightening for Deng Xiaoping and the party elders was the fact that the protests that began with a small group of students soon brought to the scene hundreds of thousands of workers, ordinary citizens, government office workers, teachers, other professionals, and even party cadres. The call for change was universal. The declaration of martial law, and the arrival of fully armed PLA soldiers in key areas of Beijing, failed to frighten the protesters.

More people arrived on a daily basis. Among them were also journalists, and the employees and editors of CCTV (China's official television network), radio stations, and some of the most prestigious official newspapers and magazines, including Yue Haitao's *Beijing Review*. From lay people to intellectuals, the country was united in calling for political change. And for the first time since 1949, not a single member of the top party leadership was in charge of this momentous movement. For a time, the party could not even rely on its otherwise obedient soldiers to break it up. Joining the protesters at the square, the younger PLA soldiers sang revolutionary songs, mingled with the cheering crowd, and refused to shoot. Older and more experienced soldiers were herded to the capital for the final crackdown.

Rallying behind the students' call for more democracy in China, the *Beijing Review* devoted five issues to coverage of the protests. "At that time, most leaders in the media were pro-democracy. We thought it was our duty to be the objective observers of the events," Yue Haitao said.

The Communist Party reasserted its control over the capital and cleared the square on June 4. Some three hundred civilians died according to official reports; independent sources claim the deaths of 2000–7000. Most of the deaths occurred in the streets of Beijing, when PLA soldiers opened fire on workers and ordinary Chinese who had set up barricades to prevent the army from reaching the square. A wider political cleanup followed immediately after.

Angered and alarmed by the government-backed media's support for the protesters, the army seized control of the *Beijing Review*, CCTV, CNR (China National Radio), and the Xin Hua News Agency. Soldiers destroyed all the remaining copies of the *Beijing Review* from the days of the protests.

The military demanded that Yue Haitao's boss at the *Beijing Review* write a public statement declaring allegiance to the Communist Party. He agreed. "They still fired him even after he agreed to cooperate." Two thousand journalists and staff of different media outlets were told to write letters of allegiance. All apart from Yue Haitao obliged: "I refused. I could not write the letter."

Had Yue Haitao agreed to follow the example of the others, he would have been promoted to chief editor of the *Beijing Review*, he told me. "The representative of the military told me I was the only person out of 2000 who disobeyed. I lost the promotion."

The punishment for failing to write the statement was imprisonment. Yue Haitao's refusal to write the letter touched many people, he told me. They came to his rescue. "Many of my colleagues wanted to do the same, but they were afraid. They admired me for my action and came together to help me avoid imprisonment."

They reached an agreement with the army to allow Yue Haitao to remain at the *Review* as a columnist. Yue Haitao was not interested, and pleaded with the army to let him leave for Shenzhen. The army agreed. "This is when I jumped into the sea," he said, using a common expression about those who moved to coastal areas to join the world of business after the reforms. With that, Yue Haitao's career as a journalist ended in 1989. A new Yue Haitao, the business strategist, was born.

"Do you regret any of these things?"

"No. We would have not met if I had remained in the media. I would have refused to meet you and talk to you so openly. I would have been under the strict control of the authorities."

OWN A PIECE OF AMERICA

Yue Haitao's parents returned to Beijing from the May Seventh Cadre School to find a changing China. Soon after, the political campaigns that banished them for six years and destroyed the lives of many of their friends were features of the past. Those scorned earlier were now heroes in the emerging China. It was a dizzying situation. Taboos were broken. Old friends and long-time comrades would be leaving political life in Beijing and going south, and settling down in Shenzhen. Using their influence and connection with the government, they would become the pioneers of China's new capitalism.

China was beginning a new journey. The Communist Party now embraced profiteering and other bourgeois habits scorned in the past. Zealous communists would now enrich themselves and their families, setting up businesses in Shenzhen and along China's southern coasts. They would be building "socialism with Chinese characteristics." The U-turn was puzzling at first, especially for those who had paid a heavy price during the anti-bourgeois campaigns of the party. Nevertheless, the change came with opportunities that were tempting even to the most faithful communists.

Aged, relatively frail, and out of work for a long time, Yue Zhenhong sat on the sideline watching the changes. His wife, the younger and more ambitious Shan Ying, however, embraced the new China with great enthusiasm. Her first step into the China of economic reforms was as early as 1979, when Deng Xiaoping commissioned the creation of the country's first investment bank, the powerful China International Trust and Investment Corporation (CITIC). Shan Ying joined ranks with some of the most influential Chinese figures in founding the bank. "My mother worked with Rong Yiren," Yue Haitao boasted.

The son of the richest Chinese capitalist in the 1930s, Rong Yiren remained in China while others in his class fled to Taiwan and Hong Kong after the victory of the Communist Party in 1949. Like thousands in his position, he was denounced and punished as an enemy of the people during the Cultural Revolution. Threatened with death by the Red Guards, Rong was saved by Zhou Enlai. Following Mao's death, Deng Xiaoping rehabilitated Rong Yiren, and appointed him to set up CITIC and serve as his economic adviser on opening up to the West. His new power in China made Rong the wealthiest man in the country by 1999.

Working with Yiren put Shan Ying in the company of some of the most influential men in the new China. The connection could not have been more useful when she "jumped into the sea" and joined the ranks of China's new entrepreneurial class in Shenzhen in later years. By then Yue Haitao was on the road to make *his* mark in the world of business.

*   *   *

Shenzhen's Nanshan District is scattered with state-of-the-art high-rises, impressive corporate headquarters, government buildings, five-star hotels, and fancy shopping malls. A tall glass building on the main road along the sea features a 125-ton sculpture of Neptune, the god of the sea, riding a horse carriage. Unlike other sculptures standing tall on the ground, the horse carriage cuts through the middle of this impressive constellation of metal, glass, and concrete like a sharp arrow piercing the heart of the rider's enemy. It is an awe-inspiring sight demanding respect from passersby and visitors. "This might be the second largest sculpture in the world," Yue Haitao told me, nursing a pint of beer in a German beer garden in Beijing. "It is a reminder of the grand Italian sculptures," he said.

The building is the Neptunus Mansion, the giant headquarters of Neptunus (Shenzhen Haiwang Group). It is a large holding company built on a 64,000-square meter piece of land in one of the most expensive quarters of Shenzhen. The Neptunus Mansion stands against the backdrop of the sprawling small and large uniform-looking labor-intensive export-processing factories in the industrial districts of Shenzhen.

Neptunus was founded in 1989 by none other than Yue Haitao's parents, with the help of contacts Shan Ying had made earlier in CITIC.

When Yue Haitao went south after losing his position at the *Beijing Review*, he joined the family business as vice-president. Some 20 years later, he reminisced about his time at Neptunus, and his role in building the giant company. "I was the one who chose the name Neptunus," Yue Haitao told me. "I chose the names of many products, like the popular Gold Oyster." Producing marine health products, the company grew in size and product lines to become one of the top Chinese manufacturers of Western medicine, Chinese herbal medicine, and other health products. It opened branches in China, Hong Kong, and Australia. Yue Haitao was working for his parents' company when he chanced upon "Own a Piece of America." This is how the story evolved.

*   *   *

"Sooner or later someone was going to discover a way to make money from the Chinese craze for America. Now it looks as if someone has—perhaps at the expense of thousands of naive Chinese. All across the country, from the ice-glazed terrain of Harbin in the north to this moneyed metropolis in the south, Chinese people are talking about the chance to buy a 'Piece of America,'" said a short news story by Suzanne DeChillo on the January 29, 1993 issue of *the New York Times*. That "someone" was none other than Yue Haitao. *The New York Times* did not mention his name, but "others did," Yue Haitao told me. "*Time Magazine, Voice of America*, and 15 other media outlets mentioned me by name," Yue Haitao told me. This is how it all began.

While the United States was preparing for the celebration of America's 500th birthday, Scott Moger, a former entertainments industry promoter, was planning a brilliant way to make money by selling people a square inch of land in each state. Scott Moger founded American Acres Inc. as the corporation in charge of the land transfers in America, and purchased one acre of cheap land in every state. The total bill was $250,000. Once the purchase was completed, he divided the land everywhere into one-inch parcels and sold them to enthusiastic buyers who received only a certificate from Moger's website. Scott Moger sold the certificates for $10 or $29.95, depending on whether the buyers wished for generic or personalized copies. He made a fortune in the United States, more around the world. And his biggest triumph was in China, through a local distributor in Shenzhen.

In an unusual frenzy, Chinese of all walks of life rushed to buy a piece of America and grabbed more than two-thirds of all the deeds sold around the world. Soon, the deeds had a lucrative secondary market. Like gold in times of economic crisis, they changed hands, and rose in price: $468 in Guangzhou, $700 in Beijing, and $1700 in Shanghai. By all standards, these were large sums of money for most Chinese. There was no limit to the Chinese hunger for these worthless pieces of paper.

Some bought them as collector's items, others as speculative stocks. In those simple land deeds, others saw a badly wanted green card, a chance to visit their land in a long-awaited journey to America. At last, a real chance had arrived to lay foot in America, the buyers thought. And nothing could change that belief. The United States Embassy in Beijing issued a warning, telling the over-zealous buyers that the deeds were not a prelude to a visa. Appearing on the BBC and Voice of America, Scott Moger issued his usual disclaimers, telling the Chinese that they could not build, live, or retire on their land. They could not visit their one-inch pieces of America. None of this stopped the flood of buyers already packing to meet their uncles and cousins in the United States. Even if they could never visit their property, there were those who were simply happy to own land in America. "I want to be a landowner in America! How many Chinese people can say that they own American land?" a buyer told *the New York Times*.

By the time I arrived in China, the "Own a Piece of America" bonanza was all but forgotten, even by those Chinese enthusiasts who, for a short time, saw the dream of visiting America within their reach. One person, however, remembered those days with mischievous joy and pride. Yue Haitao used his parents' new company in Shenzhen and made a fortune from "Own a Piece of America."

* * *

I visited Yue Haitao in his office one afternoon in October, when he showed me a framed Chinese certificate and told me the story of the first quick and effortless money he made after he jumped into the sea in 1989. He was jubilant. "I was already rich from working at Neptunus. But this was fast money. It took no effort on my part," he told me. The certificates hit the market on October 12, 1992. He made a lot of money in no time. "It was surreal," he said.

With Neptunus behind him, Yue Haitao took on the exclusive distribution of the certificates in China. He possessed all that was necessary to make this a quick success story: a giant modern company in Shenzhen, deep connections with influential people across the country, and the media. His years at the *Beijing Review* now came to his help in the world of business. "Own a Piece of America" became a national obsession only days after it was launched in China. "My friends in the media helped me publicize it, for free, of course. In those days, people believed in newspapers." The American dream was now a Chinese dream.

Like any good thing, this too had to end. It did not take long before some Chinese newspapers began criticizing the enterprise. "American dream is a bubble that will burst," they wrote. The buying frenzy continued despite the warnings. "The Chinese people had been chasing the American dream for 200 years. Before liberation, the Chinese thought there was gold everywhere in America. They called America the 'Gold Mountain,'" Yue Haitao told me. The economic reforms and China's opening up to the West created a new American attraction among the Chinese, especially its youth. Three years after the violent repression of the Tiananmen Square protesters by the army, the Chinese were even more fascinated with all that was American. They had a new American Dream. "Own a Piece of America" provided an easy way to realize this dream. And it made Yue Haitao a richer man in a short time.

*   *   *

The success of "Own a Piece of America," made a name for Yue Haitao among American businessmen hoping to make fast money in China. One such businessman paid him a visit in Shenzhen in 1993. "That was the first time I had met an American capitalist." He recalled the meeting.

"He was very fat and took up two seats." The American businessman had a goatee and wore suspenders. He had "a five-carat diamond ring," and smoked cigars throughout the meeting. A real estate developer in California, he had come to recruit Yue Haitao to sell American property, large estates, to the new rich Chinese looking for opportunities to invest their wealth. "The stock market was not that developed in China in those days. There were a lot of rich people who did not know what to do with their money."

Although flattered, Yue Haitao could not accept the offer. "I didn't know anything about the American real estate." But he knew China and the Chinese quite well. Emboldened by the remarkable ease and success of "Own a Piece of America," Yue Haitao began working on a Chinese version. By the spring of 1993, he had completed the plan for "Have a Homeland," a project that would bring him yet more fortune.

Yue Haitao targeted Chinese around the world, including the millions of expatriates in America and Australia, and sold them one square *cun* (1.3 square inch) of land in 36 areas in return for a "Have a Homeland" certificate. Unlike the "Own a Piece of America" project, this time, the Chinese buyers could actually visit their property.

"I bought land in each of the 33 provinces, the autonomous regions, and Taiwan," he told me. Yue Haitao purchased land in or around big cities and planned to turn each piece into a People's National Park and make them available for visits by the owners of "Have a Homeland" certificates free of charge. The owners' names were to be permanently engraved on the granite walls of a tall tower in the main garden in Beijing. The certificates were transferable, and could be inherited. Neptunus had agreed to a yearly raffle with a top prize of 1,000,000 yuan for the next ten years. The list of benefits continued.

"Own a Homeland" officially started on June 26, 1993. This was a major undertaking. "Considering the special situation in China, I could not have done this alone," Yue Haitao told me. He recruited partners from China's ruling elite. "Very famous people participated in the project. I gathered a consortium of influential people and organizations, including seven ministries."

"Own a Homeland" came to life through the partnership of the Neptunus Group and the National Science and Technology Commission, the State Education Commission, the National Physical Education Committee, the Ministry of Construction, the Ministry of Land and Resources, the China National Tourism Administration, and the China Disabled Persons' Federation. Four vice-chairmen of the Chinese People's Political Consultative Conference, four vice-chairmen of the Standing Committee of the National People's Congress, the Minister of National Defense, and other influential figures attended the founding meeting and put their names behind the project, Yue Haitao told me. All documents had their signatures.

A founding meeting was held on June 26, 1993 to announce the formal issuing of the certificates. This was an unusual business meeting. The meeting was not in the boardroom of a corporation, but in the Great Hall of the People, a place reserved for the most important official gatherings in China. "There were 200 dignitaries, vice-ministers, and people above them," Yue Haitao boasted. "But I was the commander in chief."

Organizing the meeting was a special challenge, Yue Haitao recalled. "It was difficult to decide who to put on the first table and who on the second or third. These were powerful people. Chinese officials care about how they are treated by others. I had to be very careful. After considering many options, I decided to use only one table, a very long table that would seat all 200 dignitaries. It was over 150 feet in length." He leaned back on his chair, took a long puff from his cigar, turned to me and said, "Let me tell you who else was at that meeting." Pausing after each name, he told me a brief history of the men and women who sat around the long table on June 16, 1993.

Deng Pufang, Deng Xiaoping's son, was imprisoned and tortured. He was paralyzed when the Red Guards threw him out of the window of a three-story building at Beijing University in 1968. He came to the June 16 meeting as the president of the China Disabled Persons' Federation. Having the son of the "Paramount Leader" at the long table was a guarantee for success.

"Wang Qishan also joined the meeting," Yue Haitao said. The vice-governor of the People's Bank of China at the time, Wang Qishan was promoted to governor of the bank in 1994. In 2004, he became Beijing's mayor. In 2008, he was promoted to vice-premier of the State Council and member of its Leading Party Members' Group. Yue Haitao recalled, "Bo Xilai also came." Bo Xilai was minister of commerce in 2007. "Shen Guofang sat at that table." Promoted to secretary of the Ministry of Foreign Affairs in 1993, Shen Guofang became assistant minister of foreign affairs in 2003.

With the participation of some of the most powerful people in China in the project, the financial success of "Own a Homeland" was guaranteed. Some 9.6 million certificates were sold worldwide in less than a year. Within 80 days or so, the project generated 160 million yuan. Yue Haitao had discovered a goldmine.

Then, as if disaster had struck the project from the sky, the government issued an order for the immediate termination of "Own a Homeland." Even the Paramount Leader's son could not save it. "You know, there were different factions in the CPC," Yue Haitao said. "My faction did not have the upper hand." He sipped the red Bordeaux and took a long puff from his half-burnt cigar, and told me about factional wars, and the fate of his "Own a Homeland" cash-cow.

When "Own a Homeland" hit the market, Prime Minister Li Peng had five vice-premiers. Among them were a famous anti-corruption tsar, Zhu Rongji, and a conservative, Zau Jiahua. Zhu Rongji and Zau Jiahua were political adversaries, competing for the future premiership of China. In 1994, Zhu Rongji began a campaign against financial corruption and used the campaign to crack down on his political opponents, Lipeng and Zou Jiahua. "Those were my supporters," Yue Haitao said. Hoping to undermine his opponents, Zhu Rongji targeted "Own a Homeland." In March 1998, Zhu Rongji became prime minister. "My supporter lost the fight." The new prime minister ordered "Own a Homeland" closed. Authorities came after Yue Haitao and his family. They were accused of funding "Own a Homeland" through Initial Public Offering (IPO) without having obtained permission from the government. "I found the charges ridiculous." Yue Haitao was raising money through normal sales operations, not funding the project through stock offerings, he told me. "We have a saying in China, 'You can always find a stick to beat a dog.' That's what happened to us."

As with all other factional wars in China, the penalties for the losers were severe. The authorities condemned Yue Haitao to 20 years in jail, and the president of Neptunus to death. For 15 days, "and without any sleep," Yue Haitao visited different ministries, pleading for help from his influential supporters. "The forces on my side were very strong." Yue Haitao's supporters and their adversaries reached a compromise in the end. The sentences were not carried out. Yue Haitao was pardoned, and the president was put on probation. "He was not killed and I did not go to jail."

The committee could no longer sell the certificates to the Chinese. "We could still sell them to foreigners." The founding committee refunded 80 million yuan to the Chinese owners of the certificates. "This was half of what we earned. We still had 80 million left. After all, Zhu Rongji could not go after me and those ministers."

Not long after, Yue Haitao left his family business and "went north to explore oil."

BASTILLE DAY

The world was grappling with the most serious economic crisis since the Great Depression in the summer of 2009. Unemployment was on the rise in most countries. China was, however, marching ahead, with a rapidly growing economy. The country was breaking new boundaries. It was surpassing others in technologies and productions that were to shape the future of China and the world. Yue Haitao's Everthriving Investment Group was among the leaders in China's march into the future.

These were exceptionally busy times for Yue Haitao. Having recently acquired the majority stock of a mineral company in Inner Mongolia, he was away from Beijing most of the time. He had arrived directly from the airport when we met again in Beijing. "I will be back in Inner Mongolia in two days," he said. "I am too thinly spread these days.".

In 2009, the Everthriving Investment Group was at the peak of its success. With 13 national and international subsidiaries, it was making major inroads in the fields of clean energy and environmentally friendly production. It was engaged in final negotiations with the government to start a landfill cleanup project. The company would take garbage out of the landfill, reclassify and separate the trash, and recycle its different parts. "We had no environmental regulations in the old days. We created massive landfills in lowland areas, dumped our garbage, and polluted the land and the underground water sources. But the Chinese government is paying more attention to this problem now."

The work was to begin in the giant Haidian landfill in northern Beijing. The Haidian landfill attracted much controversy and protest when the community stood up to the government, and opposed its plan to build garbage incinerators in the area. Yue Haitao's cleanup project was a lucrative enterprise that cleaned the environment and defused the political crisis at the same time. "We will recycle the steel, compress the construction material into bricks, use the organic trash to produce fertilizer, and burn only what is not usable," Yue Haitao said.

By 2009 China was leading the world in clean energy technology, and the Everthriving Investment Group was among the clean energy leaders in China. It was the first Chinese company to invest in Convertible Static Compensator (CSC) clean energy source development. The Everthriving Investment Group "was one of the first companies in the world" with the patented technology and facilities to produce biodegradable plastic. The company was planning to produce 150,000 tons of this plastic every year. "China is the most advanced country in this field. And we will be one of the biggest producers," he said in our last meeting on July 14, 2009.

*   *   *

July 14, 2009 was hot and smoggy. Pollution was high, and breathing exceptionally difficult. It was Yue Haitao's 58th birthday. We met in the garden of a spacious restaurant decorated with antique furniture and elegantly carved wood pillars, near the Workers' Stadium in Beijing. I made a toast and wished Yue Haitao a happy birthday. "Birthdays are not important to me," he said. "But this is an important day in history. I will toast to that," he said and raised his glass. "To Bastille Day," he said.

Two hundred and twenty-two years earlier, on July 14, 1789, the citizens of Paris stormed the notorious Bastille prison in an act that became the symbol of the French Revolution and the struggle against monarchy. Outraged by the injustices of the feudal system, a heavy tax burden, and the rising price of bread, the peasants joined the workers and townspeople in a bloody revolution against the monarch, and for the Republic. Every year on Yue Haitao's birthday, millions across France commemorated the fall of the Bastille, an event that changed France, and gave rise to a new social order and new politics. The storming of the Bastille marked the beginning of the fight against the arbitrary and despotic rule of the king and the feudal order, and the beginning of the republican era in France. For Yue Haitao, however, Bastille Day was a reminder of China's failures to follow in the footprints of developments that had changed France and much of the world.

"The peasants overthrew feudalism and made France a model of modernity. We never had anything like that in China. Thousands of years of feudalism are haunting China. The feudal mindset is still with us," Yue Haitao said. "Chinese people are easily satisfied with the status quo. They are pragmatists without a dream."

"Do you know the difference between the Eastern arbitrary society and the Western democratic society?" Yue Haitao asked. "The most obvious difference is that in the Eastern arbitrary society, the emperor is like the father, and the ministers are his sons who have to be on their knees in his presence. In the Western democratic society the emperor is the elder brother and the ministers don't have to be on their knees. It is common for brothers to fight each other. It is not normal, however, for sons to rebel against their father. That's how feudalism survived in China but not in the West. We are still paying the price for that."

China was undergoing epic changes, yet it lacked what countries in the West had mastered, Yue Haitao lamented. "Market discipline! Chinese people don't have discipline." To create the required discipline Chinese bosses demanded that their employees stand to attention and take part in military-like drills at the start of every shift. Some went as far as wanting their employees to receive actual military training. "An army man" managed Everthriving Investment for two years before Yue Haitao joined the company. "I was not used to that at the beginning. Employees watched me with no emotion on their faces when I gave speeches. I did not know what they had in their minds. It was like I had no audience. Everyone wore black uniforms like hotel managers. Men and women had their different uniforms. The first day I went to the company I thought I was in a hotel."

There were short-term gains, however. The military discipline increased efficiency. Profits rose. But something more important was sacrificed. "Creativity," he said. To correct the ills of feudalism, Chinese bosses sacrificed creativity for discipline. "How can we compete in the world without creativity?" he said, and took out his medicine kit from the brown leather bag and gave himself an insulin shot in his belly.

*   *   *

For the first time in two years that I had known him, Yue Haitao was showing signs of fatigue. He sat silently before me, stared away for a few long minutes and smoked his cigar. "I think I will leave this company and start something new soon," he said, and put out his cigar.

"I have done my job," Yue Haitao said, and became quiet. "I am like a missionary. I know there is tough work waiting for me. Another group of people is waiting for my preaching. The next project may be my last. I am reaching the end of the road," he said. "But before I die, I will buy a boat and take a long journey. There is a saying in Chinese that means 'better to disappear in the sea, than to die in the desert.'"

"For thousands of years, Chinese intellectuals contemplated the end of their life in advance. I am no exception."

We embraced and said farewell.

Conclusion

China shook the world when the Communist Party defeated the Kuomintang and established the People's Republic of China on October 1, 1949. Some 30 years later, China astonished the world again when the Communist Party embraced capitalism. With that, China became an integral part of the global economy. It made possible the emergence of a global economic system that relied, in part, on nineteenth-century labor standards and wages in the final years of the twentieth century. China's low-wage capitalism became an important building block of contemporary globalization. Meanwhile, China prospered and rose from an economically backward country to a financial powerhouse and the factory of the world.

Now, once again, China is making its mark on the world by slowly abandoning its low-wage and waste-producing capitalism. It is on the road to a more high-tech and environmentally friendly model of growth, and is slowly emerging as a leader in green capitalism. Meanwhile, the Communist Party is using the country's newly gained economic power as a foundation for building a middle-class society, and narrowing the income gap created in the past three decades. China continues to change, and the state remains the driving force behind that change.

China relied on a mix of market and non-market relations throughout the process of economic change. The state played a central role in designing and directing the country's economic journey, and its road to successes. It selectively used free markets in some cases and violated them in others, subsidized some industries, and guided China's reform and economic transformation through trial and error. It tested uncharted waters and moved the country from economic isolation to a powerful player in contemporary globalization. Thirty years ago the Chinese state launched a process of guided globalization. China is now entering the second phase of its state-led globalization.

The first phase of China's globalization resulted in remarkable success. China broke norms and historical records in speed of economic change. Many prospered. Others, however, paid a heavy price. They carried the burden of China's economic reform. China's prosperity had its sacrifices.

From the outset of its victory in 1949, sacrifice by various sections of the population played a key role in the Communist Party's design and implementation of economic and social change. The targets of sacrifice varied during the turbulent period that followed. The Communist Party and its fractured leadership, however, remained in charge of choosing the sacrifice for their vision of progress. Sacrifice became ideology, a weapon with which to mold the population and transform society.

The Chinese peasantry was granted land rights after the victory of the revolution. For millions of impoverished peasants, land reform became the greatest achievement of the revolution. Decades later, despite all the turmoil that the country had endured, many peasants remained grateful to Chairman Mao, and faithful to his legacy. Meanwhile, the Communist Party saw the peasantry as instrumental in winning the industrialization war in the populous and economically backward China. The party fueled its industrialization drive by restricting the peasants' movement, and through harsh and inflexible procurement policies. China's peasants became the sacrificial goat for the country's industrialization in the first 30 years of the revolution. They remained the sacrifice for China's new model of industrialization after the 1980s—this time, however, as migrant workers.

China's economic opening up and its model of low-wage export processing required not only change in laws and practices, but also a vast working class willing to work at any wage and under any working conditions. The impoverished peasantry was the natural candidate. Millions of peasants were allowed to leave their farms and fill the jobs in the export-processing factories that were mushrooming in the sprawling cities of southeastern China. They were to fuel the first phase of China's globalization.

To make China attractive to foreign investors and contractors, the government allowed forms of labor exploitation long banned in the West and many parts of the world. The low wages, long hours of work, and primitive living conditions endured by millions of migrant workers allowed Chinese subcontractors to become the manufacturers of choice for foreign corporations. In less than three decades, China became the manufacturing hub for low-end exports in the world. By the end of the twentieth century, it was a celebrated sweatshop of global capitalism. Migrant workers shouldered the burdens of China's rise to power.

The low-wage export-processing model required a strict system of labor control at the factory and in society. The state banned strikes, and enforced labor control through intimidation and threats of imprisonment. Beijing and various local governments also closed their eyes to similar abusive practices by the management of export-processing firms. To maintain uninterrupted production and a steady flow of foreign capital, local governments gave impunity to factory managers to control their workers and punish disobedient employees. Many subcontractors built private prisons in their factory compounds, and jailed, and physically punished their disruptive workers. Intimidation and physical assault by factory guards occurred regularly.

Strict control of migrant workers, and their sacrifice for economic growth, required social acceptability of these practices in the larger society. The state gained the consent of the new middle classes by delivering the promised benefits of economic change. Economic opening enriched many, and created a new middle class that saw its chances for a better future in sustaining the practices that were the hallmark of China's low-wage capitalism. The new middle class saw the sacrifice of the migrant workers as a necessary condition for the country's progress, and their position in the emerging China. No doubt, in many cases, political repression and fear played an important role in creating this social consent. Equally important, however, were the visible achievements of the economic reforms in molding a generation that stood behind the state and its policies in return a share of China's new riches.

"What could unions do other than destroy the stability China is enjoying now?" a young graduate student told me in Beijing when I made a case for independent unions to improve the living conditions of migrant workers. Unions lead to "chaos and revolution," he told me. China could not help all its citizens at the same time. Someone had to get rich first; others—migrant workers and farmers—had "to wait their turn," another student said.

Social stigmatization of migrant workers also played an important role in winning the middle-class consent. China's changing culture, and its new norms of beauty and standards of social behavior, fueled the further resentment of migrant workers among the middle classes. They ridiculed the workers for their dark skins and their social manners, feared them as the sources of rising theft and violence, and viewed them as outcasts. Migrant workers and their dark skins represented the China of the past, the ignorant China, the China that many resented. Even the migrant workers saw their darker skins as an embarrassing reminder of their hard work on the farm, and long hours of strenuous labor under the sun.

Despite social prejudices and the discriminatory policies of the state, migrant experiences remained complex and hybrid. Economic reform had contradictory effects on their lives. Amid exploitation and life on the margins of a changing society, migration provided opportunities unparalleled in the village. For Grandpa's nephew and many others, migration became an opportunity to escape rural poverty. After years of working in factories or on construction sites, they would return to their villages with money, live in better homes, eat better food, and enjoy a life of leisure compared to others. To the second generation of migrant workers, particularly women, migration became the ultimate escape from their stagnant and suffocating small-town life, the surgical knife that cut the umbilical cord connecting them to land and to rural China. Migration was liberation.

Migration gave Yu Xinhong the self-confidence to decline the offer to marry a rich man in the village. It gave Yu Xinhong and others financial independence, and the chance to escape the isolation experienced by their parents. Migration allowed her to feel normal, live like others, and taste some of the benefits that a globalizing China promised its middle class citizens. After nearly 30 years of routine farm work, migration gave Wang Chun Ling the chance to meet Chinese from other corners of this vast nation, travel, say no to jobs that did not satisfy her needs, and feel equal to her husband for the first time in her ten years of married life. To millions of migrant workers, migration was an exhilarating experience despite the harsh working conditions, and degrading treatment by others.

*   *   *

The earlier sub-standard working conditions and low wages experienced by most migrant workers are slowly changing. Better conditions are evident

172 THE ACCIDENTAL CAPITALIST

across the country. Wages are rising, and workers are enjoying more rights. China seems to be gradually abandoning the earlier labor practices as it moves towards the creation of a domestic market and a middle-class society, and the development of high-tech green products. The transformation calls for a new sacrifice.

It is the industries that brought China to prominence over the past 30 years that are to be sacrificed now. China is distancing itself from its past. Low-end exporters who relied on generous subsidies and repressed wages are the sacrificial goats for China's entry into a more high-tech and green capitalism. The winners of the past are the losers of the future in China.

The export-processing industries that flourished by using a system of nineteenth-century labor control and wages are now the subject of elimination. China is in the early stages of moving to a new model of capitalist growth. With that, the Chinese state is planning for a new position in the world economy. China will no longer be the sweatshop of globalization, but one of its leaders. The new strategy will have important consequences for migrant workers, their rights, and their economic status in China.

Various local governments have already allowed substantial increases in the wages of migrant workers. The central government in Beijing has shown readiness to promote improved labor standards and better working conditions. Beijing has been supporting pro-labor legislations, and workers' demands for better wages and rights. A new labor legislation passed in April 2007 requires all employers to provide their laborers with a signed contract, regardless of the size of their workforce. The law also restricts the use of a temporary workforce, and limits the ability of employers to randomly fire their workers. In effect, the 2007 law is the first piece of legislation that gives migrant workers the same legal treatment as other workers in China.

The Chinese state has followed the more labor-friendly legislation with its tacit acceptance of limited labor actions, and tangible improvement in workers' rights. China is slowly abandoning its zero-tolerance to labor militancy. The government remained on the sidelines when strikes and demands for independent unions and substantial wage increases swept through the plants manufacturing part for Toyota and Honda in late spring and early summer 2010. The strikes in 2010 were a continuation of a rising trend of labor actions by migrant workers in China. Labor disputes rose by 42 percent in Guangdong in the first quarter of 2009. Across China, there were 317,000 labor dispute cases in 2009 compared to 126,000 such cases in 2006. In all of these cases, the government demonstrated unprecedented restraint.

Beijing's new attitude towards migrant workers and their rights is an indication of broader policy changes, and a growing self-confidence about the country's position in the world. It is a sign of belief in the ability of the Chinese economy to confront challenges of global competition without relying on low wages and low-quality exports.

A June 3, 2010 *China Daily* story about the rising labor strikes provides a telling illustration of the Communist Party's new attitude towards labor relations and the future of China. The strikes are "seen as another example of how Chinese workers are growing impatient with the long hours and low pay culture that has been the bedrock of the country's reputation as the 'world's factory.' Analysts say workers—particularly those among the new generation of migrant laborers—are becoming more confident about their bargaining power and predict these actions could ultimately bring an end to cheap labor in China."

Recent titles from Pluto Press
The very best in independent progressive publishing

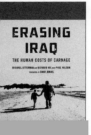

Erasing Iraq
The Human Costs of Carnage
Michael Otterman, Richard Hil and Paul Wilson

9780745328973

If I could only recommend one book that provides a comprehensive overview of both the situation in Iraq today, and the decades of US-backed policy it took to create this nightmare scenario, Erasing Iraq is it.
–DAHR JAMAIL, journalist

China from the Inside Out
Fitting the People's Republic into the World
Ronald C. Keith

9780745328546

A sophisticated analysis of Chinese thinking on the major issues of development and foreign policy. This book is an excellent alternative to the many cliched, and incorrect, interpretations of Chinese political history. Highly recommended.
–CHOICE

Obama's Economy
Recovery for the Few
Jack Rasmus

9780745332185

A trenchant critique of Obama's stimulus measures. With orthodox economics coming under strain, Rasmus' unorthodox economics is a refreshing counter-argument to the mainstream.
PAUL MASON, BBC *Newsnight*

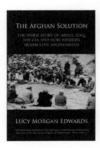

The Afghan Solution
The Inside Story of Abdul Haq, the CIA and How Western Hubris Lost Afghanistan
Lucy Morgan Edwards

9780956844903

A deeply-reported, well-argued and deftly-written account of the opportunities not taken ... based on the author's own deep knowledge of Afghanistan.
–PETER BERGEN, CNN

www.plutobooks.com